Pluralism and the personality of the state discusses the relations
between individuals, groups and the state. Set against the broad
context of philosophical arguments about group and state
personality, Dr Runciman's book tells, for the first time, the full
history of the movement in early twentieth-century English
political thought known as political pluralism. The pluralists
believed that the state was simply one group among many, and
could not therefore be sovereign. They also believed that
groups, like individuals, might have personalities of their own.
The book is divided into three parts: the first examines the
philosophical background to these ideas and refers in particular
to the work of Thomas Hobbes and the German Otto von
Gierke. The second traces the development of pluralist thought
before, during and after the First World War. In the third and
final part, Runciman's study returns to Hobbes and looks in
particular at his *Leviathan*, in order to see what conclusions can
be drawn about the nature of this work and the nature of the
state as it exists today.

IDEAS IN CONTEXT 47

PLURALISM AND THE PERSONALITY OF THE STATE

IDEAS IN CONTEXT

Edited by QUENTIN SKINNER (*General Editor*)
LORRAINE DASTON, WOLF LEPENIES,
J. B. SCHNEEWIND and JAMES TULLY

The books in this series will discuss the emergence of intellectual traditions
and of related new disciplines. The procedures, aims and vocabularies that
were generated will be set in the context of the alternatives available within
the contemporary frameworks of ideas and institutions. Through detailed
studies of the evolution of such traditions, and their modification by
different audiences, it is hoped that a new picture will form of the
development of ideas in their concrete contexts. By this means, artificial
distinctions between the history of philosophy, of the various sciences, of
society and politics, and of literature may be seen to dissolve.

The series is published with the support of the Exxon Foundation.

A list of books in the series will be found at the end of the volume.

PLURALISM AND THE PERSONALITY OF THE STATE

DAVID RUNCIMAN

Trinity College, Cambridge

CAMBRIDGE
UNIVERSITY PRESS

CAMBRIDGE UNIVERSITY PRESS
Cambridge, New York, Melbourne, Madrid, Cape Town, Singapore, São Paulo

Cambridge University Press
The Edinburgh Building, Cambridge CB2 2RU, UK

Published in the United States of America by Cambridge University Press, New York

www.cambridge.org
Information on this title: www.cambridge.org/9780521551915

First published 1997
This digitally printed first paperback version 2005

A catalogue record for this publication is available from the British Library

Library of Congress Cataloguing in Publication data
Runciman, David.
Pluralism and the personality of the state/David Runciman.
p.   cm. – (Ideas in context: 47)
Includes bibliographical references and index.
ISBN 0 521 55191 9
1. Pluralism (Social sciences).
2. State, The.   3. Political science – History.
I. Title.   II. Series.
JC328.2.R86   1997
320.1–dc21   96–46263   CIP

ISBN-13 978-0-521-55191-5 hardback
ISBN-10 0-521-55191-9 hardback

ISBN-13 978-0-521-02263-7 paperback
ISBN-10 0-521-02263-0 paperback

To my parents

Doug. Another king! They grow like Hydra's heads;
     I am the Douglas, fatal to all those
     That wear those colours on them. What art thou
     That counterfeit'st the person of a king?
King. The King himself

Shakespeare, Henry IV part I

Contents

Preface

This book is about the political thought of seven men: Thomas Hobbes (1588–1679), Otto von Gierke (1841–1921), F. W. Maitland (1850–1906), J. N. Figgis (1866–1919), Ernest Barker (1874–1960), G. D. H. Cole (1889–1959) and Harold Laski (1893–1950). Hobbes was and is the greatest of all English political philosophers; he is also one of the supreme prose stylists in the English language. Gierke was one of the dominant figures in late nineteenth- and early twentieth-century German life and thought; a jurist, philosopher and legal reformer, he was also an intellectual historian of genius. The same is true of Maitland, the founding father of legal history in England; like Gierke, he is one of the few historians whose works are still being read by other historians over a hundred years after they were written. Figgis was a follower of Maitland, and though his work has lasted slightly less well, it too has retained a readership, both among political theorists and historians. Barker, who was a political theorist and historian himself, achieved greater prominence in his own lifetime than did either Maitland or Figgis, rising to a professorship and a knighthood; his stock, however, has fallen considerably faster, and he is now something of a marginal figure in the intellectual history of this century (though a recent study in this series has attempted to reverse this trend). Barker's stock has not fallen as fast as that of Cole, who like Barker was a historian, but unlike Barker was also a socialist; once one of the most famous intellectuals in Britain, he is now fairly well neglected, if not quite so neglected as he was a decade or two ago. Laski is one of the few British intellectuals whose reputation has suffered a decline more dramatic even than Cole's, despite the brief flurry of interest that surrounded the centenary of his birth in 1993; a fellow socialist, and rival, of Cole's, his ideas are now as unfashionable as they were once fashionable; he is, in addition, generally regarded as having been something of a fraud. Viewed chronologically, this is not a sequence which follows an upward curve.

What these seven have in common is a shared interest in the concept of group personality, and it is this concept which provides the subject for most of what follows. Of these seven, the last five (and a few others) make up the movement in early twentieth-century English political thought known as political pluralism. It is the central aim of this book to tell the history of that movement, and it is in this respect that chronology is significant, because it is a history containing a clear narrative thread. The thread is provided by Gierke, from whom the concept of group personality immediately derived, and whose own work contained a narrative in which the central place was occupied by Hobbes. It is necessary to know about Hobbes if we are to make sense of Gierke, and it is necessary to make sense of Gierke if we are to have any understanding of the history of English political thought during the early part of this century.

However, Hobbes and Gierke do not appear here simply in order to explicate ideas which were in many respects pale copies of their own. The struggles of the political pluralists to apply Gierkean concepts in a modern English setting throw some light back on those concepts, and back in turn on some of the concepts with which Gierke struggled, prime among which was the concept of the Hobbesian state. In particular, the history of English political pluralism throws some light on an absolutely crucial but often ignored feature of Hobbes's conception of the state – its so-called 'personality'. It is for this reason that the book has a structure which is somewhat dialectical. The first part looks at Hobbes's and Gierke's ideas of persons and group persons in order to provide the background to the history that follows in part II; that history then provides the background for the further exploration of Hobbesian and Gierkean ideas of groups and state which makes up the substance of part III. There are thus two sets of ideas and two sorts of context involved here: there are the philosophical ideas which provide the context for what is essentially an exercise in history; and there are the historical ideas which provide the context for what is essentially (or is at least intended to be) an exercise in philosophy. It is my hope that these two exercises make some sense on their own terms. But if they make any sense at all, it is also my hope that they best make sense together.

There are two points to be made about the text. First, I am very conscious that this is a book written by a man about men, in which human beings in general are referred to by the epithet 'men', and particular groups of human beings, including all political theorists, are referred to as though they always were men. For the first two of these facts I can offer no excuses. For the third, I can only say that one of the central themes of this book is the distinction between 'persons' and what are usually referred to as 'natural men', and this is a distinction I did not wish in any way to blur. In this context, the gender-neutral term 'person' is very far from being neutral in other respects, and has to be set against what is in other respects a neutral term, which in this case means 'men'. As to the fourth, it is, I am afraid, primarily a matter of stylistic convenience, and 'he' should be read as 'he or she' wherever appropriate. However, I would add that the political theorists discussed in this book would not generally have thought of 'he' as 'he or she'. Moreover, it is one of the themes of this book that political theory should not be confused with real life. Political theory is not reality, it is simply one version of reality. It is, in other words, just a tale, full of its own sound and fury, and during the period covered by this book it tended to be told only by men.

The second point concerns the term 'state' itself. In the literature of the period (1900–33) it was almost always printed as 'State'. This convention has now died out, and the lower case is usually preferred. For the purposes of consistency I have used 'State' in all quotations from the period, even though this is not what was written in every instance. Where 'state' was used, it was purely a matter of convention, the lower case being preferred in some American publications, and in one or two English ones during the 1920s and 1930s. There was certainly no attempt to associate 'the State' with any particular philosophy (say, idealism) or any particular culture (say, Germany), nor was any distinction drawn between 'the State' and individual or historical 'states'. (Even those who wished to make that distinction tended to capitalise both.) Outside of the quotations I have used 'state', as is now conventional; again, nothing is implied by this.

I would like to express my gratitude to the people who have helped me to write this book. First of all, to Michael Bentley, who supervised the original thesis from which it derives, and who has provided much encouragement since. I am also very grateful to the Master and Fellows of Trinity College, Cambridge for electing me to the Fellowship which afforded the time and the leisure in which to write it. I have received much helpful advice in the unfamiliar areas of Roman law and medieval political thought from Magnus Ryan; all the mistakes that remain are entirely my own. Most of all, I would like to thank the three people who inspired me to write it. First, my father, W. G. Runciman, who pointed out early on the ways in which the research I was doing might be connected with Hegel. Second, Bee Wilson, who pointed out the possibility of a connection with Shakespeare. And third, Quentin Skinner, who pointed out the connection with the person without whom this book would not exist at all, Thomas Hobbes.

PART I

The personality of associations

CHAPTER I

Introduction

The question of how men form themselves into associations lies at the heart of Western political thought. An association is a group of human beings possessed of a distinct, formal identity based on the relation subsisting between its members, and it may fairly be said that it is around such groups that our political understanding has been constructed. The most prominent of these groups is the state, or civil association, and though the state can be regarded as an association *sui generis*, to be understood in its own terms, it has commonly been understood in terms of the associations that it contains. Sometimes it has literally been built out of them, a construct of the separate associations of ruling and ruled, government and people. As often it has been seen as analogous to the other associations in which men are familiarly to be found. Some of these associations have a natural existence, like the family, from which the Aristotelian *polis* is evolved. Others exist within particular systems of law, and, like the Roman or medieval corporation, may offer a model of considerable theoretical complexity to which the state can be compared. In each case, the state's identity rests on the identity of associations other than itself. And so not only must there be at least one association if there is to be a state, the character of that association will frequently depend on what is taken to characterise the business of association *per se*.

To ask questions about the personality of associations, however, is not simply to inquire into their general character. It is to inquire into their specific ability to bear the character of persons. Inevitably, this is a narrower problem than that of man's associative capabilities in general, and it presupposes a narrower sense of the word 'person' than one which renders 'personality' synonymous with 'character' or 'make-up'. Yet the problem of personality in this narrow sense was once seen as the key to a complete understanding

3

of political life in general, and of the state in particular. Within the terms of contemporary, English-speaking political theory this claim seems, at the very least, an unlikely one, if only because the terms themselves, 'person' and 'personality', have disappeared from the language of political argument in all but their broadest senses. Yet it was a claim made during this present century, and for a while it dominated political thought in England. It is the purpose of this book to describe that period in English political thought and to judge its significance. In order to do so, it is necessary first of all to explain why associations might once have been thought to be persons.

The period during which the question of the personality of associations engaged English political theorists was relatively brief, barely outlasting the first three decades of this century. Furthermore, its immediate origins lay not in England but in Germany, in the work of the German jurist and historian, Otto von Gierke, for whom the idea of associations as group persons had a peculiarly 'teutonic' significance. Nevertheless, Gierke's use of the idea of personality was anything but parochial. It provided him with the basis for one of the widest-ranging of all histories of ideas, the monumental *Das deutsche Genossenschaftsrecht*, in which he sought to organise the whole history of Western political life and thought around the problem of group personality. To that end, Gierke had to understand the arguments not just of German but of all political theorists as a response to this problem, and as a more or less successful resolution of it. Again, by present-day standards, in historiography as well as political theory, this is an unlikely and in many ways an arcane project. But it is not a spurious one. The concept of personality does constitute one of the familiar means by which European political thinkers have undertaken their character-istic engagement with the question of group identity. And though not all of those whom Gierke's history surveys may have thought in these terms, his particular form of history requires only that the thoughts of each should be comprehensible in the same terms. His is, in this sense, a distinctively German history, for it tells the story of an idea immanent in the world of ideas; what it is not, though, is merely a story about Germany, because the concept of the person was one Gierke discovered in, and used to make sense of, the history of ideas as a whole. What came to England from Gierke came to Gierke from history. And the best illustration of the part played by the concept of the person in history is provided by the part it plays at the heart of one of the most significant of all texts in the history of European ideas, written not by a German, but by an Englishman, Thomas Hobbes.

CHAPTER 2

Hobbes and the person of the commonwealth

I

Hobbes's *Leviathan,* which was first published in 1651, is divided into four parts, 'Of Man', 'Of Commonwealth', 'Of A Christian Commonwealth' and 'Of The Kingdome Of Darknesse'. Though much of the historical interest of the book resides in parts III and IV, the political philosophy on which its fame rests is located in the first two. Part I provides an account of man's natural condition, of the passions by which he is regulated, of the state of war to which he naturally inclines, and of the laws of nature by which he may still be bound. Part II provides an account of man's condition in civil society, of the covenant by which such society is created, of the sovereign by whom it is governed, and of the liberties which his subjects may yet enjoy. However, the final chapter of the first part, chapter XVI, which provides the bridge to what follows, addresses none of these themes; instead, it concerns 'Persons, Authors and things Personated'.[1] It is in this chapter that Hobbes introduces the concept which establishes the fundamental link between man's natural and his civil conditions, that of ownership, or rather the only form of ownership possible in the state of nature, ownership of words or actions. Hobbes defines his terms as follows:

A PERSON, *is he, whose words or actions are considered, either as his own, or as representing the words or actions of an other man, or of any other thing to whom they are attributed, whether Truly or by Fiction.*

---

[1] Chapter XVI of *Leviathan* continues to receive little attention in the growing mass of literature devoted to Hobbes. The most substantial account is probably still the one given by H. Pitkin in her *The concept of representation* (Berkeley, 1967). More recently, it has provided the focus for a paper in which it is argued that Hobbes's doctrine of representation incorporates the notion of 'latent "group personality"' (see M. Forsyth, 'Thomas Hobbes and the constituent power of the people', *Political Studies*, 29 (1981), 191–203). For reasons that will become clear, this is not the view that is taken here.

When they are considered as his owne, then is he called a *Naturall Person*: And when they are considered as representing the words and actions of an other, then is he a *Feigned* or *Artificiall* person.[2]

Words and actions are thus the responsibility of persons, but this does not mean that words and actions are 'owned' by whoever is responsible for them (i.e. whoever performs them). Rather, they are owned by the person who *takes* responsibility for them. This allows Hobbes to distinguish in chapter XVI of *Leviathan* between three different sorts of person: the natural, whose actions are his own; the artificial, whose actions are owned by another; and the fictitious, to whom the ability to own actions is granted by pretence.

Before asking what use Hobbes makes of these distinctions, it is worth asking how the transference of ownership on which they rest is possible at all, such that one man may act without owning, another may own without himself performing an action, and even a thing other than a man (Hobbes gives the examples of 'a Church, an Hospital, a Bridge'[3]) may own when incapable of action altogether. The answer is contained in the notion of representation, and the ability of persons to represent, personate or act the part of one another. Inevitably, this ability to act on another's behalf presupposes some prior arrangement or form of relationship between the represervter and the represented, and the most important of these is that which Hobbes describes as subsisting between an author and an actor whose words and actions the author owns. The actor is an artificial person, and is said to act on the authority of whoever owns his actions. The simplicity of this model does nonetheless allow for some significant variations, for while the relation between actor and author will frequently be founded on a covenant between them, it may also be founded on a covenant between the author and a third party binding both to treat of the actor's words and actions as though they were the author's own. This distinction is significant, not only in the development of Hobbes's own argument, but also for the diverse conceptions of authority which may follow from it, since there is a great difference between acting according to a prior agreement to be another's representative, and having one's actions taken as representing the actions of another: in the former case the actor may be quite narrowly constrained in the range of actions he can perform, while in the latter he may be not merely unconstrained

---

[2] T. Hobbes, *Leviathan*, ed. R. Tuck (Cambridge, 1991), p. iii.   [3] *Ibid.*, p. 113.

but even ignorant of the agreement of another to authorise what he does. Thus the actor bound by covenant may find himself committed to acting in accordance with the strictly laid-down preferences of his author, while the author who is represented by an uncovenanted actor may find himself committed to owning actions he could not possibly have foreseen. Neither to have authority, nor to give it, has any necessary connection with freedom of action, the scope of which is dependent on the conditions under which authority is held and the terms on which it is given.

There is, though, another form of relation besides that of actor and author for which Hobbes's concept of representation allows. A representative, or artificial person, may sometimes act on behalf of some 'thing' which cannot itself be the author of its representative's actions. Instead, these actions will be authorised by whoever owns or has dominion over the thing to be personated, in order, in Hobbes's words, 'to procure [its] maintenance'.[4] The thing in question might be a human being who happens to be without the capacity to authorise actions – 'Children, Fooles and Mad-men that have no use of Reason, may be personated by Guardians, or Curators', on the authority of 'he that hath right of governing them'[5] – but equally it might be property of a more conventional, inanimate kind, as when the owners of a bridge provide it with its own representative. The purpose of an arrangement like this would be to provide for some stability in the terms and conditions under which a bridge is used, which might not be possible if its users were held to be transacting with its owners every time they used it. Owners are not always available, nor are they always constant – they die, they disappear, they have other interests, they lose interest – and recognising this, they may seek to provide for a readily available representative of some more constant interest, and more solid thing, than they themselves embody. Yet because the act of personation is predicated on the personality of whatever is to be personated, this is not possible unless the bridge itself is conceived as a person. So it has to become a person by fiction, assuming the guise of an author but represented by an actor whose authority is derived from elsewhere. Thus while artificial persons are made from the capacity of natural persons to represent one another, fictitious persons are made from the capacity of artificial persons to be deemed the representative of almost

---

[4] *Ibid.*   [5] *Ibid.*

anything. As Hobbes himself says: 'There are few things, that are uncapable of being represented by Fiction.'[6]

The different sorts of person described by Hobbes – natural, artificial and fictitious – can thus be set apart from each other in accordance with the different number of subjects or vehicles of personality that they require: in the case of a natural person, one, the natural man himself; of an artificial person, two, author and actor; and of a fictitious person, three, owner, actor and fictitious author. However, this distinction ignores a feature common to all three types of personality, and that is the additional presence of someone in each case to raise the issue of an action's ownership. It only matters to whom actions belong if there exists an audience for the actions whose own conduct will be shaped by the answer to that question. This audience may take almost any form: it could be someone threatened by a stranger, or someone offered a contract by the agent of a third party, or someone negotiating with a government official, or someone who wishes to know against whom he has redress when the bridge he is accustomed to use is closed. In complex situations, it may even be someone who has himself helped determine the owner-ship of the actions in question: the owner of a bridge, for example, may find himself, perhaps as a user of the bridge, transacting with a representative who acts on the bridge's behalf. In each instance, the need to know to whom an action belongs presupposes the presence of some party to whom an action is addressed, or is taken as being addressed. Thus it is that 'actions' and 'words' are interchangeable in this context, and are used interchangeably by Hobbes, for actions which raise the issue of ownership are by definition communicative acts.

Though all actions performed by persons require an audience, it is not the case that the ownership of an action is determined by the audience for whom it is performed. A man who is threatened by a stranger claiming to issue his threats on another's behalf does not by disbelieving him confine those threats to the stranger's own person; if he is wrong, and has mistaken an artificial person for a natural one, his dealings will still be with whoever takes himself to own the mistakenly attributed threats. Nonetheless, Hobbes recognised that the ownership of actions was not always the result of a person's decision to give authority, and so accept responsibility, for them. The

[6] *Ibid.*

difficulty lies with fictitious persons, and in the fact that their ownership of actions is determined by a decision to which they themselves
cannot be party. That decision is made by whoever has responsibility
for whatever is to be personated, and so rests on a prior arrangement
determining ownership not of actions but of things. An arrangement
of this kind is only possible against the backdrop of civil society,
because, as Hobbes has been at pains to establish elsewhere in
Leviathan, there can be no ownership of things 'before there be some
state of Civill Government'.[7] Thus the personation of a fictitious
person depends not merely on the decision to authorise a representative but also on the conditions of ownership which precede such a
decision and give it force. And these conditions must hold for
everyone involved – authors, actors *and* audience – just because a
fictitious person cannot establish its own claim to actions undertaken
on its behalf. If the representative of a bridge is not regarded as such
by those with whom he deals, the bridge itself cannot make good his
title by some action of its own; instead, its representative must rely
on the title of the bridge's owners, and on its being upheld.

This marks an important difference between fictitious and artificial
persons. For unlike fictitious personality, artificial personality is not
contingent upon government, if only because government itself is
contingent upon the authorisation of at least one artificial person –
the person of the sovereign, without whom there can be no civil
society. A sovereign is a man, or assembly of men,[8] who, having been
authorised by a group of natural persons, has 'the *Right* to *Present* the
Person of them all, (that is to say, to be their *Representative*)'.[9] He, or
it, acquires this right in one of two ways, corresponding to the two
means of authorising an actor: either the group of natural persons

---

[7] *Ibid.*

[8] Hobbes allows that an artificial person can be an assembly. All that is required of an artificial
person is that it speak with one voice, and in an assembly this can be achieved by the simple
expedient of majority voting – 'And if the Representative consist of many men, the voyce of
the greater number must be considered as the voyce of them all. For if the lesser number
pronounce (for example) in the Affirmative, and the greater in the Negative, there will be
Negatives more than enough to destroy the Affirmatives; and thereby the excess of Negatives,
standing uncontradicted, are the onely voyce the Representative hath' (*ibid.*, p. 114). It does
not matter for the minority themselves that they have been outvoted in any instance, since
the purpose of each vote is to make decisions on behalf of whomever it is that the assembly
represents. Thus Hobbes does not have to consider one of the more familiar difficulties with
majority decision-making – that the minority are committed to something that they oppose –
since here it is not the assembly which is commited to anything, but the person on whose
behalf the assembly acts, and by whom alone the words and actions of the assembly are
owned.

[9] *Ibid.*, p. 121.

covenant with each other that they will each be represented by the same artificial person; or they covenant separately with the same person such that he becomes the representative of them all. In either case, the salient features remain the same – commonwealths arise out of the capacity of artificial persons to represent natural persons, and are properly called commonwealths only when a group of natural persons is represented by the same artificial person, making that person sovereign. It is the concept of artificial personality alone, therefore, which provides man with his escape from the brutishness of a natural existence.

The performance of this crucial task does not, though, confine the work done by the concept of artificial personality to the process of transition from the state of nature to a state of civil society. It has also to function within the life of the commonwealth, if only to allow for the creation of those fictitious persons which cannot exist without representation and cannot exist elsewhere. This is a secondary task in itself, but it raises one very important question about the nature of the commonwealth that contains it. Artificial persons make fictitious persons by providing representation for something incapable of representing itself. Is then the representation by the sovereign of a group of natural persons (which as the initial, disparate group is no person and is therefore incapable of representing itself) sufficient to create of that group the supposition or pretence of its own personality? Put in these terms the question might seem contrived, but it is one to which Hobbes provided an explicit answer. His commonwealth was indeed a person. For he writes:

A Multitude of men, are made *One* Person, when they are by one man, or one Person, Represented; so that it be done with the consent of every one of that Multitude in particular. For it is the *Unity* of the Represented, that maketh the Person *One*. And it is the Representer that beareth the Person, and but one Person: And *Unity*, cannot otherwise be understood in Multitude.[10]

The group of natural persons represented by the sovereign are one person, but only because they are represented by one person, just as a bridge is a person only because it has a person as its representative. On this account, the person represented by the sovereign – called by Hobbes 'the Person of the Commonwealth' – is a fiction. Yet this raises an obvious difficulty. Fictitious persons only come into being

---

[10] *Ibid.*, p. 114.

when an owner seeks representation for the thing he owns. No-one owns the commonwealth. How then are we to understand its personality?

The significance of this question is easily lost sight of in the face of the central polemical purpose of *Leviathan*, which was, above all, a book against civil war. The contractual basis of civil society as described by Hobbes stands in overt contrast to previous attempts to derive government from two separate contracts, one by which men make of themselves a society, a second by which that society contracts with the men who are to govern it. This double contract creates unity prior to government, and thus an association capable of judging the purposes of rulers against its own. Where the actions of government seem to conflict with the needs of society, the bonds of government may be taken to be dissolved. It was this possibility which the Hobbesian version, with its single contract, was designed to disallow.[11] For Hobbes, the unity of society was only created by the establishment of government. When men erect a sovereign, they are united in his person; without him, they are returned to the state of nature. Thus there exists no social contract with the sovereign, and no basis for judgments to be made about the civility of his conduct, for it is upon his very existence that the possibility of civil society depends. Hobbes's account of persons and things personated provides the theoretical foundation for this position: unity cannot be achieved except where a multitude is united in another person, 'and because the Multitude is not naturally *One*, but *Many*, they cannot be understood for one; but many Authors, of everything their representative saith, or doth in their name'.[12] The authority of government comes from individuals in their natural state. For a group of individuals in the civil state to claim authority against their government, and so risk a civil war, is nonsensical.[13]

---

[11] Strictly speaking, the basis of Hobbes's civil society is a covenant rather than a contract, since Hobbes understood a contract to involve 'the mutual transferring of right' at a given moment, while a covenant involved the promise of some future transfer by one of the contracting parties. Hobbes's commonwealth is instituted by covenant, not contract, because the multitude do not exchange rights with one another at the moment of its formation, but rather promise to transfer the right to present their person to the sovereign, on condition that others do the same. Nevertheless, it is fair to say that while every contract may not be a covenant, each covenant is a form of contract, and is made by parties Hobbes is happy to describe as 'contractors' (see *ibid.*, p. 94).

[12] *Ibid.*, p. 114.

[13] Forsyth has suggested that despite this Hobbes did still argue in *Leviathan* that 'the people' constituted a single entity with a single will before the institution of the sovereign (see Forsyth, 'Thomas Hobbes and the constituent power of the people'). However, he provides

The absence of any unity before there is sovereignty does not, however, answer the question posed above, which concerns the nature of the unity sovereignty creates. This is not a question about the authority of governments but about the character of the state, and the particular character of the Hobbesian state, given that he grants to it its own personality. For though the sovereign is authorised by the multitude, he does not bear a multitude of persons but only one, a person distinct from his own and also from those of his many natural authors. And it adds nothing to our understanding of that person to know that without representation it is naturally just a multitude, since the natural character of fictitious persons is immaterial; a bridge, after all, is naturally just an arrangement of bricks. What matters, for bridge and multitude, is the difference made when the non-natural capacity to own actions is attributed to their natural forms. Of what that difference might consist in the case of Hobbes's commonwealth will be discussed shortly. First, though, it is necessary to give some sense of how much of a difference the attribution to the state of its own personality can make.

II

The clearest sense of what can hang on this issue is provided by Michael Oakeshott, in his essay 'On the character of the modern European state'. For Oakeshott, the states of early modern and modern Europe have taken their character from the associational models of Roman private law, which sanctioned two distinct modes of association, and so offered two distinct models for the state. One is the *societas* (in English usually given as 'partnership' rather than 'society'), an association of individuals each of whom conditions his actions to accord with the terms of a joint agreement. The other is

little evidence to support this assertion, beyond the fact that had Hobbes held such a view, *Leviathan* would better accord with later theories of the constituent power of the people, particularly those of the late eighteenth century. All the evidence of the text itself points the other way. It is true, as Forsyth argues, that Hobbes does not explicitly deny that 'the people' are possessed of a single will; but given that he does explicitly deny that there is anything that they could do with such a will (beyond instituting a sovereign, which does not require the presence of such a will, only a congruence of individual wills) it is hard to see what relevance this has. Everything that Hobbes says in *Leviathan* about the group that institutes the sovereign is set out in negative terms: they do *not* have unity, they do *not* have authority, they do *not* have personality until they have a sovereign to represent them. Thus, as Forsyth is forced to admit, however Hobbes conceived of 'the people' before the institution of the sovereign, it is clear that after it 'he saw no role for them' (*ibid.*, p. 201).

the *universitas* (in English usually 'corporation'), an association of individuals considered collectively to form a single entity itself capable of action. The members of a *societas* share a common understanding about how each should act but they do not participate in any collective endeavour – it is 'a formal relationship in terms of rules, not a substantive relationship in terms of common action'.[14] A *universitas*, by contrast, exists to provide its members with a common identity as they pursue some collective end. As an association in private law, a *societas* is nothing more than the sum of its members and has no separate identity of its own. But a *universitas* acts in its own right, buying, selling, contracting, employing, suing, being sued; it is, in other words, possessed of something like its own personality. 'Thus', Oakeshott writes, 'it could hardly be said that any great impropriety had been committed when an association of this character was spoken of as a *persona ficta*'.[15]

The state, of course, is not simply an association in private law, but because it is an association it may be understood in analogous terms. Where understood as analogous to the *universitas*, it is conceived as what Oakeshott calls an 'enterprise association', whose members are associated in respect of some identified, common purpose. That purpose might be religious, or military, or economic; it might be directed by a monarch, by an assembly (or as likely a party) or by a people as a whole. But in each case the state is understood as a singular and purposive community. The state as *societas*, meanwhile, is a 'civil association',[16] whose members are associated in respect of some 'social' or 'civil' relation subsisting between them. It is a community of singular and purposive individuals, or groups of individuals, each pursuing their own ends, and

[14] M. Oakeshott, *On human conduct* (Oxford, 1975), p. 201.   [15] *Ibid.*, p. 204.

[16] For Oakeshott the idea of the *civitas* is itself conditional on the idea of the state as *societas*. He describes the idea of the *civitas* as 'not itself an enterprise, an undertaking, an "economy", or an educational or therapeutic organisation, and not enterprisers or groups of enterprisers associated in seeking recognition or advantage for themselves in their undertakings, but an association of *cives*; an relationship of equals, and a self-sufficient condition in being relationship in terms of the conditions of a practice (i.e. the laws of a state) which are not used up in being used and not in terms of a substantive purpose or purposes to be pursued' (*ibid.*, p. 183). For Oakeshott the *civitas* is the ideal of the state understood as *societas*, and the ideal of *civitas* is the *civitas peregrina*: 'An association, not of pilgrims travelling to a common destination, but of adventurers each responding as best he can to the ordeal of consciousness in a world composed of others of his kind, each the inheritor of the imaginative achievements (moral and intellectual) of those who have gone before and some joined in a variety of prudential practices, but here partners in a practice of civility the rules of which are not devices for satisfying substantive wants and whose obligations create no symbiotic relationship' (*ibid.*, p. 243).

united only by an agreement as to the conditions under which they may pursue them. These conditions may be broadly or narrowly defined; they may be determined by a monarch, by an assembly (or equally likely a body of judges) or by a people as a whole. But in each case the state is understood as an association of citizens who are bound to one another by their joint acknowledgment of the authority of certain 'rules', and, by extension, certain 'rulers', who, as rulers, frame, but do not always oversee, the lives of their subjects.[17] Oakeshott accepts that these two conceptions of the state, though quite distinct, are not always distinguishable in the work of particular theorists, but he does nonetheless regard Western political thought as dominated by accounts or understandings of the state which recognisably accord with one or other disposition. The states conceived by Thomas Cromwell, Francis Bacon, Calvin, Rousseau, Frederick the Great and Karl Marx were all analogous to *universitates*. Meanwhile, for Bodin, Spinoza, Kant, Fichte and Hegel the state was to be understood as a *societas*. Of this second group, Bodin's is the least and Hegel's the most sophisticated account of the state as civil rather than an enterprise association. But, for Oakeshott, it is the author of *Leviathan* – 'a work of art of superb integrity' – whose account of the state as *societas* is 'the most intrepid' and 'least equivocal' of all.[18]

There can be no doubting the intrepidity of Hobbes's work (particularly in the light of what one of his contemporaries called 'the extraordinary timorousnes of his nature'[19]), and nor can there be much doubt that Oakeshott's classification of it makes a good deal of sense. The Hobbesian commonwealth is an association of individuals who have all agreed to abide by certain rules. It is an association which has no substantive end of its own, beyond the end which its members share as individuals and which conditions the terms of their original agreement – 'namely, the Peace of the Subjects within themselves, and their Defence against a common Enemy'.[20] Peace is secured through the rule of law, and where the laws are silent, as at some points they must be, men are free to do as they please:

For seeing there is no Common-wealth in the world, wherein there be Rules enough set down, for the regulating of all the actions, and words of

---

[17] Oakeshott draws the distinction between those who 'rule' in a *societas* and those who exercise 'lordship' over a *universitas*: rulers merely establish and enforce the rules which condition the behaviour of *cives*; lords, meanwhile, 'manage' all those who live under them, and control their lives according to whichever 'policy' they have chosen to adopt.

[18] See *ibid.*, p. 252.   [19] See J. Aubrey, *Brief lives*, ed. A. Clark (Oxford, 1898), p. 390.

[20] Hobbes, *Leviathan*, p. 150.

men, (as being a thing impossible:) it followeth necessarily, that in all kinds of actions, by the Lawes praetermitted, men have the Liberty, of doing what their own reasons shall suggest, for the most profitable to themselves.[21]

But though the commonwealth described in *Leviathan* is essentially a *societas*, it is not one unequivocally. Hobbes's civil association is a person. It is not, strictly speaking, a *persona ficta* in Hobbes's own terms, for such persons must be owned or governed before they can be represented; nor, however, as Oakeshott admits, are any other states strictly equivalent to the fictitious persons of Roman private law, which could be created only by 'an already recognised superior legal authority'.[22] The members of a state might be understood literally to have associated in the manner of a *societas*, because Roman partnerships were founded upon contract. But a state could never be a literal *universitas*, since corporations were always the creatures of the state themselves. Thus the analogy of the *persona ficta* must have some fictitious elements of its own. If it is to work at all, it is because the state, whatever its origins, may at least be seen to assume a form to which personality can be attached. In the Hobbesian case, this means that it must be deemed to own actions. It does not have itself to act, any more than a bridge has itself to act in order to be a person. But its representative must be taken to be acting on its behalf, and this raises a problem for Oakeshott's understanding of *Leviathan*. On Oakeshott's account of the state as *societas*, the sovereign is a ruler who does not speak *for* the commonwealth but only *to* it, or rather to its members, through its laws. Yet if the sovereign 'beareth the Person and but one Person' of the commonwealth, then when he speaks he speaks for that person, to an audience who take his words to be the commonwealth's own. Hobbes's account of persons and things personated, resting as it does on the ownership of words and actions, allows for no other possibility. His state must, therefore, require a personal identity of its own in the world of actions that it inhabits.

III

What, though, is this world of actions that the state inhabits, and in which states may be supposed to act in their own right? The state

21 *Ibid.*, p. 147.   22 Oakeshott, *On human conduct*, pp. 203–4.

does not exist within the state, so it is not a world that can be mapped on the co-ordinates given by its laws – it has none, beyond the laws of nature, which ascribe the ownership of actions to natural persons alone. Instead, it must be described through whatever encounters take place between the sovereign representative and an audience who take his words and actions to be the state's own. This audience has only two possible constituencies: either the sovereign addresses his subjects, or he addresses the sovereigns of other states. (If he addresses the members of other states, and they listen to him, it must be presumed that they are behaving as members of his state and not their own.) However, in neither of these two encounters, as described by Hobbes, is it possible to discern the presence of the person of the commonwealth behind the sovereign's words. When a subject is faced by the words of his sovereign, he encounters them as commands, issued not on the authority of the state but on the authority, specifically, of the subject himself. Each individual subject owns his sovereign's actions, and it is this that provides the grounds for obedience, 'because it is injustice for a man to do any thing for which he may be punished by his own authority'.[23] A subject can no more disown his sovereign than he can disown his own person, and he has no more use of a contract with the sovereign than he has of a contract with himself. It is true, therefore, that a sovereign addresses his subjects bearing another's person and but one other's person, but whose that person is depends in each case upon which subject is being addressed. Meanwhile, when sovereign speaks to sovereign, the criteria determining the ownership of whatever is said are simply those applying in the state of nature, 'because the Law of Nations, and the Law of Nature, is the same thing'.[24] Like a man threatened by a stranger, one sovereign may wish to know what lies behind the threats of another. But he will never discern there the person of the state. All he will find is a group of natural persons, who cannot as a group authorise the words he hears, but may find themselves as subjects committed to carrying out the threat contained in them. Indeed, it is in circumstances like these – war, or the threat of war – that a gap appears in the argument of *Leviathan* where we might reasonably expect the person of the state to be. The personalised state is a familiar enough feature in wartime – states have honour, they have responsibilities, they need protection,

---

[23] Hobbes, *Leviathan*, p. 122.   [24] *Ibid.*, p. 244.

they require sacrifice, often to the point where the lives of their subjects can no longer be considered their own. Yet nothing like this is countenanced by Hobbes. Certainly, he acknowledges that 'when the Defence of the Common-wealth, requireth at once the help of all that are able to bear Arms, every one is obliged; because otherwise the Institution of the Common-wealth, which they have not the purpose, or the courage to preserve, was in vain'.[25] But this is a last resort, reached not by a threat to the person of the commonwealth, but by a threat to the original purpose of having a commonwealth, which is to preserve the lives of its members. Otherwise, the obligations of individual subjects are to their own safety first, the commands of their sovereign next, and the person of the state not at all. Hobbes allows no circumstances in which a subject can be called upon to sacrifice himself for the common-wealth – to run away in battle may be cowardice, but because it is done for self-preservation, it can never be done 'unjustly'. More-over, a subject has no necessary duty to serve the state in his own person – when called upon to serve, he may 'without Injustice' substitute a mercenary.[26] A subject is obliged only to condition his actions in accordance with the demands of the law, and only to do so when this does not threaten his life. Between these twin pillars of individualism – the letter of the law, and death – there is no room for the person of the state to enter.

We are left, then, with no recognisable world of actions in which to place the *persona ficta* of the state, and so with an altogether intangible fiction. But though it seems to lack any substantial presence in the world of Hobbes's political philosophy, still it is unquestionably there, haunting the pages of *Leviathan* like a ghost. For example, in chapter XV, when discussing the 'Justice of Actions' under the laws of nature, Hobbes writes: 'In Common-wealths, private men may remit to one another their debts; but not robberies or other violences, whereby they are endammaged; because the detaining of Debt, is an Injury to themselves; but Robbery and Violence, are Injuries to the Person of the Common-wealth.'[27] This is a striking passage, because it appears to use the personality of the commonwealth to pre-empt the judgment of sovereigns, to whom Hobbes otherwise grants complete licence to decide what is and what is not conducive to peace. In essence, sovereigns are being prevented

---

[25] *Ibid.*, p. 152.   [26] See *ibid.*, p. 151.   [27] *Ibid.*, p. 104.

from accommodating within civil law a right of subjects not to press charges against their assailants. Why should this be so? The answer lies in Hobbes's distinction between injury – which is the result of breach of covenant – and damage – which is the result of material hurt. He explains that a man may be damaged without injury and injured without damage, as when 'a Master commandeth his servant to give mony to a stranger; [for] if it be not done, the Injury is done to the Master, whom he had before covenanted to obey; but the damage redoundeth to the stranger'.[28] On this account, the victim of violence cannot remit his injury precisely because he has suffered none, having no covenant with his assailant. But Hobbes's argument that there is nonetheless injury done to the person of the commonwealth (allowing the sovereign, its representative, to drop charges whenever he sees fit) now makes no sense, for it suggests that each subject has a covenant with the commonwealth itself, which is then master, and the subject servant. This is impossible, because the person of the commonwealth speaks only through its sovereign representative, whom Hobbes is adamant cannot contract with a subject, and without whom, he is equally adamant, there is no person of the commonwealth with whom to contract. In fact, it is only possible to make sense of this passage if we understand the injury to be done to each of the original participants in the covenant which establishes the commonwealth. That covenant constitutes what is in essence a mutual pact to give up the right to perform, as felt necessary, actions which damage others. Only the sovereign retains this right. So, to persist in such acts is an injury, not to the sovereign, nor to the person of the commonwealth, but to the natural persons who have agreed to renounce violence on condition that all others do the same. Like a ghost, the person of the commonwealth disappears if approached too closely.

It reappears in chapter XXIII, which is an account of 'the PUBLIQUE MINISTERS of Soveraign Power' – the judges, administrators, military commanders and other officers who are to be found in every state, and whom Hobbes defines as follows: 'A PUBLIQUE MINISTER, is he, that by the Soveraign, (whether a Monarch or an Assembly) is employed in any affaires, with Authority to represent in that employment, the Person of the Commonwealth.'[29] However, we learn nothing about the person of the commonwealth from this

---

[28] *Ibid.*   [29] *Ibid.*, p. 166.

definition, which is used by Hobbes to make a particular point about the courts that gather at the seat of power. Sovereigns, as men, or groups of men, always bear their natural as well as an artificial personality, and have therefore what Hobbes calls 'two Capacities, one Naturall, and another Politique, (as a Monarch, hath the Person not onely of the Common-wealth, but also of a man; and a Soveraign Assembly, hath the Person not onely of the Common-wealth, but also of the Assembly)'.[30] Both persons will require service, one from ministers, the other from personal attendants, and Hobbes wishes to distinguish the two, so that no 'Ushers, nor Seargeants, nor other Officers that waite on the Assembly . . . nor Stewards, Chamberlains, Cofferers, or any other Officers of the household of the Monarch' can claim to speak for the sovereign.[31] The person of the commonwealth is invoked here merely to establish that public ministers represent persons who are themselves representatives, and it implies nothing about the sort of service the person of the commonwealth might itself expect. Indeed, this is another instance where the person of the state is noticeable above all by its absence. The distinction between the private and public capacities of rulers has often been drawn in order to claim for the state ownership of property in its own right, and so to protect public property ('the family silver' in a famous recent coinage) from rapacious governments. But Hobbes will have none of this, insisting that 'the setting forth of Publique Land, or of any certaine Revenue for the Common-wealth, is in vaine; and tendeth to the dissolution of Govenment'.[32] The sovereign must be free to take what he thinks is needed when he thinks it is needed, as he must be free to issue whatever commands he sees fit, and to enforce them. In the prosecution of these tasks sovereigns require ministers, and lackeys are distinguished from legitimate officers of the state precisely in order to establish that it is the sovereign representative that these ministers serve.

Nevertheless, chapter XXIII does mark a considerable fleshing out of the state's personality in one important respect. It is here, for the first time since bringing persons and things personated into the argument, that Hobbes reintroduces to *Leviathan* its presiding motif, which is not of a person, but of a man, 'that great LEVIATHAN called a

---

[30] *Ibid.*   [31] *Ibid.*

[32] *Ibid.*, p. 173. For a fuller discussion of the distinction between Hobbesian and other views of state 'property', see pp. 99–102 on the 'corporation sole'.

COMMONWEALTH, or STATE (in latine CIVITAS), which is but an Artificiall Man; though of greater stature and strength than the Naturall, for whose protection and defence it was intended'.[33] A man need not be a person (unrepresented 'fooles' are not persons), any more than a bridge, because a person, must be a man. But in this and later chapters, Hobbes seems to conflate the two: ministers who represent in their different employments the person of the common-wealth are also described as 'parts Organicall' of the commonwealth, to be compared by analogy to the parts of the body. So, for example, Hobbes writes of 'all those, that have Authority from the Soveraign, to procure the Execution of judgements', that 'every act they doe by such Authority, is the act of the Commonwealth [i.e. they represent the person of the commonwealth]; and their service, answerable to that of Hands in a Bodie naturall [i.e. they represent the hands of the Leviathan]'.[34] These are two very different forms of representation: one, in Hobbes's terms, literal, a personation, albeit of an intangible fiction; the other metaphorical, a personification, albeit of something flesh and blood. By conjoining them, Hobbes identifies the person with the man, and so cloaks the state's personality in the more familiar, and more substantial, language of the living body.

But if the person is to be a man, then the Leviathan, assuming it is neither a child, a madman or a fool, must be a person – which means that Leviathan must be capable of performing its own actions, and its parts must be co-ordinated in the performance of each action. To look to the sovereign to act on its behalf is entirely question-begging at this juncture, since the image of the Leviathan is being asked to provide the state with an identity apart from the identity of its representative. The sovereign must be a part of the body, so that the body as a whole can perform its own actions, thus providing the man with neither a fictitious nor an artificial but what might best be described as a metaphorical natural personality. Unfortunately, however, in Hobbes's analogy, the sovereign is not a recognisable body part at all; instead, he compares it to 'the Publique Soule, giving Life and Motion to the Commonwealth'.[35] This analogy contrasts with the more familiar image, so often found in medieval political thought, of a ruler as the head of the body politic. The head may govern the rest of the body, but it is still part of an organic

---

[33] Hobbes, *Leviathan*, p. 9.   [34] *Ibid.*, p. 169.
[35] *Ibid.*, p. 230. Hobbes is making a play here on the Latin, in which 'soul' becomes *anima*: it is the *anima* that 'animates'.

whole, and it cannot be said alone to give it life. Like the hands, the head has a part to play in the performance of an action. But the soul represents nothing less than action itself – without it, the body of the commonwealth is entirely lifeless, a mere 'Carcasse of a man'.[36] It is true that the soul, in Hobbes's materialistic world, is naturally a part of the living body, and can have no natural existence apart from it.[37] But the Leviathan, it must equally be remembered, is not a natural man. It is artificial, an automaton, or machine, which is able to replicate the living man only because, for Hobbes, 'life is but a motion of the Limbs'.[38] The commonwealth lives because it moves, and it moves because of its sovereign.

In truth, Hobbes's analogy is an unsatisfactory one. Natural men, unlike machines, are subject to two sorts of motion: one Hobbes calls '*Vitall*', which is the activity of the body 'begun in generation, and continued without interruption [its] whole life through',[39] exemplified by the motion of the blood through the veins; the other he calls '*Voluntary*', which is motion begun in the 'Imagination', depending 'always upon a precedent thought of *whither, which way* and *what*'.[40] In natural men, the origins of motions of this second kind are in 'the Act of Willing', which can be understood (though Hobbes himself does not put it in these terms) as the process whereby the activity of the body is turned into actions. If artificial men are to be distinguished from natural men (and the word automaton has no meaning unless they are), it must be because in their case this distinction no longer holds. Machines are simply the sum of the activity – the vital motions – of their component parts. To speak of the soul of a machine, therefore, is to invoke a peculiarly unhelpful image. If machines are simply activity, then the soul is simply that which activates them, and machines are activated by whomever sets them up. No machine, as Hobbes would be the first to admit, is self-starting, so no machine can contain its soul. Meanwhile, if machines are to be taken to perform actions, then they must be provided with a will, and since no machine possesses a will 'naturally', each machine will be possessed of an artificial soul. In this sense, artificial men and natural men are quite distinct, as Hobbes acknowledges, when he speaks of the sovereign as the Leviathan's 'Immortall

---

[36] *Ibid.*
[37] For Hobbes, the idea of 'a Naturall Immortality of the Soule' was one of the absurdities of Aristotelianism, an instance of 'the Error of *Separated Essences*' (see *ibid.*, pp. 430ff.).
[38] *Ibid.*, p. 9.   [39] *Ibid.*, p. 37.   [40] *Ibid.*, p. 38.

Soule'.[41] The souls of natural men, on Hobbes's account, share their natural deaths. But the souls of machines are separate from the motion of their bodies, with the result that any actions performed may be said to be the soul's own. All of which makes Hobbes's organic imagery, in the case of the Leviathan, somewhat anomalous. The organs of the commonwealth – not just its hands, but the judges who are its voice, the ambassadors who are its eyes, and so on – all facilitate the performance of actions. As such, they collectively embody not the artificial man but its soul, the sovereign: when judges speak, they speak for the sovereign; when ambassadors observe, they observe for the sovereign; and, as Hobbes himself puts it, 'those that are appointed to receive Petitions and other informations of the People, and are as it were the publique Eare . . . represent the Soveraign in that office'.[42] The ears of a man do not represent his soul in a listening capacity. The fact that they do, as it were, in an automaton is just what determines that it is not an organism but a machine.

It is possible to make more sense of Hobbes's organic imagery as it is subsequently applied in chapter XXIX, where he depicts the 'Infirmities [that] tend to the dissolution of a Common-wealth'.[43] The infirmities that afflict a natural man can be divided into two categories: those (like, say, blindness) which impair voluntary motion, and so threaten a man's capacity to act; and those (like, say, heart disease) which impair vital motion, and so threaten a man's capacity to live. Many of the diseases to which Hobbes compares the afflictions that can beset a commonwealth are of this second kind, for example 'Pleurisie' (otherwise 'Farmes of the Publique Revenue'), and 'Ague' ('Want of Mony').[44] Both these ailments play on Hobbes's earlier description of money as the life-blood of the commonwealth, its most vital motion, which if 'congealed' or 'inflammed' can lead to death. Thus the Leviathan does not have to be seen performing actions in order to be seen to live and die. However, there are other diseases which threaten its life and which are, for Hobbes, if anything more dangerous. These are the afflictions which introduce to the body not an impairment to vital motion but rather alternative motions to those activated by the sovereign. One he likens, somewhat bizarrely, to '*Hydrophobia*',[45] which results from the prevalence of

---

[41] See *ibid.*, p. 230. [42] *Ibid.*, p. 169. [43] *Ibid.*, p. 221.
[44] See *ibid.*, p. 229. [45] See *ibid.*, p. 226.

seditious opinion. The most dangerous of all has no technical name; it is the analogue of 'mixt Monarchy', and Hobbes writes:

> To what Disease in the Naturall Body of man, I may exactly compare this irregularity of a Common-wealth, I know not. But I have seen a man, that had another growing out of his side, with a head, armes, breast and stomach, of his own: If he had another man growing out of his other side, the comparison might then have been exact.[46]

Of course, like much of the argument of *Leviathan*, this is highly rhetorical. Nevertheless, it has important bearings on the conceptual premises of that argument as well. For the type of 'body' whose life is most immediately threatened if it contains separate or disjointed vital motions is not an organism at all, but an automaton: a man, after all, could conceivably survive (as we now know) with more than one body, but a machine pulled in different directions must by definition break down. And though the image of a diseased machine is perhaps an obscure one, it makes sense in Hobbes's terms: machines, like men, and other animals, die when they cease to move, and anything in the workings of a machine that will eventually terminate movement constitutes a terminal illness. Ultimately, then, Hobbes's organicism is as applicable to the watch to which the Leviathan is first of all compared as it is to the commonwealth itself: both may suffer from what he calls 'intestine disorder', in which case both, unless repaired, will die.[47]

IV

At first sight, Hobbes's organic imagery, like his attribution to the state of its own personality, is hard to reconcile with Oakeshott's claim that the Leviathan is an unequivocal *societas*, for it was the corporate *universitas*, not the impersonal partnership, that was commonly described in corporeal terms. Yet Hobbes's peculiarly mechanistic organicism, like his peculiarly intangible state personality, hardly of themselves suggest an alternative to Oakeshott's reading either. If the Leviathan, like a watch, lives and dies, then so does a *societas*, which ceases to exist when its internal contractual arrangements break down[48] – and as a result Hobbes's corporeal language

---

[46] *Ibid.*, p. 228.   [47] See *ibid.*, pp. 9 and 221.

[48] A partnership is dissolved either when one of the partners dies (i.e. when one of the parts stops working) or when one or more of the partners refuse to accord to the terms of the original contract (i.e. when the parts cease to work together). When this happens the

of bodies and their motions need not lead to the corporate language of persons and their actions. One insuperable problem remains, however, for Oakeshott's characterisation of Hobbes's state. For even if it is true that *corpus* and *universitas* – the Leviathan and the corporation – might be counted as distinct concepts in Hobbes's work, it is also true that the author himself, in one famous instance, fails to distinguish them. Of all the infirmities to which common-wealths are prone, perhaps the most memorable is the one that results from 'the great number of Corporations; which are as it were many lesser Common-wealths in the bowels of a greater, like wormes in the entrayles of a naturall man'.[49] Again, these words are primarily memorable *as* an image, and a purely historical study of *Leviathan* would look to their rhetorical significance, and to discover which particular corporations might have provoked the deployment of such striking language.[50] Yet whatever Hobbes's polemical purpose here, the image only makes sense if commonwealth and corporation can be understood in equivalent terms – if the corporation is but a lesser commonwealth, then the commonwealth must be but a greater corporation. Moreover, this is not simply a terminological issue. It bears upon one of Oakeshott's most important distinctions, between the state seen as a *societas* and the state seen as a *universitas*. Of the latter, Oakeshott writes:

Just as [it] cannot tolerate performances eccentric or indifferent to the pursuit of the purpose which constitutes the association, so it cannot accommodate other purposive associations [i.e. *universitates*] whose purposes are eccentric or indifferent to its purposes. There can be unregulated variety of self-chosen associations only where the state is not itself a purposive association. What we call 'minority' associations can exist only where the state is recognised in the terms of civil association [i.e. as a *societas*]; and there they require no authorisation.[51]

remaining partners, if they wish to continue in partnership, must draw up a new contract and thereby create a new *societas*. A *societas* can only endure so long as each of its parts remain in a fixed relation to one another. Otherwise it 'dies'.

[49] *Ibid.*, p. 230.

[50] In fact he was thinking of the great city corporations, such as the Corporation of the City of London, which supported parliament against the king during the civil war; in the Latin *Leviathan* he gives 'the great number of Corporations' as '*oppidorum incorporatorum multitudo*' (see Hobbes, *Opera philosophica*, ed. W. Molesworth, 5 vols. (London, 1839–45), vol. III, p. 239). However, it is also true that in the original English *Leviathan* Hobbes uses the word 'Corporation' to describe any group of merchants who have formed themselves into an association (in the Latin he simply calls such groups '*systema mercatorum*'). In the Latin *Leviathan* he reserves the word '*universitas*' to describe what in English he calls, and we should still call, universities.

[51] Oakeshott, *On human conduct*, p. 316.

Hobbes's state does not allow for unregulated corporate activity, and the reason is precisely that the state itself is of the same species of association as the corporations that it contains. Hobbes's state cannot, therefore, be understood as a *societas*. Of course, this would be a large claim to rest solely on the basis of one exceptionally visceral image. It does, however, have a solid conceptual grounding also. Oakeshott argues that where the state is conceived as a *societas*, other associations require no authorisation. But Hobbes, in chapter XXII of *Leviathan*, argues that other associations than the common-wealth can only exist on the 'Authority Soveraign'.[52] This statement, as we shall see, is integral to the whole argument of the book. And as a result of chapter XXII of *Leviathan*, Oakeshott's division of European political thought into two categories, and his subsequent categorisation of Hobbes, finally collapses.

The subject of chapter XXII is 'systemes', which Hobbes describes as follows:

'By SYSTEMES; I understand any numbers of men joyned in one Interest, or Businesse. Of which, some are *Regular*, and some *Irregular*. *Regular* are those, where one Man, or Assembly of men, is constituted Representative of the whole number. All others are Irregular.

Of Regular, some are *Absolute*, and *Independent*, subject to none but their own Representative: such are only Common-wealths . . . Others are Dependent; that is to say, Subordinate to some Soveraign Power, to which every one, as also their Representative is *Subject*.

Of Systemes subordinate, some are *Politicall*, and some *Private*. *Politicall* (otherwise Called *Bodies Politique* and *Persons in Law*) are those, which are made by authority from the Soveraign Power of the Common-wealth. *Private*, are those, which are constituted by subjects among themselves, or by authoritie from a stranger . . .

And of Private Systemes, some are *Lawfull*; some *Unlawfull*: *Lawfull* are those which are allowed by the Common-wealth: all others are *Unlawfull*. *Irregular* Systemes, are those which having no Representative, consist only in concourse of People.[53]

To summarise this passage in less Hobbesian language: groups of human beings are of two kinds – crowds (irregular) and associations (regular, having a representative); associations can be constituted in two ways – either in law (political) or independently of it (private); private associations can be constituted in two ways also – either by their members (subjects) or some foreign power (a stranger); all associations in law are by definition legal, but some private associa-

---

[52] See Hobbes, *Leviathan*, p. 156.   [53] *Ibid.*, p. 155.

tions may be illegal. In fact, later in the chapter, Hobbes allows only one example of a legal private association, which is the family.[54] The rest of the chapter is devoted to demonstrating that all other associations must be sanctioned by the sovereign (i.e. they must be 'bodies politique'). The reasoning behind this is clear. All groups of natural men apart from crowds accord to one model – they are associations with a single representative. The sovereign is such a representative of such an association. Therefore, all representatives of all associations are potentially sovereign. But if any other association than the commonwealth has a sovereign there can be no commonwealth, because no commonwealth can contain more than one sovereign. Hobbes expresses it thus:

> In Bodies Politique, the power of the Representative is alwaies Limited: And that which prescribeth the Limits thereof, is the Power Soveraign. For Power Unlimited, is absolute Soveraignty. And the Soveraign, in every Common-wealth, is the absolute Representative of all the subjects; and therefore no other, can be Representative of any part of them, but so far forth, as he shall give leave.[55]

Hobbes's state cannot allow unregulated association, because all associations follow the model of the state.

This argument would inevitably have had a particular significance for Hobbes's contemporaries, and he is not slow to point out that among the representatives who can act only where and when permitted to do so by the sovereign are 'the Deputies' authorised by the sovereign 'to enforme him of the conditions, and necessities of the Subjects, or to advise with him, for the making of good Lawes';[56] that is, parliaments. Hobbes accepts that a parliament may 'represent every Subject of [the] Dominion',[57] but for precisely that reason it can meet only when summoned by the sovereign and only to discuss matters put to it by the sovereign; 'and when it shall be declared that nothing more shall be propounded, or debated by them, the Body is dissolved'.[58] Hobbes is quite clear that a representative assembly must be the entire creation of the sovereign if it is not itself to be sovereign (though of course the sovereign itself might still be an assembly). It is equally clear, however, that his argument does not apply simply to what we should now think of a 'representative

---

[54] See *ibid.*, pp. 162–3. Here Hobbes relies on the familiar argument that families are associations in their own right because 'the Father, or Master [is] before the Institution of Common-wealth, absolute Soveraign in their own Families'.

[55] *Ibid.*, pp. 155–6.   [56] *Ibid.*, p. 162.   [57] *Ibid.*   [58] *Ibid.*

assemblies'; it holds for all manner of associations, among them 'Bodies Politique for the ordering of Trade'[59] – what we should now think of as 'corporations'. Hobbes writes that 'the variety of Bodies Politique is almost infinite', by which he means to convey both the 'unspeakable diversitie' of purposes which lead men to form associations, and also the fact that every association is distinct, because every association is constituted by the sovereign, its 'times, places and numbers, subject to many limitations'.[60] Almost any group of men *might* form an association, but no group *may* do so except where authorised. In fact, Hobbes allows two distinct modes of authorisation, one by the granting of 'Letters Patent . . . withall sealed, or testified, with the Seales, or other permanent signes of the Authority Soveraign', the other through 'ordinary Lawes, common to all Subjects'.[61] Hobbes is not insisting, as earlier jurists often had, that a corporation can only be created by an explicit act of 'concession' on the part of the sovereign.[62] But this is essentially a practical consideration. The setting of limitations on the actions of every representative is 'not alwaies easie, or perhaps possible to be described in writing'; so more general laws 'must determine, what the Representative may lawfully do, in all Cases, where the Letters themselves are silent'.[63]

The letters, or laws, of association shape bodies politic; they also shape them into persons. For this is the one certain point in *Leviathan* where bodies and persons are the same – 'Bodies Politique' are otherwise called 'Persons in Law', and when their representatives act, they act 'in the Person of the Body'.[64] In truth, the personality of these bodies is set out by Hobbes in essentially negative terms. When a representative performs some act which is not warranted by the terms of association, then it is 'his act, not the act of the Body, nor of any other Member beside himself'.[65] (In this respect, it is a form of representation quite different from that undertaken by the sovereign, whose every act is the act of those he represents.) The person of the authorised association cannot behave unlawfully because it is by definition lawful – it is a person in law. (The person of the commonwealth cannot behave unlawfully either, but for a very different reason – its representative, as sovereign, is outside the law.)

[59] *Ibid.*, p. 160.   [60] *Ibid.*, p. 158.   [61] *Ibid.*, p. 156.
[62] For a more detailed discussion of the 'concession theory' see below, pp. 49–50 and pp. 93–4.
[63] Hobbes, *Leviathan*, p. 156.   [64] *Ibid.*   [65] *Ibid.*

But still, Hobbes does allow for two sorts of punishment of representatives which is also punishment of the bodies they represent. One is 'forfeiture of their Letters, (which is to such artificiall and fictitious bodies, capitall)'.[66] The other, applicable where there is a 'Common stock' which does not belong to the individual members of the association, is 'pecuniary Mulct'.[67] Thus bodies politic have a life apart from the lives of their members (who do not die when they do), and they may possess property independently of their members (who do not pay penalties when they do). Here we have tangible, if fictitious, group persons inhabiting an identifiable world of actions. A person of this kind is not a fiction in the original sense Hobbes gives that term in chapter XVI, because the members of a body politic do not own the body and then appoint a representative for their property. (They may form an association in order to own property in common, but they cannot own property in common before they form the association.) Rather, it is a fictitious person as the commonwealth is a fictitious person – a multitude of men made one person when they are by one person represented. And in contrast to the case of the commonwealth it is not hard to discern the uses that bodies politic might make of their own personality. If their representatives act lawfully, bodies politic can own a name, reside at an address, enter into contracts, accumulate property, even do work overseas.[68] Members can also make use of the personality of their associations – because representation must be limited, the liability of members must be limited also. Unlike the commonwealth, therefore, bodies politic inhabit a recognisable world: it is what we might understand, in the broadest sense, as the world of corporate activity.

So we are returned to a familiar problem. Hobbes's account of 'systemes' provides us with substantive group persons, but only within the state. The 'fiction' of their personality can be given substance there by 'artifice' – Hobbes states explicitly that persons in law are bodies both 'fictitious and artificial'[69] – and the artificer is the sovereign. Indeed, the sovereign is 'author' of these fictions in a

---

[66] *Ibid.*, p. 157. [67] *Ibid.*
[68] Among the systems Hobbes discusses in chapter XXII are 'Bodies Politique for Government of a Province, Colony or Town'. These include the 'Companies' that were set up 'when there were Colonies sent from England, to Plant Virginia, and Sommer-Ilands' (see *ibid.*, p. 159). For an account of Hobbes's first-hand experience of the workings of one of these companies see N. Malcolm, 'Hobbes, Sandys and the Virginia Company', *Historical Journal*, 24, 297–321.
[69] See Hobbes, *Leviathan*, p. 157.

non-technical as well as a technically Hobbesian sense, because, like a writer, and moreover in words, the sovereign determines the fictitious world they inhabit. Of the commonwealth we learn only that it is a fiction, and to learn only that Emma Bovary, say, is a fiction is to discover only what she is not (she is not real). But in the case of bodies politic, we are presented with the act as well as the fact of creation – artifice as well as fiction – and in consequence we know where to look to discover what these persons are, as we know to look to the book to discover the facts about Madame Bovary. Associations are described in 'letters'. In this sense, the state remains distinct from the groups it contains, because the state cannot be given a comparable identity. The sovereign 'authorises' in the person of the state, so for the state to play the part of a person in law is for the fiction to write the book (*Madame Bovary* cannot both be a novel and also an autobiography ghosted by Flaubert). Nevertheless, this distinction between the state and 'minority' associations in no way accords to the distinction drawn by Oakeshott. If Hobbes's commonwealth is a different entity from the corporations within it, it is because their corporate personality lies in its gift. In other words, the Hobbesian state establishes an identity distinct from that of the *universitas* in the very act of regulating associational life, and not, as Oakeshott argues, by leaving it unregulated. And the reverse is equally true. If the commonwealth is to have a tangible personality of its own, then it must be allowed that corporate persons can come into being without prior authorisation by the sovereign. The Hobbesian state can only be understood as a *universitas* if *universitates* are seen to exist independently of it. Oakeshott suggests that the existence of unauthorised corporations is the best possible evidence that the state can be understood as a *societas*. In Hobbes's case, it is the best possible evidence that the state can be understood as something else.

This second possibility, that unauthorised corporate personality can be attained outside the law, is not ruled out by the argument of chapter XXII, despite its emphasis on the necessity of proper authorisation. By allowing that illegal associations do exist, even if their existence is to be curtailed wherever possible, Hobbes seems to accept that subjects can replicate the conditions of group personality without invoking the mechanism of legal recognition. Moreover, his later identification of corporations as the 'wormes' of state presupposes just this possibility – after all, were all corporate activity strictly controlled by the terms of association drawn up by the sovereign, no corporation could ever constitute a threat to the state. There are, then, some associations, other than the family, which are able to generate their own personality. Three things can be said of such groups. First, their personality must be a fiction that the group's members create for themselves. They 'authorise' it in the non-technical sense outlined above – they invent and give definition to a person distinct from their own persons and also from the person of their representative. This fiction will not be described in 'letters'; therefore, it must be a fiction which the members already understand. The members must believe in the group. Second, if private associations can have such a personality, then so can the state. Its members too can comprehend a separate person of the commonwealth without that person having a technical 'author'. The state can be a person, but only if its members are already prepared to believe in the personality of the state. Third, if the state does not have such a personality, its members may notice the lack. They may feel towards the associations in whose personality they believe a loyalty which the state, unless possessed of its own personality, cannot match. The state will always have more power, in the person of the sovereign, who can command as he sees fit, and so outlaw any association. But loyalty is more than obedience to command (an obedient dog is not necessarily a loyal one). If the state does not generate its own personality, its members will still have to obey their sovereign; but they may place their untapped loyalties elsewhere.

v

Ultimately, Hobbes's account of the personality of associations, including the state, is equivocal. It equivocates between two conceptions of order (or, in Hobbes's terms, peace). The first, and dominant conception is that of juristic order – by which peace is understood as the absence of war. Juristic order rests on sovereignty, and is exercised through law. It does not require that the state be a person, only that the sovereign should represent the persons of his individual subjects. It is a conception compatible with an understanding of the state as a *societas*. It is, however, a narrow idea. It involves the regulation of all group activity. And it creates a state resting on the principle of command, and so at the mercy of whoever happens to be in command. A second, and fuller conception is that of moral order – by which peace might be understood in terms of virtue. One guarantee of moral order is a dutiful sovereign, and the duties of sovereignty are set out by Hobbes in chapter XXX of *Leviathan* ('Of the Office of the Soveraign Representative'). Another is the granting to the state of its own personality. Where the state is understood as a person distinct from the persons of both sovereign and subjects, both sovereign and subjects share a common understanding of the state. As a result, conditions of reciprocal loyalty may arise, so guarding against the moral chaos that the unfettered exercise of sovereign power can bring in its wake. Unfortunately, however, the personality of the state does not make sense in the terms of juristic order; as we have seen, the essentially juristic account of persons and things personated given in chapter XVI is insufficient to generate a tangible person of the state. Instead, it must arise out of the understanding that groups come to have of themselves. Thus it is possible for the state to generate its own personality, but only if other groups can do likewise. And this means that moral order will be opposed to juristic order, for the latter depends upon a categorical distinction between the state and all other groups. Where the state has a personality alongside that of other groups, it must compete with them for the loyalty of their members, and it is not a competition that it is certain to win. It is, of course, certain to win any competition based on power, but victory in such a contest is no guarantee of virtue. *Leviathan* represents perhaps the most rigorous of all attempts to reconcile virtue with power – indeed, Hobbes manages to derive both from one basic rule, '*to seek Peace, and follow it*'.[70] Yet with regard to the personality of the state, and the associations within it, they remain unreconciled.

Personality is also the issue on which Oakeshott's categorisation of *Leviathan* founders. This does not mean that the state described by Hobbes, because capable of being understood as a person, is in the wrong category. Rather, the terms of Oakeshott's argument are simply not applicable in Hobbes's case, and to view *Leviathan* in those terms is to misrepresent it in two distinct ways. First, though it is true that Hobbes's commonwealth, like a *societas*, is founded on a contractual arrangement among individuals to abide by certain rules, the contract itself stipulates only one rule, which is to authorise the sovereign. Oakeshott argues that a civil association must rest on the 'loyalty [of its members] to one another'; a loyalty determined by

---

[70] See *ibid.*, p. 92.

their common acceptance of certain 'rules of conduct'.[71] But the conduct of Hobbes's *cives* is shaped by the relation of each to the commands of their sovereign, not by their relation to each other. A common loyalty requires something more, and that something is provided by the personality of the state. Second, Hobbes's state cannot be understood as analogous to one or other of the associations of private law, for the simple reason that Hobbes's political philosophy includes an account of these associations. In *Leviathan*, all groups apart from crowds are constituted by the artificial person of their representative. Thus all associations are analogous, and the character of the state depends on the degree of difference between it and the other bodies to which it might otherwise be compared. Oakeshott's conceptual framework cannot accommodate this fact. Yet without it, it is impossible to account for the character of Hobbes's civil association, which is both less tolerant, and more equivocal, than Oakeshott would allow.

[71] Oakeshott, *On human conduct*, p. 201.

CHAPTER 3

Gierke and the 'Genossenschaft'

I

Parts of Otto von Gierke's *Das deutsche Genossenschaftsrecht*,[1] to which we may now turn, bear a superficial resemblance to Oakeshott's survey of European ideas of the state. Like Oakeshott, Gierke placed great emphasis on the competing claims of the *societas* and the *universitas* as modes of conceptualising the state. And like Oakeshott, he found a special place at the heart of his story for the writing of Thomas Hobbes. But here the resemblances end. Gierke's story is quite different from Oakeshott's, and the Hobbes who emerges from it shares with Oakeshott's hero only the virtues of his intellectual courage (Gierke calls it 'his Radical audacity'[2]); in other regards, he is an equivocal figure, and his ideas are treated by Gierke with circumspection bordering on regret. Above all, Gierke's Hobbes is historical, and his character is determined by the particular sort of history he inhabits. For Oakeshott, the basic models of *societas* and *universitas* serve to divide up the history of political ideas, and then to transcend differences between theorists on one or other side of this divide. Thus the language of political thought might change – Hegel's civil association is not described in the terms of Bodin's – but the ideas being described remain essentially the same. But for Gierke ideas can never be understood in such static terms, and nor can they be understood apart from the historical conditions surrounding their

---

[1] *Das deutsche Genossenschaftsrecht* was published in four volumes in Germany, the first appearing in 1868 (under the title *Rechtsgeschichte der deutschen Genossenschaft*), the second in 1873 (*Geschichte des deutschen Körperschaftsbegriff*), the third in 1881 (*Die Staats- und Korporationslehre des Altertums und des Mittelalters und ihre Aufnahme in Deutschland*) and the fourth in 1913 (*Die Staats- und Korporationslehre der Neuzeit*). It is only portions of volumes I, III and IV that have been translated into English, and these are the translations listed in the bibliography, to which detailed reference is made in what follows.

[2] O. von Gierke, *Natural law and the theory of society, 1500–1800*, trans. E. Barker (Cambridge, 1934), p. 37.

formation. For Gierke was himself a Hegelian. The history provided by *Das deutsche Genossenschaftsrecht* is dialectical, and its primary concern is with the ways in which ideas change. In it, models of political thought are seen to react upon each other, and these models not only shape but are shaped by the language in which they are expressed. Thus ideas and themes which Oakeshott must keep distinct Gierke renders interdependent. Both men, of course, recognise Hobbes's genius. But whereas for one it is transcendent, and issues in integrity, for the other it remains contingent, and it issues only in accelerated change.

The overall process of change described by Gierke is a highly complicated one, and it involves many different dialectical relations. This can readily be illustrated by the part played within it by the two associational models of Roman private law, the *societas* and the *universitas*. After the demise of the Empire ruled from Rome, but more particularly with the revival of Roman law at the beginning of the twelfth century, these conceptions were employed in a variety of different contexts, and for a variety of different ends – by Romanists, by canonists, and later by natural-law theorists, in the formulation of what Gierke calls publicistic doctrine, and we should call political theory. These new intellectual enterprises often made use of both of the Roman models together, with the result that the two conceptions reacted upon each other. Still it remained possible, in Gierke's terms, to identify each conception with one of two distinct modes of theoretical discourse – the *societas* with the language of the mechanism, the *universitas* with the language of the organism – with the result that juristic concepts came increasingly to be expressed in other than juristic terms. Meanwhile, Roman ideas in general were involved in an altogether separate engagement with what Gierke calls 'Germanism'. Most significant of all Germanist ideas was the *Genossenschaft* of Gierke's title (usually translated as 'fellowship') which provided an alternative understanding of group life to that given in Roman law. The nature and significance of this alternative will be discussed below. For now, it is sufficient to point out that the dialectical relations of the concepts of *societas* and *universitas* to each other, to contemporary disputes in political theory, and to the language of political argument were all played out in the broader context of a cultural struggle between Romanism and Germanism. Unsurprisingly, the resulting dialectical complexities are formidable. Nevertheless, it remains possible to establish three dominant themes in Gierke's work. The first is what he calls the 'intimate connection . . . between legal philosophy and political theory'.[3] The second is the equally intimate connection between theory in general and the contingencies of changing historical circumstance. And the third is an on-going, all-encompassing struggle between two different, and irreconcilable, conceptions of order.

Each of these themes must be understood dialectically, but in the case of the most significant, the third, the dialectic is of a particular kind: it describes the interplay of ideas between which Gierke, quite explicitly, took sides. To put it at its simplest, Gierke sought in *Das deutsche Genossenschaftsrecht* to champion Germanist conceptions of order against their Romanist counterparts. But it would be wrong to characterise Gierke's argument simply in terms of a conflict between Roman and German ideas. The struggle between the two different conceptions of order which dominates his work also permeates all parts of it: it can be discovered both within Roman thought (in the contrast between the *societas* and the *universitas*) and within German thought (in the contrast between *Herrschaft* and *Genossenschaft*) as well as in the clash between them; it might be discerned in economic and social as well as juristic and political history; and it could be described by Gierke both in miniature, within the work of a single theorist (like, for example, Hobbes), and also on the broadest scale, in the clash between what he calls 'antique-modern' and 'medieval' thinking. None of these conflicts of ideas is independent; each must be viewed in the light of its relation to the idea of the work as a whole.

It is possible to summarise this idea, which is the focus of each of these conflicts, in terms of a distinction already drawn in relation to Hobbes – the distinction between juristic and moral conceptions of order. Gierke was always on the side of the latter, which he believed to be characteristic of, though not exhausted by, Germanic life and thought, and against the narrower, more legalistic notions which were typically derived from Roman law. Again, though, this risks oversimplifying the issue. Gierke's insistence on the interdependence of political theory and jurisprudence means that he understood *all* conceptions of order to have a juristic basis – including all conceptions derived from the moral life of the 'teutonic peoples', for which Gierke found juristic expression in what he calls 'folk-law'. For this reason, the argument of *Das deutsche Genossenschaftsrecht* is better

---

[3] *Ibid.*, p. 36.

summarised in terms of a struggle between two different, if somewhat abstract, conceptions of group unity. Each of these conceptions is applicable to any of those groups Hobbes called 'systemes' and to a good many others besides, and though they are mutually exclusive, neither has any exclusive connection with a particular body of law. By the first conception, groups are seen to have what Gierke would call a 'unity-in-plurality': that is, a unity which is consequent upon some arrangement between a group's individual members, such that the parts come before the whole. By the other, groups have a 'plurality-in-unity': that is, a unity which is prior to, and in some senses determinant of, the individuality of a group's members; the whole comes before the parts. 'Unity-in-plurality' is the 'antique-modern' conception, the typical preference of both Roman and natural-law theorists, exemplified by the model of the *societas* and usually couched in the mechanistic language of contract. 'Plurality-in-unity' is the 'medieval' conception, typically Germanic, exemplified by the *Genossenschaft*, and associated with the language of organicism. (The *universitas*, which can be opposed to both the *societas* and the *Genossenschaft*, and which is a concept both quintessentially Roman and quintessentially medieval, stands, as we shall see, uncertainly between the two.) There is, however, one further distinction between 'unity-in-plurality' and 'plurality-in-unity' which is of particular significance: in Gierke's terms, groups possessed of the former could only have an artificial or fictitious personality; but groups possessed of the latter might be understood as persons in their own right, in the manner of the natural man. Clearly, Gierke's terms here are not Hobbes's, for whom the idea of natural group person-ality is essentially a contradiction in terms. Moreover, Gierke tended to speak of group personality not as something 'natural' but as something 'real', a category of person for which Hobbes had no use.[4] But Gierke's terms do still apply to Hobbes, as they do to each aspect of the story he tells. In order to make satisfactory sense of that story, it is necessary to say something more about the manner in which it unfolds. And the easiest place to start is somewhere towards the end, with Gierke's interpretation of the argument contained in *Leviathan*.

---

[4] 'Real' stands in opposition to 'fictitious' as 'natural' stands in opposition to 'artificial' (an artificial lake may not be 'natural' but it is still 'real' in a way that a fictitious lake is not). For Hobbes, persons which were not fictitious were either natural or artificial. It went without saying that both natural and artificial persons (which were always men or assemblies of men) were real, i.e. that they really did speak and act.

II

Gierke's account of Hobbes's thought[5] comes in the fourth, and final, volume of *Das deutsche Genossenschaftsrecht*, which was published in 1913, though written twenty years earlier. The theme of this last volume is 'the theory of the State and Corporation in modern times', and the major part of it is devoted to an exposition of natural-law theory. Gierke divides the history of natural-law theory into two sections: the first covers the period down to 1650; the second, the period from the middle of the seventeenth to the beginning of the nineteenth century. His choice of this dividing point is not arbitrary. It marks the decisive moment in the development of natural-law theory – the point at which Hobbes, 'wielding a remorseless logic', altered its course for ever, when 'he wrested a single State-personality from the individualistic philosophy of Natural Law'.[6]

The period before this breakthrough is characterised by Gierke as one of intellectual conflict, driven by the conflict between its two dominant themes. The first of these is the problem of sovereignty, by which natural-law theorists were required to identify the pre-eminent authority within the state; the second is the language of the *societas*, which is essentially contract; and the issue between them (before Hobbes resolved it), that the language of contract was unable to generate a sovereignty that was single. Instead, sovereignty was permanently divided between the two parties to the contract of government, the people and their rulers, each of whom, as partners in contract, had rights against the other. The result, as Gierke saw it, was confusion. On the one hand, the requirement that sovereignty be founded on the basis of contract left the state in a condition of

---

[5] Gierke's sources are in fact the Latin *Leviathan* (drawn up by Hobbes himself in 1668) and also Hobbes's earlier work *De cive* (first published in its original Latin in 1642). I have based my account on *Leviathan* because it is there that Hobbes gives by far his fullest account of persons and things personated. How and why he arrived at this developed position is an interesting question in its own right, which cannot be discussed here. Gierke himself makes little of the differences between the two works, invariably citing one alongside the other. The only direct contrast he draws concerns the question of whether or not the person of the commonwealth can 'sin'. This question is not discussed in *Leviathan*, but in *De cive* Hobbes argues that the state cannot sin, since sins are offences against natural law, which hold for natural men only. This Gierke compares to the argument contained in chapter XXII of *Leviathan*, where Hobbes allows that a delict can be attributed simultaneously to a 'systeme' and to its individual members. The difference between these two positions Gierke explains as the difference between *peccatum* (sin) and *delictum* (legal offence): one, as a 'natural' matter, cannot hold for any system; the other, as a civil matter, can hold for any system except the commonwealth, which is not subject to civil law.

[6] Gierke, *Natural law*, p. 61.

ever greater disunity, riven by the rival claims of the contracting parties. On the other hand, attempts to unify the state by claiming pre-eminence for one or other of these parties often had little or no contractual basis, and natural-law theorists incorporated within arguments ostensibly resting on the concept of the *societas*, ideas drawn from other, less 'natural' sources. In essence, the search for a single sovereignty left natural-law theorists still dependent upon ideas which originated in medieval corporation theory, where alone was generated the unity on which single sovereignty seemed to depend. Thus the state as *societas* depended upon the idea of the *universitas* to prevent it from falling apart.

Gierke explains this dependence in terms of personality; and personality he understands in terms of rights. Sovereignty, for Gierke, as for many German jurists, is one of the rights of public law, and rights, in German jurisprudence, are always borne by persons. There can be no single sovereignty, therefore, without a single person to bear it, and contract cannot generate single personality. For just as the contract of government cannot unite the state, so contract cannot create a unified person within the state to whom sovereignty can be ascribed. It only creates *societates*, which are, as Gierke puts it (in terms of which Hobbes would approve) 'mere systems . . . of individuals'.[7] Thus attempts to render either the people, or their rulers, a single person tended to fall back on the non-natural 'fictions' of corporate unity,[8] and to embrace the organicist terminology in which such unity was commonly expressed. The presiding spirit of natural-law theory was mechanistic – its political structures were built out of nature rather than by nature – and yet, Gierke points out, 'there was hardly a single system of political theory which entirely escaped [the] "organic" tendency of thought'.[9]

Hobbes, who did most of all to bring this era to a close, was also himself a part of it. The conceptual language of *Leviathan* is the mechanistic language of contract; yet, as Gierke acknowledges, the

---

[7] See *ibid.*, p. 45.

[8] These include, for example, what Gierke calls the 'fiction' of majority-voting – that is 'the identification of majority-will with the common will of all' (see *ibid.*, p. 47). This idea was consistent with the principles of the Roman law of corporations (*universitates*), but it was not consistent with the Roman law of partnerships (*societates*), which required that all decisions be agreed unanimously. The 'fiction' of majority-voting was utilised by Hobbes in order to allow for sovereign assemblies, but Hobbes did not depend upon it, since his commonwealth could (and, wherever possible, should) be built without recourse to it, utilising instead the unanimous contract in the state of nature in order to authorise a monarchy.

[9] *Ibid.*, pp. 51–2.

Leviathan itself is frequently presented as an organism, such that Hobbes is able 'to expound, in minutest of detail, its analogies with a living being'.[10] What distinguishes Hobbes from earlier natural-law theorists is that this conceptual and terminological confusion was in his case unnecessary: he does not need to fall back on organicism because his argument makes sense in purely mechanistic terms. Of course, this raises the interesting historical question of why Hobbes nevertheless chose to employ the imagery of the living body. But Gierke is not really interested in this point. What concerns him is Hobbes's remarkable achievement in rescuing natural-law theory from the apparently irreconcilable tensions within it – between *societas* and sovereignty, partnership and personality – by providing a purely contractual basis for the unified state. He showed that the state did not have to be understood in the terms of the *universitas* in order to be a person, nor to be described in the language of the organism in order to be whole.

This achievement, as Gierke interprets it, was doubly significant. First, it solved the problem of single sovereignty. But second, it revealed how little was achieved by doing so. For Hobbes was only able to arrive at the single personality of the group through the artificial personality of its representative, and artificial personality, in Gierke's terms, was an inadequate basis on which to rest the personality of the state. Indeed, Gierke argues that it inevitably generates an empty conception of the state's personality because it affords to the state no personal existence apart from the personality of the sovereign, and so no 'real' personality at all. Gierke finds evidence for this lack in the complete disjunction he discerns in Hobbes's theory between the supposed 'whole' of the state's person-ality and the 'parts' which all group persons must contain. Like all natural-law theorists, Hobbes begins with the individual, as the only 'whole' (with the possible exception of the family) provided in nature. But unlike all previous natural-law theorists, he is able to construct from these individual components a greater whole by which each is transcended. However, such transcendence as Hobbes manages is for Gierke equivalent to annihilation – 'he had made the individual omnipotent, with the object of forcing him to destroy himself instantly in virtue of his own omnipotence, and thus enthroning the "bearer" of the State-authority [i.e. the person of the sovereign] as a

[10] *Ibid.*, p. 41.

mortal god'.[11] Hobbes attains a state whole, therefore, but at the cost of the parts. There is no plurality-in-unity in *Leviathan*; there is only unity, in the unified person of the sovereign.

It is important to emphasise at this point that the Gierkean concept of plurality-in-unity, though it gives conceptual priority to unity, does not grant to the group unit the capacity ever to do without plurality. The group unit, or group person, must contain other units, or persons, including the persons of other groups. This the Leviathan, in so far as it is an automaton, does not do. Gierke acknowledges that Hobbes's organicism allows him to portray individuals and groups within the state as though parts of a living whole.[12] But he also recognises that this is incidental to the central issue of the state's 'personality', which is contained exclusively in the person of the sovereign. The 'systemes' within Hobbes's commonwealth are not parts of its person; they stand apart from it, and in need of regulation by it, just because the state's person is represented by the sovereign, and sovereigns do not contain any other persons than their own. So Hobbes's single state personality is seen to emerge from an argument which starts with the natural person of the individual, concludes with the artificial person of the sovereign, and allows nothing in between. His commonwealth has, in Gierke's words, a personality that is 'purely external'.[13]

This extremely narrow conception of the state leads Gierke to suggest that the move from the personality of the sovereign to the personality of the commonwealth is in fact nothing more than a 'technical designation' – if one moves beyond the person of the sovereign, one finds nothing there but 'mere, naked power'.[14] Unsurprisingly, Gierke also suggests that the Hobbesian 'solution' to the problem of sovereignty might have been expected to lead other theorists to question the value of the whole tradition which threw up such a problem in the first place. But it did not, and 'instead of falling into a premature death, [the natural-law theory of the state] drew a new and unexpected vitality from the very crisis that threatened its life'.[15] This crisis has to be understood dialectically. Hobbes's reconciliation of sovereignty and contract represented a 'materialistic and mechanistic consummation' of natural-law theory,[16] but it also

---

[11] *Ibid.*, p. 61.
[12] Hobbes says at the start of chapter XXII of *Leviathan* that 'systemes' are to be understood as resembling 'the similar parts, or Muscles of a Body naturall' (see Hobbes, *Leviathan*, p. 155).
[13] Gierke, *Natural law*, p. 61.   [14] See *ibid.*   [15] *Ibid.*   [16] *Ibid.*

meant that there was now much to which natural-law theory itself could no longer be reconciled. To put it in technical terms, Hobbes's 'solution' represents a synthesis within the natural-law tradition but also the antithesis of all those ideas which stood outside that tradition (including some of the 'organic' ideas which found their way into *Leviathan*). Thus a choice had to be made between the ideas which could no longer be reconciled, which meant in essence a choice between the juristic and moral conceptions of order contained in Hobbes's thought.

A choice was made. Natural-law theory did not die, and European political thought continued its fixation with the juristic conception of sovereignty. What is more, sovereignty soon revealed itself to be anything but a narrow idea, and within the framework established by Hobbes it proved possible to challenge many Hobbesian assumptions. Despite his preference for monarchy, Hobbes had not 'solved' the issue of the best form of government, and sides might still be taken by apologists of aristocracy, democracy and even, within the confines of single sovereignty, those 'mixed' (or, as they were later called, 'constitutional') forms of government which had been anathema to Hobbes himself. Meanwhile, with Rousseau came the possibility that the conditions of single sovereignty could be met without the abnegation of the individual entailed by the authorisation of a sovereign government. Like Hobbes, Rousseau argued that the state was a single person; but unlike Hobbes, he believed the state's single personality could, and should, be attained without representation. Rousseau's sovereign is formed of the individuals who contract with one another in the state of nature. This was, of course, a hugely significant difference, and it marks a further turning-point in the development of natural-law theory. But Gierke remains insistent that the ideas of Rousseau and Hobbes constitute variations on a single theme – Rousseau's state was still, as Rousseau himself recognised, an 'artificial person'.[17] So long as artificial, the

[17] The difference between Rousseau and Hobbes lies in the fact that it is the state itself for Rousseau that is artificial, not just the sovereign. Rousseau is therefore quite clear that though artificial, the state is not to be understood as a fictitious person, a point he makes explicitly when he writes of the duties of citizenship: 'For every individual as a man may have a private will contrary to, or different from, the general will that he has as a citizen. His private interest may speak with a very different voice from that of the public interest; his absolute and naturally independent existence may make him regard what he owes to the common cause as a gratuitous contribution, the loss of which would be less painful for others than the payment is onerous for him; and fancying that the artificial person which constitutes the state is a mere fictitious entity (since it is not a man), he might seek to enjoy

state's personality could never be understood as unitary in itself, but only as a whole founded upon some prior arrangement among unitary individuals, 'either on the Collective basis of unanimous agreement [in Rousseau's case], or on the alternative basis of Representation by a single person or body [in Hobbes's]'.[18] Even as it developed, natural-law theory after Hobbes continued to revolve exclusively around the relation between individuals and the sovereign state they had created for themselves, and it is for Gierke no coincidence that Hobbes and Rousseau shared, among other things, a mutual antipathy for unregulated group activity.[19] There was no place for group life within their states, because there was nothing 'within' their states at all – the natural-law theory of the state was, and was to remain, 'external'.

III

It is the clear implication of Gierke's argument that the choice described above was the wrong one. Inevitably, choice is an ambivalent concept in the context of a Hegelian history. Yet Gierke does at least suggest that there was an alternative to the path on which Hobbes took natural-law theory. For if Hobbes's conception of the state's personality represents a 'solution', it is fair to say that by Gierkean standards there must have been something wrong with the problem. The problem which Hobbes solved was the problem of single sovereignty, and to do so he adopted premises which Gierke describes as 'arbitrarily assumed'. His argument, though consistent, was contingent, and it was contingent upon the issue of single sovereignty. Without the priority given to that issue, it might have proved possible to generate a conception of the state containing that diversity and vitality among its 'parts' which Hobbes was to deny. Moreover it did prove possible for one theorist, the jurist Johannes Althusius,[20] to build from the contractual foundations of the natural-law tradition a political theory which assured for all groups what

the rights of a citizen without doing the duties of a subject' (J.-J. Rousseau, *The social contract*, trans. M. Cranston (Harmondsworth, 1968), pp. 64–5).

[18] Gierke, *Natural law*, p. 136.

[19] Rousseau famously insisted that 'there should be no sectional associations within the state' (Rousseau, The *social contract*, p. 73).

[20] Johannes Althusius (1557–1638), who although born in Germany lived and worked in the Netherlands, was effectively 'discovered' by Gierke. His writing had been more or less entirely neglected until Gierke devoted a monograph to him in 1878, entitled *Johannes Althusius und die Entwicklung der naturrechtlichen Staatstheorien*.

Gierke calls 'an organic place in the structure of civil society'.[21] In two treatises published more than thirty years before *Leviathan*, Althusius argued that the state was but one of a series of associations – the others are the family, the fellowship (*Genossenschaft*), the local community (*Gemeinde*) and the province – each with its own particular functions. The state could still be distinguished from lesser associations by virtue of its being sovereign; but other associations were not to be understood as the creations of the state in virtue of that sovereignty. Each association, including the state, was the product of a contractual arrangement among lesser associations seeking the security of a broader community (families in fellowships, fellowships in local communities, and so on). Every association, therefore, was assured of its existence within the state, because the state, as conceived by Althusius, could not exist without them.

The fundamental assumption which lay behind this argument is a simple one. Gierke sets it out as follows: 'If a contractual agreement between individuals had power enough to produce a sovereign commonwealth, it must also possess the power of producing Fellowships and local communities.'[22] It is a line of thought (disregarding the specific forms of association involved) which has some resonance for all theorists in the natural-law tradition – even Hobbes acknowledges that associations other than the state can be constructed along similar lines, since all groups of men can be represented by artificial persons. Where Hobbes differs from Althusius is in his insistence that the state's sovereignty depends upon all other groups in fact being constructed along different lines than the state – the sovereign representative is authorised by a group of individuals, whereas all other representatives must be authorised by the sovereign. This is the condition of what I earlier called juristic order. But for Althusius, the authority of associations was not conditional in this sense at all. Each association in his juristic scheme had an authority derived solely from its members, and the result was a scheme which accommodated the conditions of what might be called juristic disorder. This is in part a consequence of his reliance, like all other natural-law theorists before Hobbes, on a contract of society preceding the establishment of government, such that sovereignty within the state was essentially divided. Althusius insists, in Gierke's terms, that 'it is the community of the Ruled which is the true "Subject" or owner of the common

---

[21] Gierke, *Natural law*, p. 71. [22] *Ibid.*, p. 76.

authority . . . and as the true "Subject" of the common authority the community is superior to the officer entrusted with its actual exercise'.[23] However, this conception of authority does not hold for the state alone. Every association in Althusius's scheme is generated by a 'contract of society', and there is thus provided in every association the grounds for communal disobedience of its officers. What is more, every association in Althusius's scheme (except the family, which is created by individuals) is created by other associations. So, not only can the ruled of every association resist their rulers, but there can be no rulers of the state, or civil society, without the existence of a whole range of lesser societies, each with rulers of their own. This was the state of affairs that Hobbes dreaded. It remains consistent with a conception of sovereignty, to the extent that the association with which this process stops, the state, is distinct from the rest, because part of no association greater than itself. But by Hobbesian standards, this is a purely technical designation. For Hobbes, the state is sovereign because other associations are its creation. For Althusius, the state is sovereign because the reverse is true – his state is created by other associations, and sovereign because it creates no other associations itself.

This does not, of course, mean that Althusius was championing disorder. His system allowed for resistance,[24] but it did not encourage it, and it was naturally assumed that in a well-ordered state resistance would be unnecessary. A well-ordered state on the Althusian model was one in which every group, including the state, exercised authority in its own appointed sphere, and the officers of every group, including the officers of the state, dutifully served the group that had 'elected' them. This conception of political existence, embracing every aspect of social existence, and every group in society, closely corresponded to Gierke's conception of a genuinely unified society, in which every part is an aspect of the whole. Crucially, however, Althusius still had to rely on ideas drawn from outside the strict terms of his natural-law system to generate that degree of order on which this social unity ultimately depended. One of these was the idea of 'divine order' – what Gierke calls 'that divine order of the world which is *ex hypothesi* revealing itself naturally in this

---

[23] *Ibid.*, p. 74.
[24] Richard Tuck has recently described Althusius as 'setting out many of the fundamentals of Calvinist resistance theory' (see R. Tuck, *Philosophy and government, 1572–1651* (Cambridge, 1993), p. 158).

natural-law system'.[25] The other was the idea of the *Genossenschaft*, or fellowship. These were essentially 'medieval' ideas (in Gierke's sense of that word), and they do not accord with the juristic basis of the Althusian system, which is contract. Yet Althusius makes use of them for precisely that reason. His juristic system, though compatible with order, does not describe order. What it describes is a series of contracts leading from the individual to the state *via* the groups in between. Juristically, the parts must always precede the whole, and therefore unity cannot reside within the system, but must come to it from outside. Gierke recognises this, and he recognises, in consequence, that Althusius, for all his efforts, cannot achieve the synthesis from which true plurality-in-unity might be derived. A contractual partnership could not, even by Althusius, be reconciled with 'anything more than a collective sum of associated individuals'.[26] Thus Gierke is forced to conclude:

> The Teutonic idea of the freedom of corporate bodies is introduced [by Althusius] into the sphere of the Law of Nature; an inherent existence is vindicated for associations over against the State; and yet, in spite of every effort to attain the idea of a true and organic Group-being by the use of the Teutonic conception of 'Fellowship', there is a failure to make either the State or the corporation a whole which is really one, and can assert itself against the individual in the strength of its own inherent existence.[27]

Althusius fails to create a unity which is anything more than unity-in-plurality, and where Hobbes gives us the whole without the parts, Althusius in the end can only give us the parts without the whole.

This failure is a failure of natural law, and it demonstrates that the failures of natural law are not simply contingent upon the issue of single sovereignty. The Althusian 'solution' cannot be the whole answer, any more than the Hobbesian solution can. What both lacked was the one thing that natural law was unable to provide: a conception of 'real' group personality. The genuinely unified group persons of natural law, like the Hobbesian commonwealth, were fictions, and thus lifeless. Meanwhile, the apparently vital groups of natural law, like the Althusian fellowship, were ultimately just as lifeless, for they were artificial, and had no real personality of their own. Real group persons had to be both unified and vital, like a true organism, and true organicism was only to be found in the political thought of the middle ages. This Gierke had established in the third volume of *Das deutsche Genossenschaftsrecht*, first published in 1881 and

---

[25] Gierke, *Natural law*, p. 74.   [26] *Ibid.*, p. 76.   [27] *Ibid.*

dealing with ancient and medieval doctrines of state and corporation. Real group personality is contingent on what Gierke calls in that volume 'genuinely medieval' thought, and it is here that an alternative to both Hobbes and Althusius can be found.

IV

Political thought, Gierke writes, 'when it is genuinely medieval starts from the Whole, but ascribes an intrinsic value to every Partial Whole, down to and including the Individual'.[28] This is the true plurality-in-unity, and its distinguishing characteristic is the reciprocity between whole and parts denoted by the concept of the 'Partial Whole'. If each part reflects the whole, then not only must each part be a whole in its own right, but the whole must share a purpose or end with the purposes or ends of each of its parts. For just as a corporation cannot be a lesser commonwealth unless the commonwealth is capable of acting as a corporation, so no individual or group can be a partial whole unless the whole is capable of acting in the manner of the parts it contains. The whole, therefore, must be a purposive organisation, containing individuals or groups with purposes of their own. And this is only possible, as Oakeshott recognised, if the purposes of whole and parts are broadly aligned. Yet the reciprocity between them means that the purposes of the parts cannot be regulated by the purpose of the whole, as Oakeshott believed was inevitable, since the purpose of each part has to be allowed an intrinsic value. Nor, moreover, can the purpose of the whole be conditioned by the purpose of its parts, since the idea of plurality-in-unity must start from the whole. Instead, both require a shared end outside themselves. In medieval political thought, that end was God, and plurality-in-unity was founded on what Gierke calls 'a divinely instituted Harmony which pervades the Universal Whole and every part thereof'.[29] For natural-law theorists, the universal whole was either the individual, or his nemesis, the state. But in this earlier tradition it was literally the Universe – 'that *Civitas Dei*, that God-State, which comprehends the heavens and earth' – and everything might be identified with it, not just every individual, but every group, every 'component part of that ordering of the world which exists because God exists'.[30]

---

[28] Gierke, *Political theories of the middle age*, trans. F. W. Maitland (Cambridge, 1900), p. 7.
[29] *Ibid.*, p. 8.   [30] *Ibid.*

This vision of the world naturally lent itself to organic imagery, whereby the organisation of the universe and of each group within it might be compared to the literal 'organisation' (the arrangement of organs) displayed by the living body. Yet, as we have seen, the use of such imagery was not of itself sufficient to denote a genuinely medieval conception of group life, any more than an reliance on the divine ordering of the world was sufficient to render Althusius a genuinely medieval thinker. What was needed, beyond a metaphorical or a metaphysical understanding of the plurality-in-unity of human society, was just what Althusius and other natural-law theorists lacked: a juristic conception of this unity which rendered groups both equivalent to and independent of the individuals they contained. The *societas* of Roman law proved incapable of generating such a conception, but this was not true of Roman law as a whole, for in the *universitas* the Romans had created a form of association which escaped the mechanistic constraints of contract, and could take its place in the legal firmament alongside the individual, as a unit in its own right. It was to the *universitas* that medieval thinkers turned, once Roman ideas again became prevalent, in order to convey in juristic terms their sense that groups, like individuals, were aspects of a universal whole, and therefore, in some sense, universals themselves.

Because of its origins, however, the idea of the *universitas* also contained within it the seeds of destruction of the medieval world. Conceptions of group unity only had what Gierke would consider a secure juristic foundation when they could be expressed in terms of personality. It was certainly possible to think of *universitates* as persons, and the characteristic social units of medieval life – its guilds, cities, churches and colleges – were often described in the language of personality at the same time as being described in the language of universality. But the personality so described could only be of a particular, limited kind. For the *universitas* remained what Gierke calls 'an instrument forged in the laboratory of Private Law'.[31] This is a pregnant phrase, and it contains a mass of controversy. Yet the essential point that Gierke was making can be expressed quite simply: *universitates*, because constructs of private law, could only be possessed of a personality which was a construct also. A *universitas* was not a construct in the mechanistic sense that

---

[31] *Ibid.*, p. 68.

contractual partnerships are constructs; rather, it was a creation of the law itself, a group person independent of the personality of its members but dependent on the legal framework within which its personal identity is formulated. It was, in other words, a *persona ficta*. In time, this line of reasoning developed into what became known as 'the concession theory', by which it was determined that corporate personality depended in each case upon the explicit sanction of the ultimate arbiter of private law, who was sovereign. In Hobbesian language, the concession theory insisted that it was in specific 'letters', not in 'general laws', that the personality of a *universitas* must be described. If so, the *universitas* could hardly stand as the model for the complete range of associations which populated the medieval landscape, if only because, as Hobbes himself conceded, the setting down in letters of every group's personality is not always easy, nor even possible. In fact, much of the controversy surrounding medieval corporation theory relates to the issue of concession, and to the question of whether it was a doctrine formalised in medieval juristic thought to the extent that later jurists, including Gierke, were to suggest.[32] Yet even if Gierke did overstate the importance of formal concession at the expense of other, more generalised means of acquiring corporate personality, his fundamental point still holds. No conception of group unity which operated exclusively in the domain of private law could satisfactorily account for those groups which existed in the public sphere, any more than the 'systemes' existing within a Hobbesian commonwealth, whether authorised by laws or by letters, could serve as a model for the commonwealth itself. A truly medieval conception of group life had to accommodate within a single juristic scheme all associations – guilds *and* cities, churches *and* the universal Church, natural families *and* the Family of Man – and so required a conception of personality which could contain the whole world of men, not just that area mapped out by the laws men happened to have made. Because identified with an entirely man-made world, the *universitas* remained a fiction, as its Hobbesian

---

[32] A number of medieval jurists accepted that various groups could form themselves into corporate associations without having to secure the specific sanction of a higher legal authority. All that was required was that they be associated for some 'just cause'; where this was so, corporate status could be said to derive from the authority of the group themselves. It is now generally accepted that in his keenness to emphasise the contrast between Romanism and Germanism, Gierke ignored much of this middle ground (see, for example, A. Black, *Guilds and civil society in European political thought from the twelfth century to the present* (London, 1984), pp. 20–4).

equivalent, the person-in-law, remains a fiction, whether possessed of its own letters or not. The *universitas* could not, therefore, be counted a universal model of group personality, unless the universe was to be deemed a fiction itself.

Though suited to the organicism of medieval thought, the concept of the *universitas* could not escape the conditioning of its Roman origins. It remained an antique-modern, rather than a medieval, conception, and its inability to bridge the gap well illustrates the fundamental distinction between these two modes of thought, resting on the strict distinction that antique-modern thought alone draws between public and private law – between the laws which hold within states and the laws which also hold for them. This distinction found various forms of expression, from its Roman origins in the contrast between *Ius Civile* on the one hand and *Ius Gentium* and *Ius Naturale* on the other, through to the quintessentially modern contrast between positive and natural law. In it lay the source of that characteristic engagement of antique-modern thought with the individuals or groups who were taken to be bound by one set of laws but not by the other – those individuals or groups who came to be known as sovereign. It was a distinction which reached its apogee in the form provided for it by Hobbes, whose sovereign was, by Gierke's standards, freed from the constraints of law altogether.[33] And it was a distinction which genuinely medieval thought could not recognise, since a medieval conception of the universe could allow no substantive distinction between the rules governing any of its parts, whether individuals, states or groups within states. This was the reason why the medieval world was finally unable to accommodate Roman ideas, even those ideas like the *universitas* which avoided the individualistic bias, and divisive effects, of contract. In the end, genuinely medieval thought required recourse from Romanism, and recourse from Romanism, Gierke believed, was best to be found in the life and thought of the Germanic peoples.[34]

---

[33] Gierke writes of Hobbes's political philosophy: 'With a logical inevitability all public right is absorbed, in every possible form of State, by a Sovereignty of the Ruler which is absolutely unlimited and illimitable, irresponsible and omnipotent, *free from all obligation of law and duty*' (Gierke, *Natural law*, p. 60, my italics).

[34] Of course, the man who played the most prominent part in shaping medieval political thought was neither a Romanist nor a Germanist. But because Aristotle does not fit easily into Gierke's contrast between antique-modern and medieval thought (he was both antique and medieval) his place in all this cannot be discussed here (which does not mean that Gierke did not discuss it).

v

Gierke's history of Germanic conceptions of group life occupies the whole of both the first and second volumes of *Das deutsche Genossenschaftsrecht*, which he published in 1868 and 1873 respectively, and no summary of it can be attempted here. What can be attempted is an outline of the manner in which such conceptions represent an alternative to the antique-modern ideas with which volumes III and IV deal. For it is essential to an understanding of Gierke's work as a whole to recognise that the reception of Roman law into the intellectual world of medieval Europe did not mark the effective beginning of medieval juristic thinking about associations. Rather, Roman law was received into a continent which, in parts, already possessed a juristic scheme within which to frame group activity. Those parts lay to the north, in Europe's 'teutonic' regions, and the scheme was that of the *Genossenschaft*, or fellowship. To call this scheme medieval is in one sense a misnomer, since it was also timeless, at least to the extent that its origins were lost in time. As Gierke writes, evocatively, at the start of the first volume of *Das deutsche Genossenschaftsrecht*:

When they first entered history, the Germanic peoples had already long ago developed beyond those earliest beginnings of communal life which we can still observe among primitive peoples. The family connections, which among [Germanic] peoples too at one time were undoubtedly the only organised associations conscious of their common bond, had extended to form bigger communities, in which individuals are held together by a bond other than blood relationship.[35]

These communities were fellowships, and their bonds were based not on blood but on law, albeit of a primitive kind. Thus Germanic conceptions of the group had a juristic basis which was not specifically medieval, and which was independent of those twin colossi, Church and Empire, by which specifically medieval jurisprudence was overshadowed. And yet the *Genossenschaft* can still be counted a distinctively medieval idea, for the simple reason that it was based on a conception of plurality-in-unity. The idea of the *Genossenschaft* postulated a world in which men formed, and were loyal to, groups which were neither mere collections of individuals nor mere creations of a superior legal authority. Fellowships were groups in their own right, and in consequence might be deemed 'real' group

[35] Gierke, *Community in historical perspective*, ed. A. Black (Cambridge, 1990), p. 13.

persons. A *Genossenschaft* was a person because it was a legal entity – it was a subject of rights. It was real, however, just because it was not an entity created by law – it was not the product of some contingent legal arrangement, whether contractual or concessionary. It is possible to draw a comparison here with the account of persons and things personated provided by Hobbes, even though Hobbes's account is couched in different terms (it does not speak of rights). The 'right-subjectivity' of the Gierkean fellowship makes of it a basic unit to which legal capabilities (such as ownership) can be ascribed, as personality, in Hobbes's terms, determines the basic juristic units to which the ownership of words and actions can be ascribed. Yet it is to the natural person in Hobbes's account that the *Genossenschaft* must be compared. It does not, unlike either the artificial or the fictitious person, depend for its personality on some prior arrangement between persons to determine its legal capabilities. Law applied to the *Genossenschaft*, as it did to the individual. But it did not create the *Genossenschaft*, any more than it created the individual man.

There remains, though, one important difference between individuals and fellowships, which helps to set apart Hobbes's 'natural' persons from Gierke's 'real' ones. The fellowship, unlike the individual, contains individuals, who are themselves persons, or subjects of rights. There is thus what might be called an internal as well as an external aspect to the legal status of the *Genossenschaft*. Its internal aspect takes the form of a set of legal relations between individual subjects of rights; and these relations must reflect the external aspect of the group as a whole, which is itself a subject of rights. It is this reciprocity between the personality of the group and the personality of its members which renders the *Genossenschaft* a true conception of plurality-in-unity. It requires that every right exercised, or action owned by a group (a whole) must be reflected in the rights exercised and actions owned by each of its members (its parts). The unity of the whole is manifested in the legal relations of its parts, and this generates the one thing which antique-modern jurisprudence, both Roman and natural, could not provide: a juristically coherent organicism. This organicism held for any group, including those made up not just of individuals but of other fellowships. Moreover, it was compatible with a conception of the state – with what Gierke calls 'the old Germanic idea of the *Rechtsstaat*'.[36] The *Rechtsstaat* (a

---

[36] See Gierke, *Political theories*, p. 73.

term more or less untranslatable into English) provided the ultimate legal framework for the idea of the *Genossenschaft*, as well as itself being an extension of that idea. It postulated a state which was a subject of rights (among them sovereignty, which, it should be remembered, was understood by Gierke to be a right requiring a subject) but whose 'right-subjectivity' could only rest in the totality of the legal relations within it. No part of the state – neither ruler nor people, individuals nor assemblies – could 'represent' or in any other way stand apart from the whole. The whole, rather, was bound up with each of its parts, individual and associated, because every part was an aspect of the whole.

If the idea of the *Rechtsstaat* seems an obscure one outside of its Germanic context, it is because it represents the broadest possible synthesis of all those ideas which have thus far been opposed. Gierke himself describes it as 'the idea of a State which existed only in the law and for the law, and whose whole life was bound by a legal order that regulated alike all public and all private relationships'.[37] It does not follow from this that the distinction between the public and the private breaks down altogether – the external relations of persons within the state, whether individuals or groups, must remain private so long as such persons are capable of acting in their own right, as will be the case, for example, whenever they contract with one another. But it does follow that no distinction can be drawn between persons on the basis of the sphere – public or private – to which they belong. All persons in the *Rechtsstaat* are public parts as well as private wholes, and so no person can either be denied a public function (i.e. reduced to the level of a subject), nor claim the whole of public right as their own (i.e. raised to the level of a sovereign). Moreover, the distinction between the public and the private must break down altogether in the case of the state itself. As a whole the state has an external aspect, but because, juristically, it is the ultimate whole, it has no legal relations outside itself.[38] The external aspect of the *Rechtsstaat* can only be revealed in the legal relations of its parts. Thus the personality of the *Rechtsstaat* resides in the totality of its laws, public and private. This, then, is the ultimate synthesis. It is a synthesis of the two ideas which Oakeshott takes to divide up

---

[37] *Ibid.*

[38] Gierke expressed this point as follows: 'There exists no legally organised generality for which the State could be a mere particular' (quoted in J. D. Lewis, *The Genossenschaft-theory of Otto von Gierke* (Madison, 1935), p. 73).

European conceptions of the state: like a *societas*, the *Rechtsstaat* is an association founded entirely on rule, or law; yet it retains, like a *universitas*, a personal identity of its own.[39] What is more, the idea of the *Rechtsstaat* synthesises that which Hobbes left unreconciled, for it grants the state a personality while yet accommodating within it groups with personalities of their own. The *Rechtsstaat* is a synthesis of juristic and moral conceptions of order.

VI

The idea of the *Rechtsstaat* marks an appropriately Hegelian conclusion to what is a highly dialectical story. It is, however, at least as told above, a story different in one important respect from any Hegel might have told. It runs backwards – back not just from volumes IV and III of *Das deutsche Genossenschaftsrecht* to volumes II and I, but back in time, from Hobbes to Althusius, from individualistic natural law to unitary medieval jurisprudence, from received Romanism to primitive Germanism. Each step is towards a broader juristic conception of the associational life of political communities, and so represents a form of synthesis. Yet each synthesis precedes in time the development of those ideas which are reconciled by it. If told

---

[39] Antony Black, in the most recent English edition of Gierke, writes that what Gierke understands as '*Rechtsstaat*' is the same as what Oakeshott understands as 'state as *societas*'. This cannot be right. The passage in Gierke to which Black appends this remark speaks of 'the free system of association in German law [recognising] the lesser associations of its citizens as communities *homogenous with the greater whole*, and [allowing] them independent life *even while it uses them as building blocks for the overall structure*' (Gierke, *Community*, pp. 111–12, my italics). This is, at least in part, what Gierke understands by the *Rechtsstaat*. It has much in common with Oakeshott's *societas*. But, as we have seen, Oakeshott did not accept either that in the state understood as *societas* other associations would be modelled on the state nor that in such a state the state itself would be built out of such associations. That was the province of the state understood as *universitas*. This does not mean that Gierke's *Rechtsstaat* is to be understood as a *universitas* – that would be equally difficult to sustain, given Gierke's insistence on the independent life of associations within the state. But just what it does mean is that Gierke was attempting some synthesis of the two models that Oakeshott sets apart.

It should also be pointed out at this juncture that Gierke did not conceive of the modern German state as solely a *Rechtsstaat*. It was also to be a *Kulturstaat* – that is, a state which propagated a single cultural ideal. In this sense, it was closer to what Oakeshott understood by a *universitas*, if not quite what he meant by an 'enterprise association'. However, it must be pointed out as well that Gierke's conception of the *Kulturstaat* was wholly bound up with his conception of the *Rechtsstaat*. The culture that was to be propagated was a culture which found expression in law; and Gierke wrote that it was the purpose of the *Kulturstaat* 'to formulate as law the consciousness of right of the people' (quoted in Lewis, *The Genossenschaft-theory*, p. 70). In this sense, the culture of Gierke's ideal state was to manifest itself as law, and law was to manifest itself as a form of culture. It is to this ideal that the ideal concept of the *Rechtsstaat* refers.

chronologically, therefore, this is a story which assumes a very different aspect from that given it above. It will describe the replacement of broader conceptions by narrower ones, and the increasing divergence of ideas which had once been unified: the unitary *Rechtsstaat* gives way before Romanism, and so to a separation of the corporate from the contractual sphere; in due course, the unitary outlook of medieval jurists is supplanted by a distinction between natural and positive law, and between the rights of men in their natural and in their civil states; within the confines of natural-law theory, divisions arise between advocates of 'ruler' and 'popular' sovereignty, while the gap continues to widen between the organicist language and the mechanistic premises of theories of the state; and eventually, we arrive at Hobbes, the 'technical' unity of whose system of thought merely provides for the absolute disjunction of its parts, of subjects and sovereigns, persons and their representatives, individuals and the groups to which they belong. With each division, the idea of the *Rechtsstaat* is left further behind.

Das deutsche Genossenschaftsrecht is first of all a history of ideas and like any such history it cannot ignore the chronological sequence of the ideas it describes. Ideas follow upon each other for a reason, and new ideas replace old because they better meet the requirements of those who promulgate them. Germanic thought gave way first to Roman then to natural-law alternatives because, as Gierke acknowledges, it was unable to meet the demands that came to be placed on it. Gierke did not, in any colloquial sense, idealise the political structures of early Germanic and medieval communities, and he recognised that all such communities contained strong elements of lordship (*Herrschaft*) as well as fellowship (*Genossenschaft*). At those points where lordship escaped the bonds of fellowship, Romanist conceptions of authority were better suited to prevailing social circumstance than the idea of the *Rechtsstaat*. Nor was the conditioning of such circumstance simply a contingent political matter: Gierke also recognised that with the advent of the Church came a form of lordship – the lordship of Christ and his earthly representatives – 'which found its origin and its goal outside and beyond a mere scheme of law'.[40] The resulting claims of Papal absolutism were met by the claims of Imperial absolutism, and Roman law provided juristic ballast for both. Subsequently, as lordship gave way to

---

[40] Gierke, *Political theories*, p. 73.

sovereignty (*Obrigkeit*), and the competing claims of Pope and Emperor gave way to the competing claims of nations and their governments, it fell to systems of natural law to answer the juristic needs of Reformation and post-Reformation Europe. Moreover, it was not just on account of their greater adaptability that Roman and then natural jurisprudence superseded Germanic ideas. That adaptability was itself a consequence of their vastly greater sophistication. Early German law was for the most part rooted in local customs. Roman law, in stark contrast, was not, and its clarity and complexity suggested a range of application which no system of customary law could possibly match. Systems of natural law, meanwhile, just because they were built from first principles, had a broader scope still – Hobbes's single state personality may have been merely 'technical' and founded on premises which were 'arbitrarily assumed', but because genuinely technical these arbitrary assumptions generated a wide-ranging and intellectually compelling political philosophy. It is in these regards, and with good reason, that Gierke has to concede the 'insufficiency' of the old Germanic idea of the *Rechtsstaat*.[41]

Nevertheless, there remain two good reasons why the treatment of Gierke's history given above takes the story back from Hobbes to the early *Rechtsstaat*, rather than in chronological order, or indeed in the order of its composition and publication. First, because Gierke was primarily a historian rather than a philosopher, it is not easy to summarise the philosophical thrust of his argument when it is taken in strict historical sequence. His history of philosophy, unlike Hegel's, is not always the philosophy of history, and it pursues many incidental themes, down what often turn out to be cul-de-sacs. This willingness to accommodate both the contingency and the complexity of many of the ideas with which he deals means that the history and the philosophy contained in Gierke's work are not always to be found moving in tandem.[42] Second, and more significantly, the quintessentially modern era in political thought initiated by Hobbes does not in fact mark the end of Gierke's history. As Gierke was only too aware, the modern eventually gave way in Germany to some-

[41] See *ibid*.

[42] Certainly Gierke's reputation as a historian has outlasted his reputation as a political philosopher. Richard Tuck, in a work published in 1993, is happy to describe Gierke simply as 'a nineteenth-century liberal' (Tuck, *Philosophy and government, 1572–1651* (Cambridge, 1993), p. 158), which hardly does him justice, but at the same time refers to Gierke's historical treatment of German constitutionalism in the fourth volume of *Das deutsche Genossenschaftsrecht* as still the most reliable secondary source (see *ibid*., p. xii).

thing else – to that period of thought, initiated in part by Hegel, through which Gierke himself was living and to which his own thought belongs. Gierke believed himself to be writing during the early stages of an era in the history of ideas from which, as he put it, 'we expect the reconciliation of age old opposites';[43] and this meant, among other things, a reconciliation of medieval and antique-modern conceptions of the state. The culmination of his history, therefore, lay not in modernity but in what might be called, by his standards at least, the increasing post-modernity of nineteenth-century German life and thought. This sense that the antique-modern world of ideas was being supplanted by a new and peculiarly German synthesis provides Gierke's work with a conclusion which is properly historical as well as distinctively Hegelian, coming as it does at the end of history rather than at the beginning. It is, however, important to recognise that this was still a synthesis, and indeed a Hegelianism, of a very particular kind. For Gierke was clear that the displacement of antique-modern conceptions of group and state had only been made possible by the revival of the old Germanic ideas of *Genossenschaft* and *Rechtsstaat*.

It remains possible to characterise this revival in classically dialectical terms. Gierke did not believe that Germanic notions of fellowship had ever been entirely swamped by Romanism, and he also believed that the concept of the *Rechtsstaat* had maintained a lingering presence even during the high tide of natural-law theory (not just in the thought of Althusius, but also in the 'constitutional' ideas of some early eighteenth-century German jurists). Likewise, he accepted that medieval ideas had always contained within them the seeds of their own destruction, in the rights that were necessarily accorded to each individual human being as a 'partial whole', rights which in time came to be seen as 'natural'. What happened during the nineteenth century was that ideas which were always present but never reconciled finally began to find common forms of expression, and so became ideas that could satisfactorily be assimilated to one another: a Germanism began to develop which was juristically coherent; juristic schemes evolved that were coherently Germanic. The *telos* of this process was the 'longed-for harmony',[44] of organi-cism and individualism, unity and plurality, order and freedom – indubitably a Hegelian ideal.

---

[43] Gierke, *Community*, p. 12.   [44] *Ibid.*, p. 3.

Nevertheless, Gierke's approach to this ideal must be counted a distinctively post-Hegelian, rather than Hegelian, one. The most obvious reason for this is that Gierke began writing about it over thirty years after Hegel's death, and continued writing about it in one form or another for a further fifty years. His view of the development of nineteenth-century thought begins at the point where Hegel's ends, and leaves the Prussian state that Hegel knew far behind. Moreover, Gierke witnessed the growth, not only of German nationalism, but also of those theories of the *Volk* which were to provide German nationalism with much of its intellectual regalia. Gierke was no simple theorist of the *Volk*, and his Germanism has more in common with Hegel's expansive conception of the Germanic world[45] than with many of its later and grosser manifestations. But Gierke's idealised *Rechtsstaat* must still be distinguished from its Hegelian equivalent in one important respect. It rests, explicitly, on an idea drawn from Germany's past, and its realisation depended first of all on the resuscitation of that idea after centuries of comparative neglect. The same is true of the idea of the *Genossenschaft* on which the *Rechtsstaat* depends. Neither could return in precisely their old form, since both came to be neglected just because of the form that they originally assumed. But nor can either be said to have been entirely new. The Gierkean *Rechtsstaat*, therefore, unlike the Hegelian state, stands at *both* the beginning and the end of history, and the *Genossenschaft* likewise. Gierke believed that it was the old idea of fellowship, 're-awoken after a death-like sleep to more vigorous life',[46] on which the new Germanic state had to depend. In 1868, at the beginning of the first volume of *Das deutsche Genossenschaftsrecht*, he wrote:

The ancient German idea of fellowship [is] newborn, bringing both an incalculable wealth of new forms of association and giving new substance to the old. It is taking part in the transformation of the German community and state, which have only achieved progress in the past and will only

---

[45] For Hegel the 'Germanic realm' was the final of four 'world-historical realms', the others being the Oriental, the Greek and the Roman. Of it Hegel wrote: 'Mind is here pressed back on itself in the extreme of its absolute negativity. This is the absolute turning point; mind rises out of this situation and grasps the infinite positivity of this, its inward character, i.e. it grasps the principle of the unity of the divine nature and the human, the reconciliation of objective truth and freedom as the truth and freedom appearing within self-consciousness and subjectivity, a reconciliation with the fulfilment of which the principle of the north, the principle of the Germanic peoples, has been entrusted' (G. W. F. Hegel, *The philosophy of right*, trans. T. M. Knox (Oxford, 1967), p. 222).

[46] Gierke, *Community*, p. 12.

advance in the future by means of a return to the root of fellowship. This alone is the creator of a free form of association, becoming involved in and transforming all areas of public and private life; and although it has already achieved great things, it will achieve even more in the near and distant future.[47]

The transformation of German life was thus an open-ended process, both forward-looking and backward-looking, and Gierke made the furtherance of it his life's work.

This open-endedness ensured that Gierke's central theme, concerning the relationship between state (*Rechtsstaat*) and fellowship (*Genossenschaft*), was itself open to a number of different emphases. On the one hand, it was compatible with the view that German society was to be reformed from within and from below, as the number and variety of associations which might fit the fellowship mould began to proliferate. On the other hand, it was consistent with a desire to see large-scale juristic and political change, in order that the fellowship idea might more readily be accommodated to modern conditions. The difference between these two positions was not of itself that great, but it was exacerbated by the simple fact that the *Genossenschaftsidee* was, in the broadest synthesis, to be made manifest both in the life of the humblest associations in German society, and also in the life of the greatest, up to and including the state itself. As a result, support could be found for the concept of the Germanic fellowship in a variety of different causes, ranging from what we should now think of as a 'liberal' defence of the rights of groups within the state, to what we should now think of as a 'conservative' championing of national identity. The transformation of German society that Gierke sought might be effected by a revitalised nation-state, and then filter downwards; or it might issue from small-scale associations, leading to a new kind of state. Because history had not reached its conclusion, it was not always possible to tell.

Gierke's own intellectual development reflects some of this uncertainty. In the first volume of *Das deutsche Genossenschaftsrecht* the emphasis is clearly on change from below: Gierke devotes a substantial portion of the book to detailed descriptions of the various forms of fellowship which had grown up during the nineteenth century and in which he believed lay the roots of progress. These were, for the most part, economic associations, founded on principles of communality and independence, whose nearest English equivalent

---

[47] *Ibid.*

Gierke found in the 'co-operative' movement. His analysis of these groups draws attention, first of all, to their willingness to dispense with capitalist forms of ownership, and secondly, to the smallness of the scale on which they could operate – initially they were little more than small groups of craftsmen, in the manner of the earliest medieval guilds. Yet from these modest beginnings Gierke expected much, not just a reformulation of the role of the state, but also what he called 'economic independence for the working-classes'.[48] Unsurprisingly, this emphasis on capital, and on what might be achieved if those who lived by their labour were emancipated from it, has led to comparisons between Gierke's early ideas and those of Marx.[49] Yet it has also led to expressions of regret that Gierke did not persist in this line of thought, and instead allowed its edge to be dulled by what is described as 'an infection of mystical nationalism'.[50] For it is certainly true that in the later volumes of *Das deutsche Genossenschafts-recht*, as well as in much of his other writing, Gierke came to place less emphasis on the economic status of small groups, and more emphasis on the state, as the vehicle of national identity. The impetus behind this change of heart is not hard to find. The Franco-Prussian war, in which he fought and from which Germany emerged unified, affected Gierke deeply. As he was to recall in the inaugural lecture he gave as rector of Berlin university in 1902:

There are times when the spirit of the community reveals itself to us with an elemental power, in an almost visible shape, filling and mastering our inward being to such an extent that we are hardly any longer conscious of our individual being as such. Here, in Berlin, in the Unter den Linden, I lived through such an hour of consecration on the 15th July, in the year 1870.[51]

---

[48] *Ibid.*, p. 211.

[49] See Antony Black's introduction to Gierke, *Community*, p. xxvi.

[50] See *ibid.*, p. xxi–xxii.

[51] Quoted in the introduction to Gierke, *Natural law*, p. lxix. The fifteenth of July 1870 was the day following the publication of the so-called Ems telegram, which precipitated war between Prussia and France. In the telegram it had been revealed that the French ambassador had pressed a series of impossible demands on King William of Prussia during an interview between them in the town of Ems. It was this assault on Prussian dignity which brought the crowds out on to the streets of Berlin the following day. However, it is worth noting that the telegram, published by Bismarck, was heavily doctored by him first in order to generate the greatest possible strength of feeling, and thereby to make more likely the war that he wanted. It is something of an irony, therefore, that the elemental community spirit to which Gierke refers was, in the words of one recent history of the war, 'mobilised and manipulated' by the Prussian government (see W. Carr, *The origins of the German wars of unification* (London, 1991), pp. 196–200).

For the rest of his life, up to and beyond the defeat of the Second Reich in 1918, Gierke remained convinced that fellowship should be realised, first of all, by the nation-state.

This change of heart, and the change of emphasis that came after it, make Gierke a difficult figure to pin down. Still, the differences between the two sides of his thought should not be overstated.[52] Both are consistent with the ideal of the *Rechtsstaat*. Thus Gierke's early affinities to Marx are necessarily diminished by the fact that his was, from the outset, an idealist, not a materialist, history of the *Genossenschaft*. Gierke did not seek group-based alternatives to capitalism so that the distribution of material goods might be harmonised with the labour that produced them; rather, he hoped that alternative conceptions of ownership would produce a different understanding of the groups themselves. To concentrate on material forces meant in the end a concentration of power in the hands of those individuals or groups whose job it was to control them, and this was anathema to Gierke, who discerned in all socialist thought an expression of what he called 'the Roman tendency'. Socialism presupposed a unitary state because it insisted always on treating the state as a collective unit in need of regulation, so producing an antique-modern division between the regulators on the one side and the amorphous mass of the regulated on the other. Gierke always insisted that the unitary nature of the state could only be realised in the ideal relation of its independent parts. Even in 1868, therefore, his goal was a state which reflected the ideas behind what he called 'the modern association movement' – its communality and its plurality – rather than a state which would in due course do the material work of that movement for it. In a similar vein, his subsequent attachment to overtly nationalist doctrines should not be allowed to detract from what were, to Gierke's mind, the particular qualities of Bismarck's unified Germany, beyond the mere fact of its being unified. First, it was, ostensibly at least, a 'constitutional' state, and as such greatly to be preferred to the earlier *Polizeistaaten* of the territorial princes. Second, though dominated by Prussia, it was a 'federal' state, in which the unity of the whole was held to be consistent with the

---

[52] For example, Antony Black writes that: 'After 1868 [Gierke] made hardly any noteworthy contribution to the question of how state and association are related' (Gierke, *Community*, p. xxii). This is simply untrue. If nothing else, it was after 1868 that Gierke wrote the definitive account of how state and association have been related throughout the history of Western political thought (vols. III and IV of *Das deutsche Genossenschaftsrecht*), one of the great achievements in the history of ideas.

independent identity of each member state, or part. And third, the new Germany was a state in need of a new legal code, which suggested that the principles of fellowship might finally be provided with a secure juristic foundation. In due course, Germany did get a new code of laws – the *Bürgerliches Gesetzbuch* of 1896[53] – and though it was not as Germanistic as some, including Gierke, might have wished, its development provided the impetus for much of his later thought. German nationalism, for Gierke, was always bound up with the attempt to free Germany from the Romanist yoke, and that entailed recognising the 'right-subjectivity' of fellowships. Gierke believed in the German nation-state because he believed that in a state whose laws were specifically Germanic group life would be secure. Unity was sought for the sake of providing juristic coherence for plurality. The ideal of the *Rechtsstaat*, therefore, does not just reconcile the whole with the parts; it also reconciles change originating from above with growth proceeding from below.

VII

The result is that it is very hard to find an English word or phrase which summarises Gierke's philosophical outlook. His debt to Hegel is clear, but is complicated by the fact that his approach was simultaneously more overtly nationalistic and more overtly liberal than Hegel's. These two strands of thought are not easily reconciled in an English context, and the places where it might happen – within the confines of whiggism – are hardly amenable to the metaphysical bias of Hegelian dialectics. Nor can anything in that tradition capture the particular intensity, philosophical or otherwise, of Gierke's attachment to the group as the vehicle of freedom. The modern English term which best approximates to Gierke's vision of the state is 'pluralism', which is suggestive of a diversity founded upon coalitions of individuals rather than on individuals themselves. It is also a term which presupposes some broad setting within which diversity can be accommodated (if we speak of Britain as a pluralist society we imply that there is plurality within a basic unity). Yet

---

[53] Gierke's involvement in the drafting of this code is described in detail by Michael John (see M. John, *Politics and law in late nineteenth century Germany: the origins of the civil code* (Oxford, 1989), pp. 108–16). Gierke was a leading critic of the original draft of the code produced in 1888, which he saw as excessively reliant on Roman rather than German law, and as failing to address the 'social' issues of private law. The final draft of 1896 took account of some, though not all, of his criticisms.

'pluralism' is somewhat vague. Certainly, it conveys little of Gierke's specific, and specifically Germanic, belief that a diversity of groups can only be achieved where there is some formal identity between them, and between associations within the state and the state itself. Gierke's doctrine insists on a degree of conceptual unity which 'pluralism', as it is commonly understood, cannot be said to reflect. And it achieves that unity by means of concepts – *Genossenschaft* and *Rechtsstaat* – for which English equivalents are very hard to find.

There is, though, one sense in which Gierke's system of thought, if not overtly pluralist, is at least distinctively pluralistic. It is contained in a body of work which itself embraces a diverse range of intellectual disciplines, offering diverse approaches to the concepts with which it deals. These disciplines, as Gierke employs them, are shaped by the philosophical overview they share; nevertheless, as in any system of plurality-in-unity, they stand on their own terms also. As a result, Gierke's thought generates insights and arguments which can be applied in a variety of different spheres outside of the specifically Germanic sphere within which they originate. In particular, *Das deutsche Genossenschaftsrecht* generates historical insights, and it also generates arguments for practical legal reform. In England, in Gierke's own lifetime, there were a number of historians of a philosophical bent, but lacking Gierke's distinctive philosophical background, who had an interest in reforming the legal position of associations. It was these men who enabled Gierke's ideas, despite the technical difficulties, to be translated into England. And it was out of this process that a specifically English doctrine arose – the doctrine which came in due course to be known as political pluralism.

CHAPTER 4

Trusts and sovereigns

I

Gierke's ideas arrived in England in 1900, the year that F. W. Maitland published his translation of a part of the third volume of *Das deutsche Genossenschaftsrecht*. As noteworthy as the translation itself was Maitland's celebrated introduction to it, in which he set out what he took to be the significance for English readers of Gierke's arguments. This was to be the first of two important introductions to English editions of Gierke's work. The second was produced by Ernest Barker in 1933, as a preface to his translation of that part of the fourth volume which deals with natural-law theories of state and corporation. What follows here is a history of the period in English political thought which is spanned by the appearance of these two translations. It attempts to chart the ways in which Gierke's ideas were developed in an English setting, often in directions different from any Gierke himself might have envisaged. But it also attempts to explain what is a marked difference between the two introductions provided by Gierke's English translators. For whereas Maitland is broadly approving of Gierke's doctrine of the real personality of associations, Barker is not. In fact, Barker's introduction may be said to mark the demise of English political pluralism, just as Maitland's introduction marks its beginnings. Part of the reason why 'pluralism' is no longer a term with any specifically Gierkean resonance is that the Gierkean movement which originally adopted it ultimately failed, and Barker tries to explain why. The period in English ideas covered by this book is thus a self-contained one, with a relatively clear narrative structure: ideas arrived in England, achieved some prominence here, but failed to take root, and were eventually abandoned. To move from Maitland's introduction to Barker's is to tell that story.

64

The particular historical significance of the year in which Barker chose to produce a translation from the work of a theorist of the organic German state is hard to miss; indeed, 1933, as well as signalling the demise of Gierke's influence on English political theory, also marks the beginning of new interest in his thought in Germany, aiding his posthumous reputation there in the short term, diminishing it in the long. There is, however, nothing particularly significant about the moment at which Maitland chose to introduce Gierke to an English audience, though it was also the year in which the *Bürgerliches Gesetzbuch* finally came into force in Germany. If that event produced among Germans a keen interest in some of the practical implications of Gierke's ideas, there was no reason to expect it to have the same effect in England. The level of English interest in German law was not high, and the level of interest in the practical problems of codification was no higher. English lawyers, and English political theorists, were working with a juristic system very different from its German equivalent, with a very different history. Above all, it was not a system amenable to the sort of radical overhaul that codification entailed. In 1900 it was far from clear where Gierke's views about groups and their personality might fit into an English understanding of such things. In order to see where they did fit in, it is necessary first to describe the English position as it stood in that year, and had stood for many years before that.

II

The most immediate difference between the respective situations in England and Germany lay in the fact that in England a number of the issues which persistently troubled Gierke regarding the legal position of associations had already been resolved by parliament as early as 1862. In the Companies Act of that year parliament had dispensed with most of the formal requirements of incorporation, and it was allowed that 'any seven or more persons associated for any lawful purpose' might constitute a corporate entity. Maitland, in his introduction to Gierke, called this act 'splendidly courageous',[1] and Gierke himself, writing in 1868, acknowledged its significance, when he declared that 'regarding the status of the various personal economic fellowships [*Genossenschaften*] in the legal system, only the

---

[1] Gierke, *Political theories*, p. xxxviii.

most recent *English* Companies Act is advanced enough to comprehend all of these'.[2] What both Gierke and Maitland were applauding
was the willingness of parliament to abandon any pretence that
group personality lay in the gift of the sovereign, whose explicit
sanction was therefore in every case required. In other words,
English law was freed from what Gierke viewed as the most
pernicious consequence of Romanism, the concession theory.
Whether or not this was the consistent doctrine of the middle ages, it
had certainly persisted in the *Polizeistaaten* of Germany, where, as
Gierke put it, 'regardless of [an] association's aim the state asserted
its power to supervise the internal life of the society and (following
the prevailing theory of corporations) its right to approve [its]
existence and organisation'.[3] This was, of course, a right that
Hobbes would have recognised. Nevertheless, it was a right that
parliament had repudiated. During the last third of the nineteenth
century, associations in England were free to assume the status of
group persons as and when their members chose.

As we have seen, the attainment of corporate personality through
general laws rather than specific letters does not of itself denote that
the personality attained is a 'real' one – it is possible, as Hobbes
showed, to have a fiction theory which is not simply a theory of
concession. Furthermore, the act of 1862 was directed primarily
towards what we should now call 'businesses', a form of enterprise
which does not exhaust the range of purposes for which men
associate with one another. But for those groups – whether clubs,
charities or congregations – which did not feel themselves accommodated by the act, English law had long since provided another
resource which was denied to their German counterparts. That
resource was the trust, which Maitland called 'the blessed back stair'
of English law.[4] Its blessedness was revealed by the number of
different associations that made use of it, ranging from families and
small societies to the Jockey Club, the Stock Exchange, and even, as
Maitland pointed out, the Roman Church in England, with the Pope
at its head.

The concept of trusteeship freed group life in England over many
centuries from the constraining Roman apparatus of partnership and
incorporation. A partnership depended upon a contractual relationship between its members, and thus upon the specific identity of the

---

[2] Gierke, *Community*, p. 224.   [3] *Ibid.*, p. 188.   [4] Gierke, *Political theories*, p. xxxi.

partners involved. A trust, in contrast, could provide a legal existence for groups whose individual members remained completely unknown (as, for example, in the familiar case of a family trust, whose individual beneficiaries have no existence, legal or otherwise, while they remain unborn). This capacity to secure an identity for a group apart from its members is something that the trust shares with the corporation. But because the trust does not fall under the sway of Roman notions of group personality, it was never subject to the limitations of incorporation. At no point did trusts require the sanction of the sovereign, and they could be formed wherever a desire existed to protect those things which endure beyond the life-span of an individual man. Moreover, the beneficiary of a trust need not be construed in the conventional language of personality at all – it might, say in the case of a charity, be a 'purpose' which has no 'personal' equivalent (so, for example, the Council for the Protection of Rural England is a trust for whose beneficiary, a protected countryside, no person or persons are a convincing substitute). There were few things that were incapable of being protected by trust.

Of course, none of this means that trusts concealed the presence of 'real' group persons simply because they were relatively free from certain forms of control. Indeed, the formation of a trust is almost suggestive of the opposite: trustees act for those things which cannot act for themselves, whether they be incapable (or unborn) individuals, inanimate objects (such as hospitals) or intangible purposes. In this respect, the beneficiaries of trusteeship bear an obvious resemblance to Hobbes's fictitious persons, whose inability to act requires the appointment of a representative to act for them. But because the concept of the trust is not a conception of personality, there are important differences.[5] Trustees, unlike Hobbesian representatives, do not have their actions ascribed to whatever it is they are to benefit (when the trustees act, we do not imagine the protected countryside to have performed the action); they merely act on the beneficiary's behalf (as it makes perfect sense to act on behalf of a countryside which needs protecting). Similarly, trusts do not depend on the prior ownership of whatever it is that requires the appointment of trustees.

---

[5] One difference which is not contingent upon the issue of personality itself is that a trustee may act on behalf of a perfectly capable human being – for example, if the terms of a family trust stipulate that property is to remain in trust until beneficiaries reach a certain age, be it twenty-one, thirty or fifty – while Hobbes only treats natural men as fictitious persons when there is genuine incapacity ('Children, Fooles and Mad-men').

On Hobbes's account, representatives are appointed by whomever has dominion over the thing to be represented,[6] which invariably meant the sovereign. Trusteeship creates entities which nobody owns, and it protects them in a world in which dominion over such entities is often prized. This is why Maitland, in his introduction to Gierke, has an imaginary German jurist, asked to survey the English legal scene, begin his report as follows: ' "There is much in your history which we can envy, much in your free and easy formation of groups that we can admire. That great 'trust concept' of yours stood you in good stead when the days were evil: when your Hobbes, for example, was instituting unsavoury comparisons between corporations and *ascarides*." '[7]

There is another point to be made about the trust. Though it was a distinctively English concept, it was not English in the same way in which the *Genossenschaft*, as formulated by Gierke, was distinctively Germanic. That is, it did not form part of a coherent juristic alternative to Romanism. The English legal system contained many Roman elements. What it also contained were elements, like the trust, which had no systematic juristic basis at all. What is distinctive, and distinctively English, about the concept of the trust is that it is an essentially *ad hoc* formulation, developed without reference to the -isms, either Roman or German, of legal philosophy. For Maitland it was this above all which rendered the trust concept so serviceable – as he writes, 'behind the screen of trustees and *concealed from the direct scrutiny of legal theories* all manner of groups can flourish' (my italics).[8] It was Maitland's further conviction that the very adaptability of the trust made it unlikely that it would be able to survive the direct scrutiny of legal theorists. In a long essay he devoted to the subject of trusts and corporations, Maitland suggested that 'the Trust could hardly have been evolved among a people who had clearly formulated the distinction between a right in *personam* and a right in *rem*'.[9]

---

[6] Hobbes does not speak of purposes, but he does allow that things not merely inanimate but immaterial can be personated, such as 'an Idol, or meer Figment of the brain', even though 'an Idol is nothing' (see Hobbes, *Leviathan*, pp. 113–14). However, he is also insistent that where there is nothing to be owned, the authority for representation must proceed from the state. This was just what the English concept of the trust had managed to circumvent, allowing groups (including various dissenting religious sects) to secure for themselves some permanent organisation on the basis of their common beliefs, without their having to seek the prior consent of the state.

[7] Gierke, *Political theories*, p. xxxiii.   [8] *Ibid.*, p. xxix.

[9] *The collected papers of F. W. Maitland*, ed. H. A. L. Fisher, 3 vols. (Cambridge, 1911), vol. III, p. 325. The reason that this distinction was a block to the evolution of the idea of the trust

Later in the same piece, he asks: 'Can we have a trust for a
Genossenschaft, unless it is endowed with personality, or unless it is
steadily regarded as being a mere collective name for certain natural
persons? I believe that our answer should be that in theory we
cannot, but that in practice we can.'[10]

Here Maitland sets out the juristic alternatives: if the trust is not
to have an 'endowed' personality (like the *universitas*) or a 'collective'
personality (like the *societas*) then it would appear it must be
possessed of a 'real' personality (like the *Genossenschaft*). And yet
English law managed somehow to steer a path between Romanism
and Germanism, where in theory there is no room. If called upon
to provide some formulation for groups which did not fit the
moulds of legal theory, English lawyers were happy to describe
them as 'unincorporate bodies'. No continental lawyer, however
envious of the adaptability of this phrase, would allow it to stand
(any more, one imagines, than would have Hobbes, whose pre-
eminent example of 'a Name contradictory and inconsistent' was
'*incorporeall body*'[11]). Maitland has his imaginary German declare it
'a term which seems to us to make for truth, but also for self-
contradiction'.[12] What we are left with, therefore, is a distinctively
English, and distinctly unHegelian, form of synthesis: ideas are
assumed to be true because, when pieced together, they work; they
are not assumed to work because, when pieced together, they are
true.

In conclusion to his paper on the English trust, Maitland vouchsafes
one prediction, that 'in England *sozialpolitische* will take precedence of

was that the rights created by the idea of the trust belonged neither to particular persons
(rights in *personam*) nor to particular objects (rights in *rem*). The beneficiary of a trust was not
a 'person', but nor were trusts organised around the ownership of particular 'things' (trusts
might remain intact even though their property did not, as the things they owned were
bought and sold). Yet in theory (in Roman theory) the rights of ownership must be attached
either to the persons that do the owning or to the things that are owned. Maitland made a
similar point in a letter he wrote to an American lawyer in 1902, in which he discusses the
'unconscious' process by which the English arrived at the concept of the charitable trust: 'I
think that continental law shows that this was a step which could not be taken and should
not be taken by men whose heads were full of Roman law' (quoted in H. A. L. Fisher,
Frederick William Maitland. A biographical sketch (Cambridge, 1910), p. 134).

[10] Maitland, *Collected papers*, vol. III, p. 367.
[11] See Hobbes, *Leviathan*, p. 30. Maitland gives a different, though similar, example. In his
essay on 'Moral personality and legal personality' he writes: 'For some time past we have
had upon our statute book the term "unincorporate body". Suppose that a Frenchman [i.e.
a product of the Enlightenment] saw it, what would he say? "Unincorporate body:
inanimate soul!"' (Maitland, *Collected papers*, vol. III, p. 317).
[12] Gierke, *Political theories*, p. xxxiii.

rechtswissenschaftliche considerations'.[13] It was from this priority of the 'social-political' over the 'legal-scientific' that the trust had developed.[14] But if this was so, it is not clear what need the English legal system might be expected to have of a Gierkean *Genossenschaftstheorie*. In simple terms, it could be argued that groups in England had got by perfectly well without one. But it might also be argued that in an English context Gierke's ideas would generate a particular sort of dilemma. By the standards of legal theory, Gierke's arguments were consistently supportive of independent associations; yet as examples of legal theory *per se*, they ran against the English experience, which found freedom for groups in an environment free from pressing theoretical concerns. Clearly there are disadvantages to any system of dealing with associations which is primarily pragmatic: what appears to be flexibility at some moments may seem to be unpredictability at others, and the groups exposed to it will sometimes feel the need of the security that comes with consistency. Nevertheless, consistency entails rigidity, and excessive rigidity was the one thing which the English in their treatment of groups had managed to avoid. A new legal theory arriving in England had to demonstrate not just its superiority to other theories, but also that the adoption of any theory was worth the inconvenience.

It would be wrong to press the particularity of this situation too far. Gierke's Germanism was itself a reaction against what he perceived to be the excessive formalism of Romanist theories, and it was certainly intended to accommodate better than them social and political developments in Germany. The concept of 'real' personality is, after all, suggestive of a life lived apart from the restraining influence of legal technicality. But still, Gierke did express his convictions in highly theoretical terms. He was able to do so because of the dialectical idealism he embraced, which allowed juristic and social considerations to be synthesised within a single world of ideas. The ultimate expression of this is the concept of the *Rechtsstaat* itself: *Recht* encompasses the 'legal-scientific' domain; *Staat* the 'social-political'; together they constitute a single conception of both. This was, however, a device which was unlikely to be found satisfactory anywhere which had not been thoroughly penetrated by Hegelianism first. This was not true of England, and it was certainly not true of

---

[13] Maitland, *Collected papers*, vol. III, p. 382.

[14] The law of trusts was a matter of 'equity', and matters of equity were dealt with in the Court of Chancery, the most 'social-political' of England's legal institutions.

English jurisprudence, such as it was. There were, therefore, still particular problems to be faced, if Gierke's ideas about groups within the state were to be translated into England. It was not clear, first of all, whether there was need of any alternative to the *status quo*. And second, in the absence of any idealistic tendency to synthesise the 'social-political' with the 'legal-scientific', it was possible that the *Genossenschaftsidee* would fall somewhere between two stools.

III

Of course, the position of associations within the state was only half the problem as Gierke understood it. There was also the matter of the state itself, and here too the situation in England was somewhat different from that in Germany. First of all, there was in England no nationalist cause to which Gierke's views about group personality could be allied. Gierke own nationalism stemmed from a wish to see Germany unified, and Germanic laws of association then applied within the new nation. In England, the law regarding associations was as English as it was ever going to be, and the kingdom within which it applied had long ago been united. United is not quite the same as unified, and the fact that the state itself was not English but British meant that there remained considerable scope for nationalist politics. But this was a nationalism of a kind quite different from that countenanced by Gierke. First, it had no obvious juristic element – the British state already contained distinct national legal systems (the criminal justice systems in England and Scotland, for example) without its compromising the integrity of the nation-state as a whole. Second, it was a nationalism geared not towards unification but the reverse, a separating out of national groups from within the pre-viously united whole. In general terms, proposals for devolutionary reform are compatible with Gierke's preference for federalist poli-tical structures. But federalism for Gierke presupposed national unity. Where nations themselves constitute groups within the state, the issues are rather different, not least because of the inevitable contrast that exists between the homogeneity of the parts and the heterogeneity of the whole. If national identities are strong, the state is more likely to appear as the sum of its parts than as a unified whole. So, where Gierke's nationalism tended towards a conception of plurality-in-unity ('the German Empire'), other forms of nation-alism tended towards artificial conceptions of unity-in-plurality

('Great Britain and Ireland'), and towards the fragmentation which Gierke believed such conceptions to bring in their wake.

Nevertheless, there was at least one thing that England and Germany did share with regard to their respective experiences of the state, and that was a common heritage in the history of ideas. Though in varying degrees and with differing consequences, both nations had been the recipients of natural-law theories of the state; and in particular, both nations had been exposed to the intellectual legacy of Thomas Hobbes. As in Germany, political theorists in England had by 1900 long since abandoned any preference for the familiar doctrines of natural law. But whereas in Germany these doctrines had been supplanted by idealistic and romantic conceptions of the state, in England natural-law theory gave way to utilitarianism. Following Hume, utilitarians rejected the Hobbesian conception of a state born out of a contract between individuals in the state of nature. There had been no state of nature for the utilitarians, or at least no such state which could clearly be marked off from the state of civil society that replaced it. But this rejection of the conceptual foundations of Hobbes's thought did not entail a rejection of the ultimate doctrine in which it issued. Utilitarians accepted Hobbes's conviction that political authority was founded entirely on sovereignty, and that sovereignty was based exclusively on command. To this extent, English political thought remained squarely under the influence of 'antique-modern' thinking: it postulated a state divided between those who made the law, and those who observed it. In 1900, the most familiar version of this doctrine was still the one which had been formulated by John Austin nearly seventy years earlier. Austin's definition ran as follows: 'If a *determinate* human superior, *not* in a habit of obedience to a like superior, receive *habitual* obedience from the *bulk* of a given society, that determinate superior is sovereign in that society, and the society (including the superior) is a society political and independent.'[15] This is an altogether pared-down account of the relation which lies at the heart of Hobbes's political theory. In the gap between 'habitual' and 'constant', and between 'bulk' and 'all', Austin leaves room for that area of political existence in which command gives way to punishment. Otherwise, he ignores all extraneous considerations, beyond

---

[15] J. Austin, *The province of jurisprudence determined*, ed. W. E. Rumble (Cambridge, 1995) p. 166.

the mere fact of obedience, and the distinction that must follow between the obedient and the obeyed.

Austin's theory of sovereignty seems to provide an obvious focus for the application of Gierke's arguments in an English setting. Yet because Austin's is so pared-down a version of Hobbes's account, it is not always clear how Gierke's arguments might be related to it. For example, Austin has no great interest in the concept of personality. Certainly, echoing Hobbes,[16] he accepts that a determinate human superior may consist either of 'a sovereign person, or a sovereign body of persons', and that the obedient bulk of the population might be described as 'persons in a state of subjection [i.e. subjects]'.[17] But he uses the term in what he himself calls an 'extensive' sense, simply to signify 'physical or individual' personality.[18] It carries with it no implications about the nature of sovereign power. Austin also accepts, as a result of his identifying personality with the physical man, that there are some entities, such as 'collections or aggregates of physical persons', which may have to be deemed persons 'by figment, and for the sake of brevity of discourse'.[19] However, this too has no bearing on the question of sovereignty. It is, for Austin, simply a technical matter, related to certain issues in private law, and belonging therefore 'to the detail rather than the *generalia* of the science'[20] – the science in question being jurisprudence, and its *generalia* constituting the definition of keys terms, such as sovereignty. There is nothing in Austin's account to produce the sorts of limitations which Hobbes sought to impose on group persons within the state. Austin's sovereign has no personality at all, beyond the individual personalities of whichever human beings make it up. Groups which are formed of its subjects, and which may have a

---

[16] Austin quotes Hobbes at length during the course of his lectures on jurisprudence, and devotes an extended footnote to defending him against his 'grossly and thoroughly mistaken modern censors', writing 'I know of no other writer (excepting our great contemporary Jeremy Bentham) who has uttered so many truths, at once new and important, concerning the necessary structure of supreme political government, and the larger of the necessary distinctions implied by positive law [i.e. the distinction between the sovereign and the rest]' (*ibid.*, p. 231). Austin does, though, criticise Hobbes on two counts: '1. He inculcates too absolutely the religious obligation of obedience to present or established government . . . 2. Instead of directly deriving the existence of political government, from a perception by the bulk of the governed of its great and obvious expediency, he ascribes the origin of sovereignty, and of independent political society, to a fictitious agreement or covenant' (*ibid.*, p. 229).

[17] *Ibid.*, p. 165.

[18] J. Austin, *Lectures on jurisprudence, or the philosophy of positive law*, ed. R. Campbell, third edn, 2 vols. (London, 1869), vol. I, p. 362.

[19] *Ibid.*, p. 364.   [20] *Ibid.*

personality of their own, pose no threat, because Austin's conception of sovereignty does not provide a person of the state for them to threaten. It simply provides for commands, and for the juristic superiority of whoever issues them.

In fact, Austin did not strictly speaking produce a theory of the state at all. This is partly a matter of terminology. As illustrated above, the term Austin uses to describe an association which contains a person or group of persons who are sovereign is 'society political and independent'. He does employ the term 'state', ostensibly as a synonym for 'sovereign',[21] but also in what could be called an 'extensive' sense, to denote any associated group of individuals outside of the private domain, whether containing a sovereign or not. The Hobbesian equivalent of what Austin calls a 'state' is therefore not 'commonwealth' but any of those 'systemes' that Hobbes would describe as 'politique'. Moreover, Austin's use of 'state' in this extensive sense allows him to accommodate within his theory of sovereignty states which are federations, and federations which are made up of states, in a manner which Hobbes's use of the term would disallow. So Austin speaks of 'composite states' and also of 'systems of confederated states' (with particular reference to the newly formed system known as 'the United States of America'), and he reconciles his conception of sovereignty with both. The one usage he will not allow is the 'incongruous epithet' that styles states '*half* or *imperfectly* sovereign'[22] – this is a combination of terms he considers impossible, because it is not the state itself but only what Austin calls a 'portion' of it that is sovereign, and because sovereignty itself is an absolute quality, admitting of no half-measures or degrees. Otherwise, Austin is strictly indifferent as to the form which states may assume. And it is this indifference which distinguishes Austin from those 'antique-modern' theorists of the state with whom Gierke was primarily engaged. Austin did not believe that the distinction between the sovereign portion of a political society and its bulk had any moral or even what he describes as 'constitutional' significance. Indeed, the 'antique-modern' distinction between the obedient and the obeyed is subsumed in Austin's account by what is a more immediately modern distinction, between Austin's preferred 'science' – what we would now call analytical jurisprudence – and other, value-laden approaches to the subject. For Austin, jurisprudence was

---

[21] See Austin, *The province of jurisprudence*, p. 190.   [22] *Ibid.*, p. 199.

the study of positive law, which is the law made by sovereigns; and his definition of sovereignty was simply designed to determine what the province of jurisprudence must therefore be. Outside of that province lay questions of 'positive morality' and 'constitutional law', and these could not be resolved by reference to anything within it, but only by reference to the index of 'Divine law', which was utility. Thus Austin explicitly, and in obvious contrast to Hobbes, denied that a description of what sovereignty is could have any bearing on the question of what sovereigns should do, or of what the political societies they governed ought to be like. That was the business of a different science – what he called 'the science of political economy'[23] – and Austin railed against those who would confuse the two, reserving an especial contempt for all appeals to 'the sacred rights of sovereigns' (once again with particular reference to the formation of the United States, and to 'the stupid and infuriate majority who rushed into that odious war [and] could perceive and discourse of nothing but the *sovereignty* of the mother country and her so called *right* to tax her subjects'[24]). Austin had no wish to derive a theory of the state from his conception of sovereignty, nor a moral from his juristic conception of order, since he believed that morality and jurisprudence had nothing to do with each other.

IV

The sharpness of this disjunction takes some of the edge off a Gierkean critique of English political thought at the turn of the century, given that the place where an 'antique-modern' conception of sovereignty had most steadfastly endured was also the place where the least claims were being made on its behalf. That edge is further dulled when it is considered that the durability of Austinian ideas did not mean that English political thought was lacking a theory of the state altogether. For if English jurisprudence had proved entirely resistant to Hegelian influence, English philosophy had not. Alongside utilitarianism there had grown up during the second half of the nineteenth century an English school of philosophical idealism, and

---

[23] Austin believed not only that political economy was the science that legislators ought to study but also that it ought to be studied by the populace as a whole, writing that 'the best of moral securities . . . would arise from a wide diffusion, through the mass of subjects, of the soundest political science which the lights of the age could afford' (see *ibid.*, p. 328). He certainly did not believe that the same was true of jurisprudence.

[24] *Ibid.*, p. 55.

with it a very different perspective on the problems of political theory. The influence of this school was probably at its height during the 1870s and 1880s, under the aegis of T. H. Green, yet in a sense it was to culminate in 1899, with the publication of Bernard Bosanquet's *The philosophical theory of the State*. Bosanquet's political philosophy was anything but 'antique-modern' in Gierke's sense, for it portrayed the state as a unified whole which embraced every aspect of social existence. The whole itself Bosanquet described as 'organisation', and though the direct analogy was not with an individuated organism, it was still with an organic entity, the human mind, which Bosanquet characterised as 'a fabric of organised dispositions'.[25] Sovereignty, for Bosanquet, resided in no particular portion of society, but in the general will of the organised whole. And within that general organisation he allowed considerable scope for the lesser organisations that every such society must contain: its families, partnerships, corporations, even what Bosanquet calls (following Hegel) its 'classes', all of which are aspects of the general whole, and in each of which individuals discover what it is to be part of a particular whole. Bosanquet spent much of his life championing the cause of voluntary associations against those who would concentrate only on a direct relation between the individual and the state.[26] In *The philosophical theory of the State* he expressed these convictions with regard to what he calls there 'the Corporation or Trade Society',[27] a phrase which covers all those workers' associations that Gierke had brought under the heading of 'the modern association movement'. Of the relation of their members to these 'corporations', Bosanquet agrees with Hegel that 'it is the very root of ethical connection between the private and the general interest, and the State should see to it that this root holds as strongly as possible'.[28] He believed that in such self-formed associations men learned honour, loyalty and the other social virtues, and he also believed that without a fully

---

[25] See B. Bosanquet, *The philosophical theory of the State*, fourth edn (London, 1923), pp. 160–1.

[26] Bosanquet, along with his wife Helen, was the leading light behind the Charity Organisation Society (COS), which promoted voluntary forms of social welfare against the organisation of social welfare by the state. (An account of the work of the COS is provided in R. Plant and A. Vincent, *Philosophy, politics and citizenship: the life and thought of the British Idealists* (Oxford, 1984), pp. 94–131.) Bosanquet's theory of the state did not entail a commitment to state remedies for social ills. The apparent contrariness of this position forms the subject of S. Collini, 'Hobhouse, Bosanquet and the state: philosophical Idealism and political argument in England, 1880–1918', *Past and Present*, 72 (1976), 86–111.

[27] See Bosanquet, *The philosophical theory of the State*, pp. 258–9.   [28] *Ibid.*

developed range of these associations the state's own capacity to develop would be stifled.

Clearly Bosanquet's philosophical outlook is very close to that of Gierke, to the extent that even their respective judgments of Hobbes are almost identical (Bosanquet arguing that '[Hobbes] inherits the language which enables him to predicate unity and personality of the state, but in his mouth the terms have not recovered a true political meaning, and the social right, which they are intended to account for, remains a mere name').[29] But there is one important difference. Bosanquet's account of group life has no obvious juristic dimension. It is not simply that he gives no clue in his writing as to how the state is to secure the roots of corporate activity in law. It is more that he regards technical jurisprudence as something a philosophical theory of the state must get beyond, as it 'move[s] toward a point of view which deals more completely with life and culture'.[30] In this respect, Bosanquet's is a brand of Hegelianism which contrasts directly with Gierke's, and more closely resembles Hegel's own. He does not provide a secure juristic foundation for the part he wishes groups to play in the life of the state. He does not in fact provide what is an overtly moral conception of order with any juristic basis at all. Instead, he concentrates on the general will, which is a product of mind (essentially an ethical or metaphysical concept), not of personality (in this context essentially a juristic one). This means that Bosanquet did not have to face the problems encountered by theorists like Hobbes and Rousseau, who sought to formulate the unity of the state in juristic terms.[31] But it also means that he did not address the particular problem which engaged Gierke, that of providing groups within the state with a clear juristic expression of their own unity. Indeed, Bosanquet did not address any of those problems which are commonly understood in legal terms – the

---

[29] *Ibid.*, p. 98.   [30] *Ibid.*, p. 37.

[31] Bosanquet makes much of Rousseau's conception of the 'general will', but he also suggests that Rousseau himself could not make full use of it because he remained preoccupied with the problem of relating it to the 'will of all'. In the end, Bosanquet argues, Rousseau succeeded only in 'enthroning' the will of all, because he was fixed on the notion that the general will could be expressed in the vote taken by an assembly. We can express this argument in terms of personality: for Bosanquet, the general will was an expression of the 'moral' personality of the state; the will of all, in contrast, was an expression only of its 'legal' personality, since it was arrived at by legalistic conventions (i.e. contracts and shows of hands); and the solution, for Bosanquet, was to discount the possibility of deriving a general will from mere legal procedures, and instead look for it in the moral life of the state as a whole.

problems of representation, or of obedience, or of ownership. He does, it is true, make some reference to the law of property. But he refers to it as 'Shylock's law', and he dismisses it on the grounds that it simply produces a world 'appropriated by legal "persons"'.[32] It was precisely the purpose of Bosanquet's political philosophy to transcend such legalistic notions altogether.

English political thought at the end of the nineteenth century was thus split between two approaches to the subject, one resulting in a juristic conception of order with no moral dimension, the other a moral conception of order with no juristic dimension. Both employed the familiar language of state and sovereignty – Bosanquet still insisted on calling his state 'sovereign'[33] – but each meant something quite different by it. In one sense, there was an obvious Gierkean resolution of this situation, and that was to seek some synthesis of the two. But there was also an obvious problem. The philosophical approach on which Gierkean synthesis relied had already been annexed by one of the two sides to be reconciled – Hegelianism in England, instead of being something which might with profit be brought to bear on Bosanquet's thought, was already identified with it. So, just as there was a dilemma to be faced at the level of practical legal reform if Gierke's ideas were to take root in England, there was also a dilemma to be faced at the more abstract level of political theory. The philosophical theory of the state which most nearly reflected Gierke's own had been produced by a man who shared few of Gierke's interests, and in time the curious situation arose of Gierkean doctrines being used to attack the most visible English exponent of Germanic political philosophy. Bosanquet's emphasis on the general will, and his consequent neglect of the issues of group personality, was taken to reflect a greater concern on his part with unity than with plurality, and as we shall see, the English followers of Gierke held this against him. Meanwhile, the intellectual domain in which juristic issues were still taken seriously was also the place in which they had been denuded of all moral force. The use of Gierke's ideas to challenge some of the 'antique-modern' notions of Austinian jurisprudence did not of itself generate an alternative conception of order; that required something more, a challenge to the presupposi-

---

[32] *Ibid.*, p. 240.

[33] Bosanquet makes use of Rousseau to explain what he understands by sovereignty: 'We may, in conclusion, sum up the whole theory of state action in the formula which we inherit from Rousseau – that Sovereignty is the exercise of the General Will' (*ibid.*, p. 215).

tions of English jurisprudence *per se*, and at the end of the nineteenth century the most visible challenge to the presuppositions of English jurisprudence was being provided by Bernard Bosanquet. Hegelianism, which Gierke used to reconcile jurisprudence with other disciplines, served in England to set them apart. The result was that where Gierke might have seen an opportunity for synthesis, English theorists tended to face a series of hard choices – *between* juristic and moral considerations, and for one at the expense of the other.

v

There was one further choice available to English political theorists, of a kind unlikely to have occurred to Gierke himself. Instead of seeking to synthesise Austin and Bosanquet, it was possible that they might simply conflate the two, and then use aspects of Gierke's thought in the attempt to construct an alternative to both. To have had his ideas conflated with those of a thinker like Bosanquet would almost certainly have baffled Austin, given that he did not conceal his contempt for 'the high ideal philosophy which the Germans oppose to the philosophy of Bacon and Locke; the earthly, grovelling, empirical philosophy which deigns to scrutinise facts and stoops to observation and induction'.[34] Moreover, there is concrete evidence that it was a prospect which caused Bosanquet real concern, and he went out of his way to emphasise 'the diametrical and fundamental contrast between Austinian sovereignty, the sovereignty that is contemplated by the legal experts, and the sovereignty contemplated by a theory such as ours'.[35] Nevertheless, Bosanquet made this statement in the 1919 preface to a new edition of *The philosophical theory of the State*, and he made it in response to those who had over the previous two decades persisted in ignoring this distinction. Prime among them were the advocates of what Bosanquet was by now calling 'pluralism', and they included theorists who had been influenced, if only via Maitland, by Gierke.

What happened during these two decades was that a new split had emerged in English political thought, partly under Gierke's influence, between, on the one hand, the proponents of group-based, or what were sometimes called 'federalistic' theories, and, on the other, the traditional theorists of state and sovereignty. What this entailed is

---

[34] Austin, *The province of jurisprudence*, p. 342.
[35] Bosanquet, *The philosophical theory of the State*, p. lv.

best illustrated in the remarks made by Ernest Barker in his 1914 survey of *Political thought in England from Herbert Spencer to the present day.* Barker records in this book the growing interest that had been shown during the early years of the twentieth century in associations other than the state. He goes on to speak of what he calls 'a federalistic feeling [that] is curiously widespread'.[36] This he attempts to characterise as 'a feeling that the single unitary state, with its single sovereignty, is a dubious conception, which is hardly true to the facts of life'.[37] Yet single sovereignty, and the single, unitary state, were, as Gierke would have been the first to point out, not necessarily the same thing. A federalistic feeling might be opposed to one or to the other, but it does not follow that it must be opposed to both: Austin, who gives us a single sovereignty, is happy with all sorts of federalistic states, while Bosanquet, whose state is unitary, is content with a distinctly federalistic conception of sovereignty. In truth, many of those who shared Barker's federalistic feeling – and they included fabians, distributists, guild socialists and devolutionists – would have been uninterested in the niceties of these distinctions. But that was certainly not true of Barker himself (later to produce his own edition of Gierke), and nor was it true of some of the others covered by his survey, including Maitland, and also J. N. Figgis, who helped Maitland with his translation of Gierke, and who provides one of the later subjects of this book. It is therefore necessary to address one final question, before turning in detail to the history of the period to which Barker's remarks allude – to ask how it might be possible that two conceptions as different as Bosanquet's state and Austin's sovereign could be deemed not merely dubious, but dubious in the same way.

In essence, there are two possibilities. The first, and simplest, means of generating a common alternative to both juristic and moral conceptions of order is to embrace, or at least to accept, disorder. The political philosophy of disorder is anarchism. At first sight, anarchism is a highly unlikely refuge for defenders of real group personality, if only because of the term's extreme individualistic bias. But by the end of the nineteenth century anarchistic doctrine was starting to assume a distinctive, group-based form. This was syndicalism. Again, syndicalism is an improbable vehicle of Gierkean views

[36] E. Barker, *Political thought in England from Herbert Spencer to the present day, 1848–1914* (London, 1915), p. 181.
[37] *Ibid.*

about the role of groups within the state. Syndicalists, whose intellectual roots lay in France, believed in seeking independence for groups of workers apart from, not within, the structures of the state. Like almost all anarchists, syndicalists tended in the end to fall back on moral conceptions of order. But unlike, say, Bosanquet, whose moral conception of order subsumed juristic concerns, syndicalists were prepared to accept that moral and juristic considerations must clash. In the syndicalist scheme of things, the rights enjoyed by groups apart from the law brought them into conflict with the law, and could not be accommodated to it. This was not something which Gierke could have accepted any more than could Bosanquet. And yet, in England, there were points at which Gierkean and syndicalist ideas seem to have overlapped. Barker, for instance, writing during the 1930s, offered this reminiscence of an encounter he had had with J. N. Figgis over twenty years earlier: 'I shall never forget him taking me round the house of the community in which he lived at Mirfield [Figgis was a clergyman], and suddenly exclaiming, "Barker, I really believe I am a syndicalist!"'[38] Similarly, Harold Laski, who was to become one of the leading exponent of English political pluralism, was also, as his most recent biographers have noted, 'a convert to syndicalism' on graduating from Oxford in 1912, where he had been Barker's pupil.[39] This did not prevent Laski, any more than it did Figgis, from being receptive to Gierke's ideas, as Laski acknowledged on Figgis's death in 1919, when he wrote that 'twenty-five years ago [Figgis] was still an Austinian, and the means of escape from the cobwebs of that nightmare he did not see until Maitland told him that in Gierke's magistral book he would find the secret of political freedom'.[40] Yet in the unlikely connection they drew between Gierke's arguments and the theoretical tenets of syndicalism, Figgis and Laski also indicated a possible means of escape not merely from Austinian, but all conceptions of the state and its sovereignty.

Nevertheless, syndicalism cannot be the whole, nor even a very large part, of the answer. For if Laski did convert to it while at Oxford, it would not have been under Barker's influence.[41] Syndic-

---

[38] E. Barker, *Church, State and study* (London, 1930), p. 131.

[39] See I. Kramnick and B. Sheerman, *Harold Laski. A life on the left* (London, 1993), p. 74.

[40] Laski, 'A great churchman', *New Republic*, 20 (20 August 1919), 95.

[41] Laski made out that Barker had influenced him greatly but Barker knew better: 'Laski's dedication of his first book, *Studies in the problem of sovereignty*, in 1917 to [H. A. L.] Fisher and Barker with effusive praise for both was clearly difficult for Barker to accept. He wrote to Laski that he made too much of him' (Kramnick and Sheerman, *Harold Laski*, p. 60).

alist was not a word which Barker would ever have used to describe himself, and nor would he have used it to describe the beliefs of many of those whose feelings he characterised as 'federalistic' in 1914. Indeed, 'federalism' and 'syndicalism' are not terms which can easily be reconciled with one another: one is suggestive of order, and the other is not. Barker believed in order. He did also, it is true, include Figgis among his 'federalistic' thinkers, and syndicalism is certainly no harder to reconcile with federalism than it is with Gierke's *Genossenschaftsidee*. But Figgis's public pronouncements were, as we shall see, considerably more restrained than his private confession to Barker would suggest. It is this which made it a confession, and it is this which explains the surprised tone of Barker's reminiscence, a response which Maitland, who taught Figgis at Cambridge, would surely have shared, had he but lived to see it – whatever else Maitland might have told his protégé to look for in Gierke's 'magistral book', it would not have been encouragement for his anarchistic tendencies. But if Maitland and Barker were not prepared to countenance the radical alternatives which attracted their former pupils, there is in the very fact of this relation between them the suggestion of a different means of escape from state and sovereignty combined. Maitland taught Figgis, and Barker taught Laski, because all four were historians. Austin and Bosanquet were not – one was a jurist, the other a philosopher. There is thus a second alternative to theories of both juristic and moral conceptions of order, and it is simply history. History does not presuppose disorder. It does, however, presuppose change. Both Austin and Bosanquet, though they recognised historical change, sought to discount it, if in very different ways: Austin circumvented it in grovelling, empirical science; Bosanquet transcended it in high, ideal metaphysics.[42] But each believed that it was possible to make general claims about political existence which were not undermined by changing political circumstance.

---

[42] Neither, of course, discounted history as an intellectual exercise altogether, only as the primary determinant of the particular intellectual exercises in which they were engaged. Austin recognised that 'the specific or particular causes of specific or particular governments, are rather appropriate matter for particular history, than for the present general disquisition' (Austin, *The province of jurisprudence determined*, p. 247); Bosanquet, meanwhile, wrote that 'if we consider that hypothetical necessary or relative judgment is entirely based upon categorical judgments, that all nexus is within an individuality, we shall see that history may be received into the intelligible unity of knowledge without sacrificing its concrete import and characteristic significance' (B. Bosanquet, *Logic*, 2 vols. (Oxford, 1911) vol. I, p. 262).

Austin's sovereign and Bosanquet's state are the manifestation of that belief. A historian of changing political circumstance could be expected to question both.

The case that a historian might make against the single state with its single sovereignty can be expressed as a form of pluralism. Here, though, the contrast is not with unity but with identity: jurists like Austin and philosophers like Bosanquet look for an identity in our experiences of sovereignty and the state; historians, in contrast, study each experience on its own terms, and are able thereby to reveal the plurality of the whole. It is in this way that historians disclose the contingency of our conceptions of order. They establish the contingent relation between a particular political theory and the historical circumstances which surround it, and they also establish the possibility of different circumstances giving rise to different theories. It was as historians that the English pluralists were drawn to Gierke, and from his work they drew a clear sense of the contingency of theories of the state and its sovereignty. However, Gierke was not able to provide them with a theory of pluralism in the sense outlined above. Contingency in Gierke's history was transcended by the Hegelian concept of the *Rechtsstaat*, so that the history generated its own form of identity. His was, in Karl Popper's sense, a 'historicist'[43] account of the past: it found in historical variety a 'rhythm' or 'pattern' from which general theoretical truths might be derived. As such, it stands in contrast to what Popper calls 'historism':[44] the view that statements of general theoretical truths are simply the contingent products of particular historical circumstance. Historism, like anarchism, is a denial of all that Austin and Bosanquet jointly represent. But historism, like anarchism, was not a Gierkean, nor even a Germanic doctrine.[45] Instead, it was closer to the recent philosophical tradition of another nation, the United States, whose national

---

[43] Popper defines historicism as 'an approach to the social sciences which assumes historical prediction is their principle aim, and assumes that this aim is attainable by discovering the "rhythms" or the "patterns", the "laws" or the "trends" that underlie the evolution of history' (K. Popper, *The poverty of historicism* (London, 1957), p. 3).

[44] Popper defines historism as 'the possibility of analysing and explaining the difference between the various sociological doctrines and schools by referring . . . to their connexion with the interests prevailing in a particular historical period' (*ibid.*, p. 17).

[45] There is a famous Germanic account of historism given in Friedrich Meinecke's book of that title. However, what Meinecke means by 'historism' is closer to what Popper means by 'historicism' – it is intended to provide us with an understanding of national identities, of what Isaiah Berlin calls in his introduction to Meinecke's book 'social wholes, which develop like plants, each obedient to its own specific nature' (F. Meinecke, *Historism. The rise of a new historical outlook*, trans. J. E. Anderson (London, 1972), p. xi).

philosophy at the turn of the century was pragmatism. The American pragmatists emphasised, above all, the contingency of general claims to truth. They were not themselves historians, but their understanding of the world was historistic. What is more, one of them, William James, characterised the nature of that understanding as 'pluralism'. It was from James, not Gierke, that the English pluralists took their name.

The details of the route that English political thought took during the early years of this century to get from Gierke to William James will be set out in what follows. For now, it is important to emphasise that the historistic element in pluralist thought introduces a third level to the case that might be made against the single state with its single sovereignty. Beyond the arguments for legal reform, and beyond the arguments within political theory, there was also scope for arguments *about* political theory, taken as a whole. These last took place at the level of meta-theory, and they concerned not any particular conception of order, but rather what was involved in the business of ordering such conceptions. Of course, there was a deeply meta-theoretical aspect to Gierke's thought, as there is to all forms of Hegelianism. But in England, where Hegelian synthesis was not an option, the meta-theoretical issues tended, as they did at the other levels of argument, to resolve themselves into a series of choices. The pluralists, as historians, wished to repudiate attempts by theorists of the state to transcend history. Yet they also, as political theorists, wished at times to transcend history themselves. They had, therefore, to choose between those theories of political order which overrode historical contingency, and that sense of contingency which made political theory impossible. This was the dilemma of historism.

VI

Each of the dilemmas that were faced by the English pluralists had its roots in the same problem – how to translate Gierke's ideas into England without recourse to the synthetic ideal of the *Rechtsstaat*. In its absence, the English pluralists were to take Gierke's ideas about the personality of associations in directions that would have surprised him. But as they did so, they helped to uncover the limitations of his thought. For the lack of a synthetic, conceptual catch-all is not necessarily a handicap in the construction of political theory. It does at least mean that the hard choices which characterise political existence cannot be glossed over, as the high ideal philosophy of the Germans has a tendency to do. The choices faced by the English pluralists were, as we shall see, real ones. Unable to avoid them, and without the concept of the *Rechtsstaat* to fall back on, they discovered what Gierke's ideas about the personality of associations really entailed.

The following account of English political pluralism falls into three stages. The first explores the origins of pluralist thought in Maitland's work on Gierke. The second looks at the attempts of four English theorists to build a distinctive political theory on the back of themes that Maitland developed. These were Figgis, Barker, Laski and also G. D. H. Cole, whose guild socialism owed much to Maitland's influence. The third describes the rapid decline in the significance attached to pluralist ideas in England, culminating in Barker's reappraisal of Gierke in 1933. In truth, the period during which the influence of political pluralism can be said to have been at its peak barely extends beyond the second decade of the century. These years were, of course, overshadowed by the First World War, and the war provides a recurring theme in what follows. Gierke lived to see it, but he did not live to see many of its consequences (he died in 1921). The pluralists who did found it increasingly hard to reconcile ideas whose origins lay in the nineteenth century with the political conditions of the twentieth. This tells us something about twentieth-century politics. But it also tells us something about those theories of the state with which nineteenth-century thinkers like Gierke had been engaged. This is the theme of the last part of this book, which seeks to take the story back not just to Gierke but also to Hobbes, in an attempt to resolve the issue of the personality of that association we still call the state, and thereby to say something about the limitations of political theory itself.

PART II

Political pluralism

CHAPTER 5

Maitland and the real personality of associations

I

In 1903 F. W. Maitland, the greatest legal historian in England, delivered the Sidgwick lecture at Newnham College under the title 'Moral personality and legal personality'. His subject was the legal status of associations within the state, and also the legal status of the state itself, given that it too was an association, or 'organised group' as Maitland termed it. The question Maitland sought to address was whether such groups were to be considered to be persons in their own right. His lecture surveys the history of the law regarding associations, and also the theorising that went with it, in order to establish some of the difficulties which attached to the fiction theory that continental jurists had derived from Roman law. The view that groups were persons merely by a 'fiction of law' Maitland contrasts with what he calls 'the morality of common sense', which understands them to be something more.[1] On the question of what that something might be, however, Maitland refuses to be drawn. 'As to philosophy', he announces at the conclusion of his talk, 'that is no affair of mine'.[2] It belonged to others 'to tell us of the very nature of things and the very nature of persons'.[3] All it behove a 'mere lawyer' to recognise was that 'if *n* men unite themselves in an organised group, jurisprudence, unless it wishes to pulverise the group, must see *n* + 1 persons'.[4] And yet these disclaimers – which Maitland puts down to 'conscious ignorance and unfeigned humility'[5] – are more than a little disingenuous. For even a mere lawyer, once he insists that groups of individuals have a personality of their own, is committed to looking beyond the realm of mere law. He is, after all, insisting that the law 'see' the personality of the group, as though it

[1] Maitland, *Collected papers*, vol. III, p. 314.   [2] *Ibid.*, p. 318.
[3] *Ibid.*   [4] *Ibid.*, p. 316.   [5] *Ibid.*, p. 318.

were something already there, rather than 'inventing' it, as though it were not. It is the fiction theory which is the 'lawyerly' response to the question of group personality – it leaves the personality of the group exclusively in the hands of those responsible for the law. Maitland, in looking beyond that theory, was looking beyond the law itself to the 'reality' that lay outside it. Of what that reality might consist he refused to speculate, but that it was indeed a kind of reality he was prepared to acknowledge. And so, in 1903, in the same lecture in which he announced himself to be no philosopher, Maitland also accepted that group persons must have at the very least 'a phenomenal reality – such reality, for example, as the lamp-post has for the idealistic ontologist'.[6] Group personality, for Maitland, had come to seem 'real'; and if it was not really real, it was at least no less real than anything else.

This reluctant entry into the world of ontological speculation is evidence of the great influence worked upon Maitland towards the end of his intellectual career by the ideas of Otto von Gierke, to whom idealistic conceptions of reality came more easily. It was as a legal historian that Maitland had first been drawn to Gierke. In the letter he sent Leslie Stephen in 1902 to accompany a copy of Gierke's monograph on Althusius, Maitland wrote: 'I like all [Gierke's] books, and his history of things in general as seen from the point of view of a student of corporations is full of good stuff, as well as being to all appearances appallingly learned.'[7] The learning Maitland could appreciate as a fellow historian. But it was Gierke's willingness to derive from his historical researches an account of 'things in general' which drew Maitland into territory which his own historical re-searches had hitherto left untouched – and from speculation about things in general it was a small step to speculation about the very nature of things. The path that led from the specific concerns of the legal historian to the general concerns of the philosopher Maitland had already traced in the introduction he wrote to Gierke in 1900: there he follows Gierke from what he calls 'the legal plain' ('the point of view of a student of corporations') on through 'the middle region of sociology' ('things in general') and up finally to the 'philosophical summits' ('the very nature of things'). But he also traced it in his own work after 1900, beginning with his accounts of the history of the English corporation and the English trust, and culminating with the

---

[6] *Ibid.*, p. 316.   [7] Quoted in Fisher, *Maitland*, p. 130.

thoughts to which he gave voice in his Sidgwick lecture of 1903. The path Maitland took in his writing on Gierke and the path he took in his own work are very similar, and it is best, before following the second, first to have followed the first.

II

Maitland's point of departure for his introduction to Gierke is the Reception. Like the Renaissance and the Reformation, to which Maitland compares it, the Reception was a pan-European phenomenon, but like these others its impact in England was not entirely commensurate with its impact elsewhere. English law, at the time when Roman law was being received on the continent, had already reached what Maitland calls 'the doctrinal stage of growth'[8] – it had, essentially, turned itself into a legal profession – and it was for this reason that English lawyers were resistant to certain aspects of Romanism. Even in England there were many exceptions, and Maitland cites as 'by far the most remarkable instance the reception of that Italian Theory of the Corporation of which Dr. Gierke is the historian, and which centres around the phrase *persona ficta*'.[9] But English law, though accommodating the idea of the *persona ficta*, was not wholly dependent on it, and professional lawyers were able to find an escape in the law of trusts that they themselves had been responsible for developing. In Germany things were different. There 'folk-law' had not yet reached the doctrinal stage, and was instead 'dissipating itself in countless local customs'.[10] The Germans had no Inns of Court, and no Court of Chancery, in which they might preserve and develop their own juristic conceptions of group life. As a result, the Italian doctrine 'swept over Germany like a deluge',[11] and for centuries there was no real means of escape.

Maitland is careful to call the doctrine of the *persona ficta* Italian and not Roman because he is conscious, like Gierke, that its source lay less in the Digest itself – where, he points out, 'there is no text which directly calls the *universitas* a *persona*, still less any that calls it a *persona ficta*'[12] – than in the interpretation placed on it by Innocent IV, who became Pope in 1243. It was the Innocentine doctrine that Romanists in Germany sought to uphold. The basic tenets of this doctrine Maitland summarises as follows: it allowed that groups of

---

[8] Gierke, *Political theories*, p. xiv.   [9] *Ibid.*
[10] *Ibid.*   [11] *Ibid.*   [12] *Ibid.*, p. xviii.

individuals might be possessed of their own personality, but only
when they were incorporated; a corporation was capable of proprie-
tary rights; it was not, however, itself capable of action ('knowing,
intending, willing, acting'); instead, its actions had to be performed
by individual corporators, acting on its behalf; thus the corporation
itself could not be punished, because it could do nothing unjust (it
could 'do' nothing at all); it was simply a person by fiction, to whom
the legal capacity to 'own' actions was ascribed. This is, of course, a
familiar doctrine, for it accords, more or less exactly, with the
position that was to be adopted by Hobbes. For Maitland, the
defining characteristic of the Innocentine account of fictitious personality was a reluctance to allow corporate rights to be exercised by
'agents', since 'agency' suggested that the corporation appointed
those who were to act on its behalf. This was the one thing that a
corporation could not be supposed to have done, since if it were, it
would follow that it had been capable of performing the action itself,
and had simply elected not to. Uncoincidentally, it was also the one
thing that Hobbes's fictitious persons could not be supposed to do,
since their representatives were by definition authorised by someone
else, which is precisely what made them representatives and not
agents. Maitland suggests that anyone who wished to make fun of
this theory could argue that 'it fills the legal world with hopeless
idiots and their State-appointed curators'.[13] But in Hobbes's case,
any criticism of this kind would be forestalled by the fact that it is the
very analogy he himself would use: for Hobbes, as we have seen,
fictitious persons, whether corporations, buildings or purposes, are
no different from 'Mad-men and Fooles'.

In nineteenth-century Germany the most familiar version of this
doctrine was neither Innocent's nor Hobbes's but the version
propounded by Friedrich Karl von Savigny (1779–1861), the leading
Romanist of his age. Still, for Maitland, as for Gierke, the implications of Savigny's theory remained manifestly Hobbesian. From it
emerged a state in which corporate activity was directly controlled
by the sovereign, and thus a state in which corporations had no
rights of their own. 'The Savignian corporation', Maitland argued,
'is no "subject" for "liberties and franchises" or "rights of self-
government". Really and "publicistically" it can hardly be other
than a wheel in the State's machinery, though for the purposes of

---

[13] *Ibid.*, p. xxi.

Property Law a personification of this machinery is found to be convenient'.[14] Indeed, Savigny's views were, if anything, even starker than those put forward by Hobbes, for Savigny was adamant that fictitious personality depended in all cases on a specific concessionary act on the part of the sovereign. Hobbes, as we have seen, though insisting that the sovereign is 'author' of all group persons, does not insist in each case on an authoritative 'act'. But Savigny did, and his were therefore literally 'State-appointed', not just 'State-authorised', curators – they were required to submit themselves to the state for approval. It was for this reason that the theory of the *persona ficta* tended to appeal, as Maitland put it, to 'any Prince or princeling . . . inclined towards paternal despotism', for it implied that 'over the doings of guardians and curators the State should exercise, no mere jurisdiction, but administrative control'.[15] Where the fiction theory entailed the concession theory, corporations were liable to be seen not merely as the creations but as the creatures of the state. And in Germany, land of princelings, this is what happened.

Nineteenth-century Germanism, of the kind of which Gierke became the leading exponent, was, Maitland explains, a reaction against Savigny. The concession theory which Savigny had sought to enshrine was wholly incompatible with the Germanists' conception of the *Genossenschaft*. German fellowships were not, and had never been, creatures of the state. However, it was not simply with the concession theory, and the bureaucratic controls that came with it, that the Germanists took issue. They also argued that the very idea of the *persona ficta* itself was irreconcilable with what they saw as the essentially 'organic' nature of the *Genossenschaft*. This 'organicism' had some specific legal ramifications. For example, it challenged the Savignian (and Hobbesian) view that a corporation could not be liable for the actions of its representatives, since it had not itself authorised them; if the representatives of a corporation are understood to be its 'organs', their wrongs must belong to it, making the corporation itself in each case liable. Inevitably, though, Gierkean organicism had broader implications than these. If a corporation is regarded as an organic entity, then it must be supposed to be born, to grow, and to die, all of itself. It must, in other words, be seen to have a life of its own, and unless, during the course of that life, it displays tangible signs of madness, there is no

---

[14] *Ibid.*   [15] *Ibid.*

obvious reason why it should be provided with guardians and
curators in the first place.

It is this organic conception of corporate activity which leads
Maitland, in his pursuit of Gierke, from the legal plain to the middle
region, 'where a sociology emulous of the physical sciences discourses
of organs and organisms and social tissue'.[16] By sociology Maitland
evidently understands the sort of history which looks to uncover
patterns of behaviour in the events on which it reports.[17] Historicism
in Popper's sense – the sort of history that is emulous of the sciences
– is another way of expressing this, but there is a third, more familiar
term for what Maitland has in mind, and that is natural history. At
the close of his account of the Germanists' case against the concession theory, Maitland suggests that 'a time seems at hand when the
idea of a "particular creation" will be as antiquated in Corporation
Law as it is in Zoology'.[18] The notion that corporations are capable
of evolution clearly puts paid to the idea that their formation
depends always upon the explicit approval of some higher authority.
But it also puts paid to the idea that they are merely fictions, since it
is not easy to understand how a fiction might be said to evolve. If
groups are to be studied as though they were organisms, then the
suggestion is not simply that they have an identity that is 'natural',
but also that they have an identity that is 'real' – after all, it makes no
more sense to think of an organism as something imaginary than it
does to think of it as something artificial. Maitland recognised this,
and he recognised as a result that if, as Gierke hoped, 'the Concession Theory has notice to quit, [it] may carry the whole Fiction
Theory with it'.[19] It is not impossible to conceive of a sociological
challenge to the concession theory which does not carry the whole
fiction theory with it: for instance, it might be argued that the
tendency in Germanic societies had been to 'see' the personality of
independent associations without it following that what was being

---

[16] *Ibid.*, p. xi.

[17] The standard English example of the sort of sociology Maitland has in mind would have
been Herbert Spencer's, and in particular Spencer's detailed exploration of the analogy
between social and organic bodies in his essay 'The social organism'. It is interesting to note
that in this essay, which first appeared in the *Westminster Review* in 1860, Spencer, like
Gierke, acknowledges the significance of Hobbes's attempt to equate the state with the
human body, and also its inadequacy (Spencer's specific complaint being the entirely
justified 'If the sovereignty is the soul of the body-politic, how can it be that magistrates,
who are a kind of deputy-sovereigns, should be comparable to joints?' (Herbert Spencer,
The man versus the State, ed. D. MacRae (Harmondsworth, 1968), p. 200).

[18] Gierke, *Political theories*, p. xxxviii.   [19] *Ibid.*

seen was necessarily real; here, 'natural' would be understood in a narrow sense, to mean simply those things which have a tendency to occur and which should not therefore be seen as subject to arbitrary control.[20] But a Gierkean sociology of group life, because natural in the more familiar sense, took the extra step, and as it did so it moved from the middle region to the philosophical summits, where questions about patterns and tendencies gave way to questions about the very nature of those things whose patterns and tendencies were being described.

This leaves one further stage for the argument to go. The allusion Maitland makes to Darwin with regard the creation of corporations tells us something about the nature of the state, even if it is only that the state can no longer set itself up as the 'mortal god' of Hobbes's fancy. However, Maitland uses the language of natural history to make another, more specific point. 'For', he declares, 'when all is said, there seems to be a *genus* of which State and Corporation are species'.[21] He goes on:

Let it be allowed that the State is a highly peculiar group-unit; still it may be asked whether we ourselves are not the slaves of a jurist's theory and a little behind the age of Darwin if between the State and all other groups we fix an immeasurable gulf, and ask ourselves no questions about the origin of species.[22]

What is true of corporations, therefore, is true of the state itself, and Maitland uses this connection to make two observations about contemporary theories of the state's essential nature. The first is directed towards those who were arguing that the state was possessed of 'not only a real will, but even "the" real will'.[23] If the state has such a will, then the same could not be denied to any of the group persons within it, such that their personalities must be real also. The view that the state's will was alone the 'real' one had, Maitland

---

[20] This would be to employ something like the celebrated distinction that Hume makes in his *A treatise of human nature* (though here 'artificial' takes the place of 'fictitious'): 'To avoid giving offence, I must here observe, that when I deny justice to be a natural virtue, I make use of the word, *natural*, only as opposed to *artificial*. In another sense of the word; as no principle of the human mind is more natural than a sense of virtue, so no virtue is more natural than justice. Mankind is an inventive species; and where an invention is obvious and absolutely necessary, it may properly be said to be natural as anything that proceeds immediately from original principles, without the intervention of thought or reflection. Tho' the rules of justice be *artificial*, they are not *arbitrary*' (see D. Hume, *A treatise on human nature*, ed. E. C. Mosser (London, 1969), p. 536). Thus it might be argued that though the *Genossenschaft* is a product of human invention, still it is a necessary, or 'natural' product, and not therefore to be understood as the concession of this or that sovereign.

[21] Gierke, *Political theories*, p. ix.   [22] *Ibid.*   [23] *Ibid.*, p. xi.

notes, started 'mak[ing] some way in England',[24] and there can be
no doubt that his target here is Bosanquet, and Bosanquet's willingness to draw a line between the moral attributes of the state and
the mere legal attributes of some of the group persons within it. But
it follows that if all associations share the basic attributes of the state,
then the state must share the attributes of legal persons. So, the
reality of the state's 'life' must be seen to include a juristic dimension.
And here, Maitland turns his attention from Bosanquet, who gives
the state life but no juristic aspect, to Austin, who managed to
provide the juristic dimension, but failed to provide a life for the
state that contains it. By placing sovereignty in a portion of political
society rather than in what Maitland calls 'the whole organised
community',[25] Austin denied to the state the capacity to act as a
person in its own right. It is for this reason, Maitland suggests, 'that
the set of thoughts into which Englishmen were lectured by John
Austin appears to Dr. Gierke as a past stage'.[26] But Gierke did not
grant to the state its own personality simply in order to make of it a
legal entity (that would be to replicate the presuppositions of the
fiction theory at one remove); he considered it to be a legal entity just
because it possessed a real personality of its own. Thus, Maitland
writes, 'for Gierke it is as impossible to make the State logically prior
to the Law (*Recht*) as it is to make law logically prior to the State,
since each exists in, for, and by the other'.[27] The state is law; law is
the state. This concludes Maitland's journey, which has taken him (in
less than forty pages of text) from the medieval law of corporations to
the idealistic conception of the *Rechtsstaat*.

III

At the close of his introduction to Gierke, Maitland concedes that the
Rechtsstaatsidee was unlikely to mean much to his English readers; to
them it could only appear as something 'unfamiliar and obscure'.[28]
But if so, he remarks, it is in part because the English have had no
practical experience of its opposite, the *Polizei-* or *Beamtenstaat*. This,
then, is the other side to Maitland's story – the fact that while
Germans and Germanists were wrestling with the great concepts of
Korporationstheorie, the English, partly by luck, partly by ingenuity, had
managed to organise the life of their state in such a way as to be

---

[24] *Ibid.*   [25] *Ibid.*, p. xliii.   [26] *Ibid.*   [27] *Ibid.*   [28] *Ibid.*

more or less untouched by them. 'In the past', Maitland writes, 'we could afford to accept speciously logical but brittle theories because we knew that they would never be subjected to serious strains',[29] and though 'the trust deeds might be long and the lawyers' bill might be longer',[30] Englishmen knew that they could, if they had to, turn a deaf ear to the lectures of jurists. But although there were no serious strains, there were some strains nonetheless, and even in England the ingenuity of lawyers could not accommodate every aspect of group life. In particular, there was one association around the question of whose identity conceptual as well as practical arguments had sometimes raged. This was the 'organised group' which had been known at various times in England as 'Crown', 'Common-wealth', 'Publick' and 'State'. It was to the arguments surrounding this group and these names that Maitland's own attention, once he had finished with Gierke, came to be turned.

Maitland's point of departure for the legal history of this organised group, which he pursued across five separate articles published after 1900,[31] is itself somewhat obscure. He begins with the old English idea of the corporation sole. English lawyers, on the infrequent occasions on which they were required to give some account of the principles lying behind their law of persons, tended to fall back on the following: 'Persons are either natural or artificial. The only natural persons are men. The only artificial persons are corporations. Corporations are either aggregate or sole.'[32] The first three of these sentences represent an extremely blunt statement of essentially Romanist principles (Roman law knew other artificial persons than corporations and Romanists would prefer to call them fictitious than artificial). But the fourth contains an idea peculiar to English law – the concept of the corporation sole. That this idea existed at all was evidence that English lawyers had, on occasion, been compelled to engage in some speculations of their own in the realm of *Korporationstheorie*, and Maitland traced the source of these speculations to a particular problem tackled at a particular time. The problem concerned the parish church, and the question of who or what was to be understood as the subject of the right of which the church constituted the object; the time was the first half of the sixteenth

---

[29] *Ibid.*   [30] *Ibid.*, p. xxxi.
[31] These were entitled: 'The corporation sole'; 'The crown as corporation'; 'The unincorporate body'; 'Moral personality and legal personality'; 'Trust and corporation'.
[32] Maitland, *Collected papers*, vol. III, p. 210.

century. Why this problem tackled at this time might have produced the corporation sole as its solution is something to which Maitland devotes considerable attention, and his explanation cannot easily be summarised. However, it is at least possible to set out some of the choices that were available to those who tackled it, and also one that was not. This last was the possibility of placing the right in a corporation aggregate: a parish church, unlike say a monastery, could not belong to such a corporation because there was no organised community to form the aggregate; there was only the church, the parson and his patron, and between these last two there was no 'organisation', since their relation was in essence determined by a single act of patronage (an 'appointment'). This left four possibilities. The right might be taken to reside in the parson alone; here though there was difficulty in providing for the continued exercise of duties or obligations – what would usually be called 'offices' – as one parson died and was replaced by another. The right might be taken to reside in the patron who appoints the parson; here though there was difficulty in providing for the independent exercise of right which the office of parson seemed to demand. The right might be taken to reside in the church itself; here though there was difficulty in providing for any exercise of the right at all, since it was not clear how the church might itself perform an action. Finally, the right might be taken to reside in the parson *understood as a corporation*. The merit of this last solution was that it maintained the independence of the parson while implying that his actions were nevertheless undertaken not on his own behalf (as a natural man) but on behalf of his office (an artificial person). At any given moment, the individual parson *was* the office, and therefore there was no distinction to be drawn between the actions of the natural man and the actions of the artificial person.[33] But because at any given moment the actions of the natural man might be understood as the actions of the artificial person, there was at least some semblance of continuity in the exercise of rights and duties as one parson died and was replaced by another.

This was the doctrine of the corporation sole, and English lawyers, on the rare occasions that they had recourse to it, found it serviceable. However, as Maitland is only too happy to demonstrate, it did have one, rather English flaw: in juristic terms, it was a wholly

---

[33] Maitland points out that in the sixteenth century the words 'parson' and 'person' would have sounded the same, aiding this process of assimilation (see *ibid.*, p. 226).

meaningless concept. For a corporation sole could in fact do none of the things that corporations existed in order to be able to do. For instance, it is one of the distinguishing characteristics of what Maitland calls a 'true corporation' (a corporation aggregate) that it can undertake legal transactions with some or all of the individual corporators that are its members. A corporation sole cannot, since a man does not undertake legal transactions with himself. Similarly, it is one of the marks of a true corporation that it is able to endure when some or all of its members do not. A corporation sole, however, because bound up with the natural existence of an individual man, tended to disappear when he did. Thus at just those points where the law might have need of a corporate entity – such as in the interval between the death of one parson and the appointment of another – the corporation sole failed to deliver. And so, as he surveys its uses, and more particularly its lack of them, Maitland concludes that the concept of corporation sole is 'a juristic abortion'[34] – it is a creation which has been denied any life of its own.

Because of its fairly narrow ecclesiastical origins, the abortive nature of the corporation sole might be considered a matter of little importance. However, the office of parson was not the only one in early modern England which might be filled by a natural man in need of his own corporate identity. The same was true of the Crown. The king, who lived and died as men did, occupied an office which, it was commonly hoped, did not live and die with the king. This distinction between man and office had traditionally found expression in the language of the corporation aggregate (the *universitas*). However, by the sixteenth century there were those, in England as elsewhere, who were reluctant to accede to the suggestion that the king was a mere officer of the state, and thus in some sense its servant. Nor would they accept that the king, who was free to do as he wished with his own property, was mere guardian of that property ('the common wealth') which belonged to the state as a whole. Yet these same apologists for kingly power did not wish to suggest that the king occupied no office at all, nor that his subjects were simply obeying a peculiarly powerful natural man. Their wish was to preserve the distinction between king and Crown, while yet maintaining that at any given moment the Crown *was* the king. In England, this meant that the king was to be understood as a

---

[34] *Ibid.*, p. 243.

corporation sole. The term itself was not always used, but the reasoning which turned the parson into a corporation was the same as that which did the same for the king. Moreover, this was no obscure doctrine. It had prominent champions, and it had them over many years. Of these, Maitland uses the example of just two. One is Henry VIII. The other is Thomas Hobbes.

Maitland's view of Hobbes was not Gierke's. Certainly, he gives no impression of sharing that admiration (albeit tinged with horror) that Gierke had for the man whom he believed to have changed the course of the history of ideas for ever. In the same letter in which he wrote to Leslie Stephen about Gierke, Maitland also wrote of Hobbes (whose life Stephen was then writing): 'I rather fancy that [his] political feat consisted in giving a new twist to some well worn theories of the juristic order and then inventing a psychology which would justify that twist.'[35] This slight disdain may explain what is in fact a rather superficial comparison that Maitland draws between Hobbesian and Henrician views of the state, when he writes that 'as for Hobbes, so also for King Henry, the personality of the corporate body is concentrated in and absorbed by the personality of its monarchical head'.[36] To express it in these terms is to miss entirely what is distinctive about Hobbes, which is his recognition that the conventional language of corporate unity could not convey the particular conception of sovereignty he had in mind. Because he misses this, Maitland also misses, which is rare, the opportunity for some word-play. For it is not in its head that Hobbes absorbs the personality of the commonwealth, but in its 'soul', which is sovereign. This said, and once it is accepted that the soul of the body politic can be an assembly as well as a man, the parallels between Hobbes's sovereign and the parson of the English parish are indeed striking. Like the lawyers of a hundred years earlier who turned the parson into a corporation sole, Hobbes wished to find a formula which would render sovereignty an office but which would identify that office with the natural man or men who held it. He could not allow sovereign right to reside in the group of natural men who appoint the sovereign ('the patron') because that would make impossible the independent exercise of right which he determined that sovereignty required; he could not allow sovereign right to reside in the commonwealth ('the church itself') because the commonwealth was no more capable of

---

[35] Quoted in Fisher, *Maitland*, p. 130.   [36] Maitland, *Collected papers*, vol. III, p. 248.

action itself than was a bridge; but nor could he allow sovereign right
to reside in the natural person or persons of the sovereign ('the parson
alone') because that would be to destroy the integrity of the office. So
he made the sovereign representative of a corporate entity which
could not exist where the sovereign ceased to exist, and the considerable attention which he devoted to the problems of succession shows
that he knew just where the most pressing difficulties were likely to
arise.[37] Because it was 'representative', the position of Hobbes's
sovereign did at least rest on a coherent juristic idea, unlike the
corporation sole of English law, which was little more than a form of
words. But the remarkable use which Hobbes made of the idea of
representation could not conceal the illusory nature of the entity
whose person the sovereign was said to represent. Maitland calls the
idea of the corporation sole 'this mere ghost of a fiction'.[38] It was a
phrase which, as we have seen, he could justifiably have applied to the
person of Hobbes's commonwealth as well.

To imply, as Maitland does, that Hobbes's political philosophy
was simply a case of the corporation sole writ large is to suggest one
of two things: either that an idea with relatively humble origins had
achieved remarkable things in English political theory; or that one of
the most celebrated of English political theorists had done little more
than recast what was a very humble idea. For Maitland it is the
latter. He did not believe that the corporation sole had exercised an
enduring influence on English political thought for the simple reason
that he did not believe that Hobbes had exercised such an influence
either. Rather, Hobbes stood at the end of that period, stretching
back to Henry VIII, when, as Maitland put it elsewhere, the days
had been uncharacteristically 'evil'.[39] When that period ended in
1688, Englishmen were happy to fall back on the more comfortable
idea that public power rested with the organised body of the state as
a whole, and it was an idea that they had remained comfortable with
ever since. Moreover, the comparative freedom enjoyed by associations in England provided ample evidence that England was not, and
had never been, anything like a Hobbesian commonwealth, despite a
few uncomfortable interludes, of which the reign of Henry VIII had

---

[37] Hobbes discusses the problems of succession at length in chapter XIX of *Leviathan*.
Recognising that the doctrine of the corporation sole cannot accommodate an interregnum,
Hobbes allows that succession under a monarchy may be determined either by 'Custome' or
'by presumption' of primogeniture (see Hobbes, *Leviathan*, p. 137).
[38] Maitland, *Collected papers*, vol. III, p. 241.   [39] See Gierke, *Political theories*, p. xxxiii.

been one. But though Maitland discounted the legacy of the corporation sole in the purely public domain, he did nevertheless discern it
elsewhere. For while the ownership of public right had long since
been accorded to the state as a corporate entity, the same was not
true with regard to the ownership of property. Even as the twentieth
century was beginning, Maitland argued, English lawyers and
English legislators had yet formally to recognise the public ownership
of private goods ('land and chattels'). This did not mean, of course,
that English lawyers denied that such a thing was possible – it was
indubitably the case that the state was able to borrow money against
what it owned, and that the resulting debt belonged to the state itself,
and not to the natural man or men who held office, and who might
well have considerable debts of their own. But English law had been
unable to arrive at a consistent formula by which to express this
condition, and this, Maitland argued, for the simple reason that 'the
foolish parson had led it astray'.[40] English lawyers, having accommodated themselves to the idea of the corporation sole, found it
difficult to secure an independent identity for the state in law apart
from the natural identities of king and government. This Maitland
did not attribute to any sinister motives – a king, after all, would be
more encumbered than not if every debt he assumed brought with it
a personal obligation – but simply to 'clumsy thoughts and clumsy
words'.[41] Nevertheless, he believed that this clumsiness had produced
persistent confusion, not only in the strictly private domain of debt
and debt-collection, but also at the point where private and public
overlap, in the area of 'service'. Shackled by the wholly inappropriate concept of the corporation sole, English law had been
unable even to make clear that distinction upon which Hobbes had
insisted, between the servants of the office and the servants of the
man.[42] Until such confusions were eradicated, Maitland wished to
suggest, the subjects of the English Crown might never entirely be
certain who owned what, and what whom.

Of the possible remedies for this uncertainty, the most obvious by
far was simply to extend the corporate personality of the state from

---

[40] Maitland, *Collected papers*, vol. III, p. 266.   [41] *Ibid.*, p. 243.

[42] Maitland provides this example: 'A statute of 1887 tells us that "the expressions 'permanent
civil service of Her Majesty', and 'permanent civil service of the Crown' are hereby declared
to have the same meaning". Now as it is evident that King Edward is not (though Louis
XIV may have been) the State, we seem to have statutory authority for holding that the
State is "His Majesty". The way out of this mess, for mess it is, lies in a perception of the
fact, for fact it is, that our sovereign lord is not a "corporation sole"' (*ibid.*, p. 259).

the public into the private domain. Since it was assumed, though rarely expressed, that the state had a public life apart from the lives of its individual members, there seemed to be no reason why lawyers, whose business it was to find concrete expression for such assumptions, should not grant the state a personality comparable to that allowed to private corporations aggregate. In this way it would make perfect sense for the state, rather than the king or his government, to enter into contracts, assume debts, employ servants, and generally both to suffer wrongs for which compensation might be sought and commit wrongs for which compensation might be required. It would not matter greatly what this corporation was called – Maitland's own preference was for 'the Commonwealth', although he accepted that 'the Crown' or 'the Public' would do just as well – so long as it was recognised that it was an entity quite distinct from its titular head (the king) and from the rest of its titular and non-titular members (the government and the people). However, an arrangement like this, familiar as it was, brought with it an equally familiar problem. Private corporations aggregate in English law were allowed only an artificial or fictitious personality, which rested in each case on the authority of the state. How could it make sense for the state, or anything else, to authorise its own personality? The answer was that under English law it made no sense. Yet it was nevertheless true that English lawyers had been able to circumvent this problem for all those other associations that either could not or would not seek the state's authority for their corporate activities. As a result, a different question immediately suggested itself. If other groups had managed to secure for themselves a distinct legal identity through the concept of trusteeship, why should not the state do the same, and include itself among those unincorporate bodies in which English law abounded?

This was an option to which Maitland gave careful consideration. Though the beneficiary of a trust was not technically a person in law, lawyers, if prepared to perform what Maitland called 'wonderful conjuring tricks',[43] could make it as good as one. At the very least, the concept of trusteeship suggested a clear distinction between the individual men with whom the law dealt and the entities on whose behalf they acted. This was a distinction, Maitland argued, which might resolve the uncertainty shrouding much of English local government, where the ramshackle condition of English *Korpora-*

---

[43] Gierke, *Political theories*, p. xxxvii.

tionstheorie had left its mark.[44] Moreover, it was a distinction which he believed had already permeated everyday discourse about government in general. 'Open a newspaper', he wrote, 'and you will be unlucky if you do not see the word "trustee" applied to "the Crown" or to some high and mighty body'.[45] This was the readiest means to hand of expressing the continuous existence of the state in both the public and the private domain, even though the question remained unanswered as to the benefit of whom or what, exactly, the actions of its trustees were being directed.

There was one sense in which this was a question whose answer did not greatly matter. It was the great merit of the concept of trusteeship that it focused not on someone or thing but on the terms and conditions under which the rights of someone or thing were held by others. These terms and conditions were determined by the terms and conditions of each individual trust, and it was here that the lawyers could perform their tricks, fashioning legal entities out of the constraints which acted on the trustees themselves. However, for precisely this reason, the concept of trusteeship could not readily serve as the basic model for the relation that subsisted between state and government. The problem was that there were no trust deeds in which this relation was described. This difficulty might be overcome where new organs of government, and particularly of local government, were being established; here, 'elaborate statutes', as Maitland calls them, would determine the terms under which public positions were entrusted to natural individuals.[46] But unless the state as a whole could be provided with such statutes – that is, with a written constitution set out in the manner of a deed of trust – there was nothing for lawyers, or anyone else, to work on. And this, in turn, raises a more basic difficulty. Maitland's complaint against the condition of English *Korporationstheorie* was not that it was impractical, nor that it had produced unacceptable results; on the contrary, he believed England to have been blessed with a markedly practical and liberal means of dealing with questions of corporate identity. His

---

[44] Maitland writes: 'A natural result of this long history is a certain carelessness in the use of terms and phrases which may puzzle a foreign observer. I can well understand that he might be struck by the fact that whereas our borough is (or to speak with great strictness, the mayor, aldermen, and burgesses are) a corporation, our county, after all our reforms, is still not a corporation, though the County Council is.' He also discusses at some length the relation between the notion of corporate 'privilege', which was one of the consequences of the concession theory, and the 'rottenness' of boroughs (see Maitland, *Collected papers*, vol. III, pp. 398–9).

[45] *Ibid.*, p. 403.   [46] See *ibid.*, p. 402.

complaint was that, considered *as* theory, the English view of corporations had no juristic foundations, which led to uncertainty, as exemplified by the nonsense of the corporation sole. Where uncertainty threatened to produce impracticality or even illiberality, the trust concept was ready to retrieve the situation. But though curative, the trust concept could not itself prevent uncertainty, for the simple reason that it had no basis in legal theory either. The stated terms of each individual trust were all. Without them, there was nothing to fall back on, and the concept of the trust became just that, a matter of 'good conscience' rather than 'strict law'. Much might be achieved by trusting in conscience, but the one thing that could not, by definition, be provided was a bridge for the gap that had opened up in English law – the gap between good practice on the one hand, and good theory on the other.

Maitland never quite spells this out.[47] Yet it is a conclusion he seems, tacitly at least, to have accepted by the time he delivered his Sidgwick lecture in 1903. There, as in all his other writing on this subject, he acknowledges the great practical resourcefulness of the English legal system in dealing with organised groups. He speaks, more approving than disapproving, of the 'English contempt for legal technique', made possible by 'sound instincts' and 'convenient conclusions'.[48] But he also acknowledges that the English legal system in the end has no satisfactory resource for dealing with questions about one organised group in particular. He provides his audience with this illustration:

[The] organised group is a sovereign state. Let us call it Nusquamia. Like many other sovereign states it owes money, and I will suppose that you are one of its creditors. You are not receiving the expected interest and there is talk of repudiation. That being so, I believe you will be indignant, morally, righteously indignant. Now the question I want to raise is this: Who is it that really owes you money?[49]

Faced by this question, English lawyers have nowhere to turn. There is no trust here, either in law or in the more colloquial sense. Such legal technique as English lawyers possess is bound up in the conventional lineaments of the concession theory, which they have done their best to disregard just because it cannot stretch to cases like

---

[47] The closest he comes is at the end of his essay on 'Trust and corporation', where he acknowledges that the idea that government is a trust can never be more than a 'metaphor': 'Those who speak thus would admit that the trust was not one which any court could enforce, and might say that it was only a "moral" trust' (see *ibid.*, p. 403).
[48] *Ibid.*, pp. 318–19.   [49] *Ibid.*, p. 318.

these. All that remains is to speak of the debt being owed by certain men. But which men?

Clearly you do not think that every Nusquamian owes you some aliquot share of the debt. No-one thinks in that way. The debt of Venezuela is not owed Fulano y Zutano and the rest of them. Nor, I think, shall we get much good out of the word 'collectively', which is the smudgiest word in the English language, for the largest collection of zeros is only zero.[50]

'Collectively' must give way before 'corporately'. And if it is pointed out that corporations are the fictitious creations of sovereign states and not the states themselves, then there is only one response left: to argue that corporations cannot be the fictitious creations of sovereign states. Instead, they must be taken to exist in their own right, and the law not to create but merely to acknowledge them. If this were so, it would mean that the debt might be owed by Nusquamia itself, even though there is no evidence of Nusquamia having had an independent legal personality conceded to it. It would also mean that any other unincorporate body might be understood to be a corporation. In practical terms this might make little difference to how the vast majority of such bodies were treated. But in juristic terms it would at least mean that English law had finally arrived upon a *Korporationstheorie* that made sense.

Further than this Maitland was not prepared to go. Having posed his question, and having indicated how he believes it might best be answered, he announces his incompetence to deal with the issues of philosophy, and leaves the matter there. He has, he recognises, indulged in speculations which in Germany would be associated with jurists like Gierke, and grouped under the rather grand heading 'Realism'. But as a 'mere lawyer', and because no German, he is reluctant to make the connection an explicit one. He professes not to care greatly whether lawyers persist in thinking of the personality of organised groups as fictitious rather than real, so long as they accept that groups do have a personality of their own, and that this personality is not something to be ascribed or denied to them on a sovereign's whim. We may persist in thinking of group personality as a fiction, Maitland argues, just so long as we accept that it is, like the idealistic ontologist's lamp-post, 'a fiction we needs must feign',[51] and not something to be feigned as and when we choose. However, he cannot quite leave it at that. For though no philosopher, Maitland

---

[50] *Ibid.*   [51] *Ibid.*, p. 316.

recognises that there is something peculiar about a fiction over whose creation no-one has control. At some point, he admits, however much we might disregard the deeper issues, 'the thought will occur to us that a fiction we needs must feign is somehow or another very like the simple truth'.[52]

IV

There were thus two different routes by which Maitland was able to arrive at the doctrine of the real personality of associations, one German, undertaken on Gierke's behalf, the other English, undertaken on his own. The German route took Maitland from the Innocentine doctrine of the *persona ficta*, through the middle region inhabited by the *Genossenschaft*, and on to the idea of real group persons existing within the idealistic domain of the *Rechtsstaat*. The English route took him from the doctrine of the corporation sole, through the middle region where men formed trusts, and on to the idea that all organised groups must have a corporate personality of their own, whether we will it or no. Each of these stories follow a similar pattern, and the problems with which they deal intersect at many points. But there are also differences, and it is on the differences that I now wish to concentrate. What distinguishes these two accounts of group personality is that the English version is, at each point, more contained than the Gierkean equivalent. So, for instance, the concept of the corporation sole is an idea both more parochial and more limited in scope than the broader concept of the *persona ficta*. Similarly, the idea of the trust, though it is able to produce results similar to those Gierke extracts from the *Genossenschaftsidee*, does not of itself lead Maitland to speculate about the 'nature' of those things that trusts conceal. His middle region is more historical than it is natural historical, and it looks at how men have dealt with certain problems rather than at the species of thing that those problems address. Likewise, when Maitland arrives at the view that groups must be treated as persons come what may, his concern is more to regularise problem-solving techniques than it is to justify them with an account of the world that threw them up in the first place. For all these reasons, Maitland does not really tell us what a world made up of real group persons would be like, and nor does he tell us how it

---

[52] *Ibid.*

would operate. This, though, is itself a consequence of another difference between Maitland and Gierke, and that is the former's preoccupation with the issues of private, as opposed to public, law – Maitland is more interested in discovering what it is for a group to owe money than he is to describe what it might be for a group to exercise authority over its members. He follows Gierke from the legal plain to other regions touching on other disciplines, but at each point he remains wedded to what he would call 'merely' legal concerns. There is thus a gap in Maitland's English doctrine of real group personality, which in the German version is filled by the concept of the *Rechtsstaat*. This is the gap that exists between an explanation of what the doctrine of real group personality means in legal terms, and an account of what its political consequences might be.

To say that the political consequences of real group personality are a Gierkean *Rechtsstaat*, however, does not get us very far if the idea of the *Rechtsstaat* remains an obscure one. But it is in fact possible to say something more about what the idea of the *Rechtsstaat* entails if we say something more about the gap that exists between Maitland's own account of real group personality, and the one that he produces on Gierke's behalf. The lack of an obviously political (or, as he would term it, 'publicistic') dimension to Maitland's account leaves unanswered the question of whether the final step that Maitland takes, tentative as it is, from 'fictions we needs must feign' to 'the simple truth', is one that makes any difference to the argument. If it does make any difference, this will tell us something about what we can expect from the *Rechtsstaatsidee*. But in order to see whether it does make any difference, it is necessary to say something more than Maitland is prepared to do about the relation between the world of legal personality, and the world that surrounds it.

The first question that needs to be asked is whether Maitland's argument actually needs to take its final step, from fictitious personality to real. It is quite clear that Maitland's view of corporateness cannot be reconciled with the notion that corporations have their personality 'granted' to them by the state, with all the suggestions of patronage that that term brings. But given that the concession theory is not equivalent to the fiction theory, does it necessarily follow that an attack on the idea of 'grants', 'privileges' and 'concessions' must in the end bring down the idea of the *persona ficta* with it? It is perhaps useful to return at this point to the distinction Hobbes draws between persons-in-law authorised by a 'sealed' act (in letters) and those authorised by 'ordinary' statutes (in general laws). Hobbes would not have allowed that the sovereign should give up his right to concede fictitious personality to certain groups as he saw fit, and to take it away again as and when he pleased. But if we disregard Hobbes's own views, and look simply to the distinction, it is certainly possible to conceive of a state in which all corporations are authorised by general laws, and none have to rely on the specific approval of the sovereign power. Were this so, and were the laws sufficiently general, there is no reason why any group of individuals who form themselves into an association should not thereby acquire a personality of their own. Yet it would remain true that, in Hobbes's terms anyway, these groups would still be persons-in-law – that is, persons by fiction.

This point can be explored further by the use of a comparison Maitland draws in his introduction to Gierke. There, when discussing the thinking he takes to lie behind the Companies Act of 1862, he remarks on the case of certain of the American states, whose constitutions had come 'to prohibit the legislatures from calling corporations into being except by means of general laws'.[53] In the same vein, he points out that corporate status in England was no longer held to have anything to do with whether or not a group was 'chartered' (i.e. possessing letters).[54] Summarising these developments, he writes: 'It had become difficult to maintain that the State makes corporations in any other sense than that in which the State make marriages when it declares that people who want to marry can do so by going, and cannot do so without going, to church or registry.'[55] Clearly, marriage was not a 'privilege' bestowed by the state but rather something that the state simply 'recognised'; so, Maitland believed, for incorporation. But though marriages were not conceded by the state, still it is apparent that they were, in Maitland's words, 'made' by the state. In order that two individuals be recognised by the law to be married they have to fulfil certain criteria which are themselves determined by law. If they do not fulfil these criteria, they are not married. So for corporations. The terms of the 1862 Act – that any seven or more persons 'associated for any lawful purpose' can make of themselves a corporation – placed legal personality within the reach of almost any group. What it did not mean, though, was that almost every group therefore *was* a legal person. 'Associated' here refers to any group organised according to the formal criteria of association

---

[53] Gierke, *Political theories*, p. xxxviii.   [54] *Ibid.*   [55] *Ibid.*

(they would have to have a name, an address, certain signatures on certain documents and so on). Any 'association' which did not meet these criteria – lacked, say, the relevant documentation – was not properly associated, just as any couple 'married' without signing the register were not properly married. The existence of corporations, and marriages, though not decided by the state, was still determined by the state, through its general laws.

In fact, Maitland wishes to take the argument further than this. In the essays he wrote after 1900 his repeatedly expressed concern is for those groups that did not meet the formal criteria of incorporation, despite the 1862 Act, and who therefore remained in the uncertain condition of 'unincorporate bodiliness' in the eyes of the law. That many groups did remain unincorporate after 1862 is itself a consequence of the confusion that persisted regarding the concessionary nature of corporate status. Offered the chance to become corporations, many groups organised around the terms of a trust believed that to accept would be to compromise their independence, since it was felt (with good reason) that the state had sought to control the operations of such corporations as it had made in the past.[56] Maitland's worry was that groups such as these would, for the want of certain formalities, suffer when compared to their incorporate counterparts. Again, a comparison with marriage is useful here. Some couples may not wish, for whatever reason, to go through with a formal ceremony of marriage, yet live, in all other respects, as though married, under the same roof and with property held jointly by both partners. If the law does not regard the property likewise, the couple may suffer, particularly in the realm of taxation, but also with regard to simple convenience, whenever they wish, as a couple, to undertake legal transactions, such as buying a house. So for an unincorporate body, which may exhibit all the signs of corporateness – durability, singularity of purpose, property held 'in common', 'offices' – yet which would suffer if the law chose, say, to tax each member individually whenever property was disposed of, or to demand the signature of each member individually whenever a

---

[56] Thus Lloyd's of London was not incorporated until 1871, and the Stock Exchange not at all in Maitland's lifetime, for fear that incorporation would bring with it control by the Board of Trade over 'bye-laws' (see Maitland, *Collected papers*, vol. III, pp. 372–3). Many others – particularly clubs (like the Jockey Club) and charities – did not see why they should suffer incorporation, even if the risks were minimal, since they had got by so well without it. And, as Maitland says (he was writing for a German audience): 'In England, you cannot incorporate people who do not want incorporation' (*ibid.*, p. 374).

contract was entered into. The law has this century come increasingly to accept that couples who behave as though married should be treated as though married (a process culminating in the 1995 Family Law Bill). Maitland was hoping that something similar would happen for associations, and that the law would recognise what he calls the 'fact' of group personality whether or not the formalities of group personality had been observed.

Nevertheless, it can still be questioned whether 'facts' of this kind should be held to constitute 'reality'. For it remains true that even where there is no formal ceremony of marriage or incorporation, the condition of marriage or incorporation is still determined by law. It is in law that it is decided which 'facts' are sufficient to generate which forms of association. Thus the condition of marriage, though it may be achieved without ceremony, cannot be achieved unless certain criteria are met – the individuals concerned will have to have attained a certain formality in their relations to one another if the relationship itself is to accord to a certain type. Because there is no ceremony, these criteria may be broadly drawn, and they may be open to a variety of different interpretations. But it does not follow from the absence of any ceremony that it is the couple themselves who determine whether or not they are married, and nor does it follow that all couples are as good as married whether they go through the ceremony or not. The broader the criteria the easier it will be for individuals to form themselves into married units. But unless the criteria are so broad as to be meaningless, there will always be constraints, and the law will always be recognising marriages on its own terms. Nowhere is this better illustrated than in the ability of the law, in the absence of ceremony, to recognise 'marriages' where there is no equivalent recognition on the part of the individuals concerned – as may occur, for example, where children are involved, and the issue is one of maintenance.[57] And what is true of marriage is also true of incorporation. Where it is decided that the performance of some act of incorporation is not a precondition of a group's being seen as a corporation, many different associations may come to attain corporate status. But they do not

---

[57] The setting up of the Child Support Agency is a recent example of an attempt to look beyond the formalities of family law to what might be called the 'facts' of the matter. But because the 'facts' are of necessity formally determined themselves, the result has been in some cases to create 'familial' duties and obligations where the individuals concerned see none.

attain it on their own terms. They attain it when they meet the general criteria (of singularity, durability, communality and so on) which determine corporate status in law. In all but one respect the difference between general laws which stipulate formal means of incorporation and general laws which determine formal criteria of incorporation is one of degree not kind. The exception occurs in the case of those associations that do not wish to be treated as corporate entities. If the law stipulates that incorporation requires the performance of some act, then non-performance will ensure unincorporateness. But if the law determines that corporate status depends upon the fulfilment of certain criteria, then a group of individuals may be treated as a corporation if they behave as a corporation, whether they wish to be treated as a corporation or not. This may occur, for example, when the representative of an association acts illegally – the group as a whole may wish to see only the individual punished, but if the law is able to recognise corporateness despite the lack of formal incorporation, the representative may be counted an 'organ' of the association, and the group punished as a whole. As for families, so for corporations: if the law is to look to the 'facts', it may alight upon facts which bring with them unforeseen duties and obligations.

Many of these issues can be clarified with the aid of the distinction that H. L. A. Hart draws between law founded on command and law founded on rule.[58] Hart makes this distinction in the course of his critique of Austinian (and by implication Hobbesian) jurisprudence, which rests on the idea that all law issues from sovereign command, backed up by the threat of punishment. Hart points out that in all but the most rudimentary legal systems there are laws which do not fit this pattern, but instead take the form of rules to which no sanctions are appended. Many of these rules will apply to the legal system itself, such as the laws which stipulate in which courts which cases should be tried. (If a case is tried in the wrong court, no-one is punished; indeed, the likelihood is that the opportunity for punishment will have to be forgone.) But there are other rules which apply more generally. Hart gives the example of the law which stipulates that a will must be signed in the presence of two witnesses. If this rule is not followed, no-one is punished; the will is simply declared

---

[58] See H. L. A. Hart, *The concept of law* (Oxford, 1961), especially, pp. 26–48. In fact, Hart preferred the term 'order' (as in 'giving an order') to the term 'command', precisely because he believed that the latter had been annexed by Hobbesian and Austinian jurisprudence. I have retained 'command' in order to reinforce that connection.

invalid. What we have, therefore, is not a command, but a rule which establishes the criteria by which it is be determined what can, and what cannot, be 'recognised' in law. Rules like this do not compel individuals to behave in certain ways; rather, they provide individuals with guidelines concerning the forms of behaviour which will allow them access to the resources provided by a given legal system. If a will is to be recognised in law then it must conform to the law's idea of a will; but it does not follow from this that the law is insisting that individuals make valid wills, nor threatening them if they do not. Now if we return to the business of incorporation, we can see that the concession theory is a product of the idea that laws are commands: incorporation is here understood as an authoritative act on the part of a sovereign, compelling individuals to behave in certain ways, threatening them with punishment if they do not. It is no coincidence that Hobbes embraces this view in the account he provides of incorporation. But it is also no coincidence that chapter XXII of *Leviathan* marks the one place where Hobbes has difficulty sustaining his view that law is command. For in allowing corporations to be authorised by general laws also, Hobbes is conceding that corporate activity cannot always be conceived in the simple terms of sovereign (who commands) and subject (who either obeys or is punished). Where a corporation is authorised by general laws, individuals are provided with an opportunity to associate with one another in ways which the law will 'recognise'. They are not being threatened; they are simply being told of the rules they must follow if they wish to make use of the 'privileges' of group personality. Hobbes cannot give up the idea that such privileges accord to the model of concession, which is the model of command. But in a state in which 'letters' are replaced by 'general laws', command gives way to rule.

If the difference between command and rule is a difference in kind, there is within a state governed by rules the scope for considerable differences of degree. There may be many rules or there may be few; these rules may be permanent and unchanging, or they may stand in need of constant updating; each rule may be stated in the broadest terms, allowing for a liberal interpretation of its requirements, or it may specify the performance of narrowly defined, even of ritualistic, actions. And as for rules in general, so for any particular set of rules within the state. Thus the rules governing the creation of corporations may be flexible and relatively easy to follow, or they may be arcane, impractical and expensive, the preserve of lawyers rather than those for whom the law ostensibly exists. But though the differences between the sorts of rules that hold for a particular area of human activity may be great, still it remains possible to plot most rules on a single differential scale, ranging from the most accessible at one end to the least accessible at the other. Indeed, there is only one set of rules which cannot be accommodated on such a scale, and these are the rules which do not specify the *performance* of actions at all. The performance of an action requires some consciousness of what is being done on the part of the actor. But, as we have seen, it is possible to frame rules whose formal criteria may be met unconsciously. For example, the rules governing the creation of corporations may allow for corporate entities to be formed without the corporators being aware of it. Here it is not the performance of certain actions stipulated in law which enables groups of men to achieve corporate status; rather, it is the congruence of certain acts with the terms of law which determines that groups of men must assume corporate status. What is missing, in other words, is the element of choice, and it is this which makes it meaningless to seek to place such rules on a scale of accessibility. With such rules it is not a question of citizens seeking out the laws which best answer to their own needs and then attempting to comply with them; it is the law which seeks out the citizens.

The categorical nature of these distinctions is best illustrated with the aid of Hart's own example, will-making. It is perfectly possible to conceive of a legal system in which the business of will-making rests on an explicit command. For instance, the law might state that all persons over the age of eighteen must make a will and must expect punishment if they do not. Clearly a command of this kind will include a rule-based element (people must be told *how* they are to make their wills), but the primary motive for action remains fear of sanction and as a result the mode of action remains imperative. In the system of will-making to which Hart alludes, command is supplanted by rule alone, and the imperative mode gives way to what can be called an 'enabling' mode of legal activity – the rule which insists on the presence of two witnesses enables but does not force men to make valid wills. This rule is only one of many that could be applied to the drawing up of wills, some allowing easier access to this legal resource, others making the use of it more difficult. So, for example, accessibility would be diminished if it was stipulated that the witnesses to any will must themselves be lawyers, and it would be increased if only one or even no witnesses were deemed sufficient. Indeed, the rules governing the making of wills might be anything from impossibly easy (any statement in the hand of the deceased) to impossibly difficult (only statements sanctioned by parliament) without the mode of action itself being altered. But that mode is altered once the rules cease to demand action at all. Thus the rules which apportion someone's property among their family according to fixed principles of precedence, though having the same effect as other rules which allow individuals to apportion their property among their family, do not serve the same function. They are not enabling because they do not exist as a resource for those who live under the law but only as a resource of the law itself. They are, therefore, rules of a categorically different kind, to be classified in Hart's terms as having an 'external' rather than an 'internal' force. Rules which operate internally are those which invite individuals to mould their actions in accordance with certain patterns of behaviour; they include, among other things, the rules of all games.[59] Rules which operate externally are those which impose patterns on individual acts and occurrences; they include, among other things, the rules of science. Where the law imposes a pattern on the redistribution of property after death, its mode is 'deterministic' rather than either imperative or enabling.[60] But, of course, we do not think of such rules determining an individual's 'will'; they only apply, in England at least, when someone dies intestate.

What is striking about Maitland's arguments concerning corporate personality is that they can be tracked across a similar trajectory. In rejecting the concession theory, Maitland rejects the view that corporations must be formed where and when the law insists. Inevitably, the concession theory contains rule-based elements (people still require to be told how they are to form corporations), and it is also true that even chartered corporations take much of

---

[59] Hart points out that it is possible to view the rules of games externally, simply by observing certain patterns of behaviour. However, he also points out that it is impossible in this way to understand the rules of a game; all you will arrive at are 'observable regularities of conduct, predictions, probabilities, signs' (see *ibid.*, pp. 86–8).

[60] This does not mean that the law-maker will not have to issue commands in order to ensure that property is redistributed in accordance with the rules. Nor does it mean that individuals may not condition their behaviour in order to make use of the rules as they stand; for instance, where primogeniture determines precedence, families may seek to produce sons. But the decision to keep trying for a male heir in order to make best use of the law is very different from the decision to use the law in order to leave property to the child of one's choice.

their character from the use that their members are able to make of their charters. Nevertheless, the concession theory remains an example of law functioning in the imperative mode. As he leaves it behind, Maitland comes to embrace an alternative mode of legal activity, by which corporate status is made available to those who want it. The exemplar of this was the 1862 Companies Act, which allowed groups of seven or more access to a legal resource which had previously been kept under lock and key. Still, Maitland worried that the 1862 Act was not enough. In part, his concern turned on the question of accessibility, since Maitland believed that many groups had failed to make use of this resource because of their lingering concerns about the inconvenience and interference involved. But in another sense Maitland was taking issue with the criterion of accessibility itself. In the end, what was insufficient about the Companies Act was that it left matters in the hands of associations themselves, with the result that groups which functioned in a corporate manner might refuse to recognise their own position, leaving the law powerless. In arguing that it was up to the law to recognise what was 'really' there, Maitland moves corporation law from the enabling to the deterministic mode. No longer was it a question of men choosing to enter the legal domain in order to frame aspects of their lives to suit their own purposes; rather, law was to provide the framework for the lives men chose to lead regardless. This did not mean that the law must control those lives, any more than the laws of science must control the natural world. But it did mean that law had to pattern human endeavour, as science patterns the natural world. And this Maitland seems to have acknowledged at the end of his introduction to Gierke, where he declares that it is time 'to give scientific precision and legal operation to thoughts which are in all modern minds, and which are always displaying themselves'.[61]

It is this that makes the final step in Maitland's argument – from fictitious to real group personality – so significant, for it entails the replacement of one conception of law by another. Where group persons are fictitious entities, be those fictions founded on command or rule, the law is to be understood as an extension of the lives lived by natural persons, a distinct realm in which their actions are formalised in such a way as to suit either their own purposes or the purposes of their sovereign. But where group persons are deemed to

---

[61] Gierke, *Political theories*, p. xl.

be real, the law is nothing more, and nothing less, than an account of the life that surrounds it. The concept of real group personality closes the gap between the world described in law and the world in which men live. Of course, all laws must have some connection with the world around them if they are to be other than artificial in a pejorative sense. Moreover, it will sometimes make sense to seek to establish that relation in the language of 'reality'. Thus, for example, a real marriage might be contrasted with a marriage of convenience in order to determine where the law needs 'tightening up'. But a contrast like this still depends on the existence of the gap which the concept of real personality would close. Marriages of convenience are only possible where the law functions in an enabling capacity, as a formal extension of the arrangements individuals make for themselves. Any insistence that marriages should where possible be 'real' and not simply convenient presupposes that the law continues to function in this way, and takes issue with it on the grounds of accessibility alone. A similar argument could be made, and indeed has often been made, to apply to corporations. At the turn of the century many felt that corporate status had become too accessible and was open to abuse; in particular, attention focused on the so-called 'one-man corporations', which fulfilled the technical criteria of group personality without providing for the existence of any recognisable group to bear that personality (the purpose of such corporations being to allow individuals to escape certain forms of liability[62]).

---

[62] The problem of one-man companies formed the basis of a celebrated case in 1897, which is discussed in some detail in P. W. Duff, *Personality in Roman private law* (Cambridge, 1938). Duff writes: 'An interesting problem is presented by the "one-man company", and was discussed by the Court of Appeal and the House of Lords in the case of *Salomon* v. *Salomon and Co.* Mr Salomon sold his business to a limited company with a nominal capital of 40,000 shares of £1 each, the company consisting only of the vendor, his wife, a daughter and four sons (the seven required by law), who subscribed for one share each. Twenty thousand additional shares were issued to Mr Salomon, and also debentures forming a floating security. Bad times came, and the company was wound up, and all its assets were claimed by Mr Salomon, as debenture holder, leaving nothing for unsecured creditors.

'Vaughan Williams, J., in the Chancery Division, said: "This business was Mr Salomon's business and no one else's." Lindley, L. J., in the Court of Appeal, approving his decision, said: "It is manifest that the other members of the company have practically no interest in it, and their names have merely been used by Mr Aron Salomon to enable him to form a company, and to use its name in order to screen himself from liability . . . In a strict legal sense the business may have to be regarded as the business of the company; but if any jury were asked, Whose business was it? they would say Aron Salomon's, and they would be right"' (Duff, *Personality*, pp. 213–15). The House of Lords, however, insisted on looking at the matter in a 'strict legal sense' only, and decided unanimously for Mr Salomon. Duff concludes: 'Like most English cases and most Roman texts, *Salomon* v. *Salomon and Co.* can be reconciled with any theory but is authority for none' (*ibid.*, p. 215).

But to protest against this sort of manipulation of the system is very different from demanding that the law must, and must only, recognise corporations which are real. Under such conditions there would be no abuse, but nor would there be any access to the law either; instead, men would have to create corporations as they went about their extra-legal business. And the same would be true of marriage. In a world in which all marriages were real, what we should recognise as the legal business of marriage – formal bonds and the formal severing of bonds, weddings and divorces, ceremony and alimony – would disappear. Marriages would have to be made during the course of everyday life. A world of real marriages, like a world of real corporations, would have either to be highly moralised, or highly unpredictable, or quite possibly both.

The deterministic legal mode which is required by the concept of real group personality helps to determine the nature of the state that contains real group persons, the *Rechtsstaat*. Above all, it makes clear that the *Rechtsstaat* cannot be understood as a *civitas* (a civil *societas*) in Oakeshott's sense of that term. For Oakeshott, the state is only analogous to a *societas* where its laws condition but do not determine the substantive actions of its members. They exist as rules designed to formalise individual endeavour in such a way as to allow individuals to co-exist with one another. The endeavours themselves, which make up the substantive life of each individual, exist quite independently of the law; the law simply represents an addition to individuals' lives, giving them legal form as and when required. At times, when the conditions of co-existence become strained, rule may have to be supplanted by command, and citizens compelled to perform certain sorts of actions. But whether imperative or enabling, the law in a *societas* can never be the whole of a citizen's life, and each citizen will be aware of a line dividing his legal from his extra-legal performances, whether undertaken individually or as part of a group. In a *Rechtsstaat* this line disappears. But just because it disappears, it does not follow that the *Rechtsstaat* is to be understood as a *universitas* in Oakeshott's sense. Certainly it is true that where the state is analogous to a *universitas* all individual actions are governed by the collective life of the state. Yet it is also true that the collective life of such a state is not determined *by* its laws, but by some end outside of those laws which the law itself exists in order to further. In a *Rechtsstaat*, the law does not guide individuals towards some end that they collectively share. Instead, as Gierke makes clear, individuals and groups of individuals within the *Rechtsstaat* choose their own ends; it is simply that, as Gierke makes equally clear, the law manages to account for the world in which those choices are made. If the *Rechtstaat* has a purpose, therefore, it is simply law itself, for it is in law that the moral life of the state reveals itself.

Yet whatever Gierke might say about the 'intimate connection' that exists between legal and extra-legal forms of life, it cannot be claimed that the two are indistinguishable. Nowhere is this more apparent than in the work of legal historians like Maitland and Gierke themselves. For though both men range widely across social and intellectual history in the course of their writings, they do not do so indiscriminately. Both recognised, as anyone must, that the law, whether or not it applies to every aspect of social and moral existence, depends for its own existence on particular institutions and the men who constitute them: law finds its immediate origins in parliaments, courts and universities, and in the work of legislators, lawyers and jurists. These men, and these institutions, do not make up the entire life of any state, as Maitland and Gierke were only too aware. Yet they do still provide the focus of attention for both of them as legal historians. Each wished to maintain that legal activity was inseparable from the broader social conditions in which it occurred, but neither could claim that the two were interchangeable – it is simply not the case that a group of men are the same whether they are assembled inside or outside a courtroom. For the legal realist, therefore, particularly if he is also a legal historian, a final decision remains: how to decide an order of priority between two inseparable but nonetheless distinct versions of reality, one the version that is produced by legal institutions, the other the version to which the productions of legal institutions apply.

In essence, the choices are two: either it must be held that the life of the law determines the life of the state in general, or it must be held that the life of the state in general determines the life of the law. If the former, then it will be to the activities of the state's legal representatives that we look in order to discover the truth about the state itself; in other words, the state will be described in its laws. Of course, this is a position which closely resembles that adopted by Hobbes in *Leviathan*. There, the state is identified with the actions of its sovereign representative, such that nothing can be said on behalf of the state which has not first found legal expression in the actions of the sovereign. However, Hobbes's position differs in one crucial respect from any that might be adopted by a legal realist. Hobbes's state is not real; it is a fiction. As such, it is an addition to, not an expression of, reality. It does not itself represent every aspect of the lives of its members, but only those aspects which are given legal form by their sovereign. The difficulty with Hobbes's position, as we have seen, lies in relating this juristic conception of the state with the broader moral existence of the group of individuals who make it up. This is not a difficulty for legal realists, since they discern no gap between the two. But just because legal realists find the moral life of the state contained in its laws and law-making bodies, they have to face a separate problem, that of knowing where the moral content of the law comes from. For to claim that the law looks to its immediate surroundings for moral guidance is impossible without implying a substantive distinction between legal and extra-legal forms of life. Nor can it be claimed that the law looks to some end which exists outside the state as a whole, since the *Rechtsstaat* must not be understood as analogous to the *universitas*. Instead, the only possible end for law in a state where law is the whole of the state is the idea of order itself. This idea may assume a number of different, often highly moralised forms, including a host of variations on the theme of national identity. But each, in the end, must come down to one single, unvarying theme, that of organisation for its own sake. And organisation for its own sake, in the end, is fascism.

There is, though, the alternative possibility, that instead of seeing the whole life of the state determined by law, a legal realist might understand law to be determined by the life of the state, taken as a whole. In other words, it could be argued that it is the forms of organisation which men make for themselves – the whole panoply of their private transactions and associations – which constitute the essence of legal reality. Yet to suggest as much is necessarily to countenance a form of anarchism. Legal realism cannot be equated with anarchism pure and simple, if only because the latter hints at a willingness to dispense with legal forms altogether, whereas realists discern legality in every aspect of human existence. But if the view is taken that it is the legal order we discover in social reality, in contrast to the fascistic notion that it is social reality we discover in the legal order, then it must follow that law operates on two distinct levels, one actual, the other latent. Actual laws are those which exist in standardised form, instituted by the appropriate authorities. But there must also be present at every moment the possibility that men will institute their own legal forms apart from those already in existence, simply by associating with one another. This view is certainly consistent with the basic doctrine of real group personality. All theorists of the corporation have accepted that self-governance – the capacity of an association to exercise jurisdiction over its own members – is one of the qualities of the corporate life.[63] On the conventional account, which sees corporations as fictitious persons, this capacity is either conceded to a group in law or achieved by a group through recourse to law. The doctrine of real group personality, meanwhile, insists that the capacity of self-governance is in fact inherent in the group – it is part of what makes the personality of any group real. Legal realists may still argue that it is to the law as it stands that we must look for an account of this condition of corporate activity. But where it is suggested that the lives men lead best describe the law as it stands, then it is with the associations that men form that the essential order of the state must reside. Priority will have to be given to the ways groups of individuals choose to formalise their relations with one another, independently of the formalised accounts of those relations provided in the existing legal structures of the state. And though this may not be anarchism pure and simple, it bears a strong resemblance to the theoretical tenets of syndicalism.

To impose on Maitland, as an advocate of real group personality, a straight choice between fascism and syndicalism might seem a little unfair. Maitland was, as he reminds us, just a legal historian, and as an historian he sought constantly to emphasise the fluidity of the relation between juristic and more broadly social forms of endeavour. At no point did he seek to establish an order of priority between the two. Instead, his histories point up the possibility of either giving the lead to the other, at times finding the life of the state best expressed in its legal institutions, at times finding it best

---

[63] Corporations must be capable of exercising jurisdiction over their members because any group that acts in its own right must be able to compel its members to recognise the authority of its actions, and to condition their own actions accordingly. Hobbes recognised this, which is why he was able to compare the commonwealth to a corporation, and why he was so insistent that corporations should be regulated by the sovereign. In Britain, where a Hobbesian system of regulation was never properly established, corporations – particularly the corporations of city and local government – were able to develop sophisticated legal systems of their own, and to exercise jurisdiction by means of extensive 'bye-laws'. All theorists of the corporation have to accept the possibility of 'bye-laws' – even the representative of a Hobbesian corporation can be said to exercise a form of legal authority when performing representative actions, for it is in the performance of representative actions that the sovereign makes laws for the commonwealth. The question is how far a corporation should be able to go in determining the scope of its bye-laws for itself.

expressed in the extra-legal activities of its members. Maitland's realism was tempered by a consciousness of the variability of historical circumstance. Nevertheless, even a historian cannot entirely avoid facing up to the sort of choices outlined above. For history – that is, the productions of historians – itself constitutes a patterning of the reality it describes. History and historical reality are inseparable but they are by no means indistinguishable: no-one confuses an account of battle with the battle itself, any more than they confuse the trial of a criminal with the performance of the crime. Historians, like legal realists, wish neither to control, nor to add to, but simply to account for what is really the case. Yet, like legal realists, historians must acknowledge a distinction between patterned reality and the reality which is so patterned. Again, therefore, there is a choice to be made here, between formalised patterning of the past and a version of the past which resists patterning of this kind. In essence, it is a choice between historism and historicism. Historicists look to determine the 'laws' of historical development. The advantages of historicism lie in its ability to order the vast mass of historical circumstance. Its disadvantage is that such ordering can appear arbitrary, the imposition of formal structures for their own sake. Historists emphasise the unpredictability of historical circumstance, and they look to the ability of each historical event to generate a pattern of its own. The advantage of historism is its broadmindedness; the disadvantage, that it can make the task of ordering the past seem an impossibly wishful one. Of course, it might be said that no historian need face a straight choice between these options, any more than Maitland should face a straight choice between fascism and syndicalism. A historian might wish to move from one form of history to the other, as and when he deems it appropriate; perhaps to be an historicist when he feels he can, and a historist when he feels he must. But to allow historians this freedom is merely to reconstitute the problem at another level. For establishing the relation between historicism and historism is itself a patterning of a kind of reality, the reality that is contained in the historian's own patterns of the past. Is the formal patterning of *these* patterns to be held to determine the essence of that reality, or is each decision the historian has to make to be held to generate a pattern of its own? And if the issue is left undecided, because the answer is said to vary, then the problem will reconstitute itself at a further level still, and so on, *ad infinitum*. A choice has at some point to be made if a regress is to be avoided, and it is a choice which has its roots in the dilemmas faced by the advocate of real group personality.

V

These issues are not addressed by Maitland; they are merely suggested by what he wrote. In fact, his own politics were characterised by his friend H. A. L. Fisher as 'non-dogmatic liberal Unionism',[64] which carries echoes of the idea of 'plurality-in-unity', but in other respects conveys very little. Meanwhile, he was in his writing, as we have seen, extremely reluctant to press any of the theoretical implications of Gierke's work, and he shied away from -isms of all kinds. This reluctance has been described by one commentator as 'sheer intellectual fastidiousness'.[65] But whatever you call it, it is part of the reason why Maitland's work on Gierke proved so influential, for his writing provoked as much in what it left unsaid as in what it sought to say. As a result, Maitland's arguments came to be usurped in a wide variety of causes. His work on moral personality and legal personality, though itself profoundly apolitical, served to inspire two socialists, Laski and Cole, as well as finding its way into a recent anthology of key conservative texts.[66] In another field, his thoughts were put to a use he would likely have actively disapproved: though an anti-cleric (he was 'a dissenter from all the Churches'[67]), he was enlisted by Figgis in the cause of clerical independence. One way of accounting for this range of impact is to point to the richness of the vein of thought Maitland had uncovered. Another, however, is to point to its essential open-endedness, or ambiguity. It is the latter course which has been taken here, and will provide the theme for what follows. Maitland's fastidiousness may more politely be called a reticence on matters he felt to be beyond his expertise, and this is certainly how he wished to present it. But it may also be called an unwillingness to pursue lines of thought to which no satisfactory conclusion could be brought. It was left to others to see how far they could get.

---

[64] Fisher, *Maitland*, p. 174.

[65] S. Collini, *Public moralists: political thought and intellectual life in Britain, 1850–1930* (Oxford, 1991), p. 303.

[66] 'Moral personality and legal personality', included in R. Scruton (ed.), *Conservative texts* (Basingstoke, 1991), pp. 193–203.

[67] Fisher, *Maitland*, p. 100.

CHAPTER 6

Figgis and the 'communitas communitatum'

I

A note at the end of Maitland's introduction to Gierke records the thanks that were owed by the author 'for many valuable suggestions to Mr J. N. Figgis whose essays on *The divine right of kings* (1896) and on the *Politics of the Council of Constance* will be known to students'.[1] Figgis was a young clergyman and historian who had in 1896 returned to his old Cambridge college of St Catherine's as a lecturer in history. While in Cambridge, Figgis fell under Maitland's spell, and in due course he came to share in his mentor's enthusiasm for Gierke and *Genossenschaftstheorie*. But though the two men enjoyed the same intellectual interests, they were temperamentally rather different. Figgis was in no sense a fastidious man (Geoffrey Elton, in a bizarre introduction to one of Figgis's books, describes him as 'large, greedy, desperately untidy'[2]), and in his writing he exhibited few of Maitland's scruples about branching out into political philosophy proper. Nor did he seek to confine his historical enquiries to the legal field in which Maitland had proved himself pre-eminent. Figgis was a historian of ideas in something closer to our current sense, exploring the history of political theory and dogma for their own sakes. He was prepared, in ways that Maitland was not, to engage directly with the persistent issues of political thought, concerning what Maitland would call the state's very nature, and the very nature of such freedoms as it might contain. Figgis argued, passionately, for corporate freedom, and against that theory of the state's sovereignty which he believed to provide it with its most potent threat. In time, he sought to develop a coherent political theory of his own, a process

[1] Gierke, *Political theories*, p. xlv.
[2] G. Elton, 'Introduction' to J. N. Figgis, *The divine right of kings* (Torchbook edn, New York, 1965), p. viii.

which culminated in the publication in 1913 of *Churches in the modern State*, perhaps the most complete statement of a pluralistic position in English political thought this century. Yet this work, like most of Figgis's output after 1900, has its roots in Maitland's tentative hints about the real personality of associations. Whatever the value of Figgis's suggestions to Maitland, therefore, it is outweighed by the value of what Maitland suggested to Figgis – nothing less than the attempt to see how a Gierkean political theory might actually be made to work in an English setting.

If *Churches in the modern State* represents a significant advance on the ideas put forward by Maitland in his introduction to Gierke, it also marks an advance on the work of Figgis's to which Maitland refers in that introduction. Figgis wrote his first book, *The divine right of kings*, before he had any knowledge of Gierke. When he came to write the preface for a second edition in 1914, he explained that this product of his youth (it had started life as a prize essay in Cambridge) 'had been written under the shadow of the Austinian idol'.[3] Two things had happened in the interim to cause Figgis to revise his opinion. The first was that he had come, through Maitland, to view the problems of political theory in terms of group personality, and as a result to regard conventional English theories of sovereignty as inadequate. But in addition, the early years of the century had thrown up a number of important legal cases in which the basic premises of English corporation theory, such as it was, were put to the test. As they were put to the test, so they were found by Figgis to be wanting. The cases themselves, of which the most celebrated was the Scottish Church case of 1900–4, had taken place during Maitland's life-time, but though Maitland makes reference to them in his writing, he did not choose to discuss them in any detail.[4] Figgis did, and approaching the issues involved from a Gierkean perspective he concluded that the English ability to muddle through to convenient conclusions could no longer be relied upon. A faith in the tolerance engendered by English institutions had permeated his earliest writing, and in *The divine right of kings* he had sought to identify it with the utilitarian principles of Austinianism. But the evidence of the

[3] J. N. Figgis, *The divine right of kings* (London, 1896), p. ix.
[4] Maitland remarked at the end of his Sidgwick lecture: 'I cannot think . . . that it was a brilliant day in our legal annals when the affairs of the Free Church of Scotland were brought before the House of Lords, and the dead hand fell with a resounding slap on the living body' (Maitland, *Collected papers*, vol. III, p. 319). That, though, was all he was prepared to say.

years that followed persuaded him that antique-modern conceptions of state and association led, unavoidably, to illiberality. In Maitland, Gierke's influence had brought about a change of direction, drawing him further and further into the previously unexplored field of corporation theory. But in Figgis it produced a change of heart, both about the nature of the state itself, and about the immediacy of the threat faced by the groups within it.

II

Figgis's *The divine right of kings* is not, at first sight, an obviously Austinian work. Austin treated all questions of right analytically; Figgis's is a history book, and its treatment of right is not analytic, but historical. Moreover, because it is a history of political thought, it is opposed to the purported timelessness of all political theory. In it, Figgis writes:

No system of politics can be immutable. It is impossible in framing a doctrine of government to lay down eternal principles which may never be transgressed. A universal theory of the State is a chimera, for historical development and national character are the most important of all considerations in investigating the laws of historical development.[5]

If this statement forms part of an Austinian work, then Austin's theory of sovereignty clearly cannot be counted a universal or eternal principle. In fact, Figgis is not concerned anywhere in the book with Austin himself, but only with what he describes, the sovereign. This institution he takes to be compatible with the absence of theory, for he postulates a non-, or even anti-theoretical sovereign. The central theme of the book is the manner in which modern political life has escaped from the absolute claims to authority of the early modern era. These claims, paradigmatic among which is that of divine right, Figgis identifies with contingent historical conflicts, primarily religious, in which the participants formulated the political end they sought in universal terms. One possible consequence of this for the historian is a distrust of political theory; the consequence for the participants was an eventual diminution of the role of political

---

[5] Figgis, *The divine right of kings*, p. 153. By speaking of universal theory as 'chimerical', Figgis is embracing a form of historism in the sense that I have used the term. By speaking of 'national character', Figgis is embracing a form of historism in something like Meinecke's sense. By speaking of 'the laws of historical development', Figgis is embracing a form of Popperian historicism. Whether these are consistent, and which of them might be said to prevail, is discussed below.

theory, as the claims of its proponents evolved means of co-existence with one another. This evolution Figgis associates with the end of the religious strife that had characterised the Reformation and Counter-Reformation, and with the rise of rationalism, which he describes in terms of utility. And of this process, Figgis writes in the historical present of its future culmination in 'the abandonment of the attempt to find an immutable political theory; and politics will become, as they are at the present day, purely utilitarian or historical'.[6] The result is a state which contains sovereign authority, but not a sovereign whose ability to secure obedience follows from a theory of its authoritativeness. It will be, as Figgis puts it, possessed of a 'historical' sovereignty – it will command where it can, or possibly where it must, but not, as immutable theories postulate, where it will.

This, then, is a conception of a limited state, something that best is illustrated by Figgis's treatment of the question of religious tolera-tion, which was always his own main concern. Figgis argues that the only surety of religious freedom derived from the failure of doctrines of religious absolutism, for it was from this failure that there arose 'the doctrine of toleration, by which alone, as a practical limit upon State action, religious freedom can be secured without clerical supremacy'.[7] Figgis makes clear that the growth of this doctrine was in some sense inadvertent: it resulted from the competition of absolute claims necessarily leading to the recognition of a plurality of claims as much as from the independent triumph of an absolute insistence on plurality.[8] As a result, it is possible to specify the particular Austinian shadow under which Figgis could be said to be labouring: the limit on state action was that provided by the historical triumph of 'utilitarian' politics; therefore, the exercise of sovereignty was conditional upon the sovereign standing in thrall to the laws of utility. Figgis was happy to secure the state of its sovereign authority because of the uses to which he believed such authority must in the end be put – in the cause of toleration, and against authoritarianism *per se*.

---

[6] *Ibid.*, p. 162.   [7] *Ibid.*, p. 262.

[8] Figgis summarised the process as follows: 'In the first stage, the State prescribes a religion of its own and compels all men to worship the Emperor. In the second stage, the State recognises that it is incompetent to decide upon questions of religious belief, and must go to the spiritual authority to find truth; but still it regards enforcement of truth as a duty, and persecution as its proper function. The third stage is that of complete toleration of all forms of belief, when the State has given up its claim to meddle with opinion, and regards religious questions as beyond its competence' (*ibid.*, pp. 215–16).

This counts, in two senses, as a rather special reading of Austin. First, it postulates a historical state of affairs which Austin himself did not postulate; indeed, Austin continually emphasised that, though there was a moral, there was no necessary historical connection between the divine law of utility and the positive laws of a given sovereign. Second, the purpose of Austinian jurisprudence was to circumvent the need for these sorts of historical conclusions, and to establish a scope for sovereign authority which was not dependent on what was by the lights of jurisprudence a moral accident. Austin's sovereign derives its authority from the necessary fact of obedience, not the contingent fact of the coincidence of its purpose with a higher one. Figgis drew together the analytical and historical sides of Austin's account of sovereignty, while Austin himself set out the reasons why they should be kept apart. In this sense, Figgis's early Austinianism was dependent on a historicist impulse transcending his broader historism – that is, on a belief that history follows a particular law of progress, overriding the sense that general theories are the product of historical circumstance. Without the more specific, teleological belief, two consequences might be expected to follow, revealing the gap between Figgis and Austin which the specialness of Figgis's interpretation obscured. On the one hand, unallied to utility, the sovereign might appear as the potential enemy of freedom, for its authority may serve other purposes. On the other hand, freed from a pre-determined dialectic, the theory of sovereignty might appear as one of the chimerical doctrines of immutability against which Figgis's latent historism had warned.

By the time Figgis came to publish his second major work on the subject of theories of the state, his historicist convictions had been undermined. That work was *Studies of political thought from Gerson to Grotius, 1414–1625*, which started life as a series of lectures delivered at Cambridge in 1900, but which Figgis did not see fit to publish until 1907. In the audience for the original lectures was Maitland, and it is to Maitland's memory that their heavily revised final version is dedicated.[9] Like its predecessor, *Studies of political thought from Gerson to*

[9] Maitland had died at the end of the previous year. Figgis writes in the preface: 'While the book was being rewritten, nearly three years back, I asked [Maitland's] permission to dedicate the lectures to one who had taught me so much. At the very time when he accepted this suggestion with his accustomed graciousness, I felt that the end might come before my task was accomplished. It has come. And now I can only say how unworthy of his memory is this bungling treatment of a subject some aspects of which he himself illuminated' (Figgis, *Studies of political thought from Gerson to Grotius, 1414–1625* (London, 1907), pp. vi–vii).

Grotius approaches its subject from a historical perspective (it is, as its title would suggest, a history of late medieval and early modern political thought); here, however, the emphasis is definitely historist. Figgis reiterates his belief that 'we must not study political theories apart from political conditions',[10] and moreover, he states again that 'out of conflict and controversies, in essence religious, modern politics have developed themselves'.[11] However, in this work he does not draw the further conclusion that modern politics have achieved a special status by dint of their standing at the end of such development. Instead, a 'solidarity' is insisted upon between present and past disputes in political theory, and this is a solidarity which constrains rather than liberates. Modern political argument is seen to use the same concepts as were used by those who formed the terminology of European political thought in the late medieval and early modern era. As a historian, Figgis appreciates that the evolution of these concepts links them to particular historical controversies; he no longer believes, however, that this appreciation is itself constitutive of a new, modern conception of political life. Thus the theme of inadvertence appears in *From Gerson to Grotius* in a new guise. In *The divine right of kings* claims to clerical or secular supremacy had, by their incommensurability, inadvertently laid the groundwork for the doctrine of toleration. For the later work, in contrast, these purportedly immutable theories have an inadvertently divisive effect – because they linger in political argument longer than the conditions for which they were designed remain, they perpetuate claims to supremacy beyond the conditions with which the historian should like to identify them. These claims do then acquire an immutability, undeserved perhaps, but real, for their historical contingency has been transcended. The result is that political authority is conceived in terms which are absolute, and furthermore which are tied to historically relative rather than morally imperative requirements. The sovereign is then become, as Austin originally conceived it, not the vehicle of utility, but only the vehicle of command, for its apologists are destined to describe it as the vehicle of those contingent interests they wish to secure.

In one sense, this loss of faith in the ability of 'historical' politics to secure group freedoms serves to move Figgis away from Gierke. His earliest work had, if nothing else, sought to locate freedom at the end

---

[10] *Ibid.*, p. 30.   [11] *Ibid.*, p. 5.

of history, as narrower conceptions of political life became reconciled in the broader context of historical progress. This was a dialectical understanding of the past, if more whiggish than Hegelian. But however it is understood, the telos of this dialectic remained a profoundly unGierkean one – the tolerant Austinian sovereign. It was *From Gerson to Grotius* which, for all its emphasis on the contingency of political ideas, revealed the extent to which Figgis was willing to embrace a Gierkean view of politics. By the time of its publication, he had come to understand the modern idea of sovereignty as little more than a historical accident. This meant he could no longer plot the history of political thought as a progression towards the ideal of the tolerant sovereign. But it also meant that he was free to search the history of political thought for an alternative to that ideal. That there was such an alternative provides Figgis with the central theme of his book. Like Gierke, Figgis had come to regard the modern fixation on the sovereign state and its individual citizens as the antithesis of 'the medieval theory of community life'.[12] Modern sovereign states allowed rights to individuals, and individuals often used those rights to form themselves into associations (indeed, as Figgis points out, many groups, particularly churches, have championed the rights of individuals for this very reason). But associations within modern states did not have rights of their own, and as a result they did not constitute integral or 'organic' parts of those states. This they had in the medieval *communitas communitatum*. Unlike Gierke, Figgis did not believe that the modern theory of sovereignty and the medieval theory of community were to achieve synthesis in a new ideal of the *Rechtsstaat* – he was still no Hegelian. But he did now believe that something of the medieval conception of the state could, and should, be rescued within a modern setting, and this he took to have been demonstrated by one man in particular, Johannes Althusius.

Although Figgis's book concludes with the essentially modern figure of Hugo Grotius, it is his compatriot and contemporary Althusius who occupies pride of place. Following Gierke (beside whose work, Figgis suggests, everything else on the subject is 'but prattle'[13]), Figgis argues that Althusius must not be understood as a champion of resistance – his was not simply a *Vindiciae contra tyrannos*. Rather, he was a theorist of what Figgis calls 'the ordered life of the

---

[12] *Ibid.*, p. 205.   [13] *Ibid.*, p. 201.

community as a whole'.[14] The linchpin of this order was the legal theory of sovereignty. But the form it was to assume embraced much more than a purely legalistic understanding of the life of the state; it also embraced the idea of fellowship. The Althusian state is made of associations, by associations, for associations – it is, in Figgis's words, 'a true *Genossenschaft*'.[15] These associations, and the state that contains them, are still dependent upon the quintessentially modern notion of contract for their formation. But it is, Figgis says, a contract 'far less artificial' than any of its conventional equivalents,[16] and it was used to generate a state which resembled an organism more than it resembled a machine. In Althusian political theory Figgis recognised an attempt to 'combine elements which one commonly finds opposed'[17] – that is, to discover the medieval ideal of social organisation in the modern idea of juristic order.

In the end, Figgis has to accept, with Gierke, that this attempt was a failure. Althusius was unable to make the final break from mechanistic conceptions of group life, which might have 'prepared the way for the true theory of the corporation, in which authority and self-dependence are inherent essentially, and not dependent on an agreement, since they arise from the nature of the case'.[18] More importantly, he was unable to diminish the appeal of atomistic conceptions of the state for those who had to live in them: groups of individuals continued to seek the assurances of juristic order long after it had become apparent, to the likes of Gierke anyway, that juristic order assured the groups themselves of nothing. Before Maitland introduced him to Gierke, Figgis had been one of those who identified freedom with the tolerant exercise of sovereignty. But by 1907 he found it a source of regret that 'the modern unitary state is still conceived as a *Herrschaftsverband* rather than a *Genossenschaft*'.[19] Althusius had been unable to break the contingent hold of juristic conceptions of sovereignty on European political life. But he had at least shown that it was contingent, and that there was an alternative. How to realise that alternative was for Gierke a complex, dialectical and highly idealistic business, the work of a life-time. Figgis summarised his solution in a single sentence:

What is needed nowadays is that as against an abstract and unreal theory of State omnipotence on the one hand and artificial view of individual independence on the other, the facts of the world with its innumerable

---

[14] *Ibid.*, p. 210.   [15] *Ibid.*, p. 206.   [16] *Ibid.*, p. 202.   [17] *Ibid.*, p. 207.
[18] *Ibid.*, p. 202.   [19] *Ibid.*, p. 204.

bonds of association and the naturalness of social authority should be generally recognised, and should become the basis of our laws, as it is of our life.[20]

What Figgis did not do in *From Gerson to Grotius* was seek to elaborate these new-found convictions in terms of group personality. He simply asks 'whether the State creates or whether it only recognises the rights of communities . . . whether in modern German phrase the corporate union be not real rather than fictitious'.[21] However, he had already attempted to give something like a full answer to these questions in a paper he delivered to the Church Congress of 1905 under the title 'The Church and the secular theory of the State'. As its title would suggest, Figgis's concern in this paper was the place of religious associations within the political community at large, and as in all his other writing he declares that 'the tolerant State is the true State'.[22] Here, though, he makes an explicit connection between the conditions of toleration and the non-conditional recognition of corporate personality. The 'secular' theory of the state was for Figgis what Gierke would call 'antique-modern': it rested on narrow juristic premises, pushed moral considerations to one side, and perceived all group life as nothing more than the product of artifice. Where the state was understood in these terms (and Figgis now understood these terms to be Austin's), the life of groups within the state might be a precarious one. But it was not simply on consequential grounds that Figgis took issue with the 'secular' view of associations; it was also, he believed, demonstrably false. For he writes: 'The fact is, to deny to smaller societies a real life and meaning, a personality in fact, is not anti-clerical, or illiberal, or unwise, or oppressive – it is *untrue*.'[23] The truth was that all associations had a personality of their own, and it was truth in this sense which Figgis set in contrast to the claims of mere 'legality'. Certain things, he argues, may be true legally which are nonetheless false in a broader sense, as, for example, the statement that 'legally, the State could establish Mohammedanism tomorrow'.[24] So it is with

---

[20] *Ibid.*, p. 206.   [21] *Ibid.*, p. 204.

[22] Figgis, 'The Church and the secular theory of the State', *Report of the Church Congress* (1905), 191.

[23] *Ibid.*

[24] *Ibid.*, 189. In fact, Austin used a similar example to make a similar point about the subordination of notions of 'legality' to wider concerns. He argued that 'no man, talking with a meaning, would call a parliamentary abolition of either or both of the Churches [English or Scottish] an illegal act', but that it would nevertheless be 'unconstitutional' (Austin, *The province of jurisprudence determined*, p. 255). Austin's point was that the semantics of

the claim that 'legally' the rights of group persons 'can be treated as the grant of the State'.[25] This might have a juristic basis, but it cannot be the whole truth of the matter, for the simple reason that groups also have rights 'in a practical sense' and 'actually', as determined by the lives that they themselves choose to lead. Where these practical truths are denied, associations can be nothing more than facades for the authority of the state; they must not therefore be denied, if 'the Church is not to vanish into a royal benevolent fund, or dissolve into an academic debating society'.[26] This may look like a consequential argument, but in truth it is something more. For Figgis's point is that a benevolent fund or a debating society are two things that his church emphatically is not, and that no church can ever be.

Figgis could not have written this paper without having read Gierke first – his defence of religious freedoms rests entirely on the idea that all associations, whether religious or not, are persons 'in reality'. However, as in *From Gerson to Grotius*, this is a version of Gierkean *Genossenschaftstheorie* which greatly simplifies the original. Gone is the dialectical complexity, which discerns law in every aspect of life, and life in every facet of law. Instead, we are presented with a straight contrast between what Figgis calls 'the facts of life' on the one hand, and 'mere' law on the other. The advantage of such an account lies in its very simplicity – it is not hard to see the point that Figgis is trying to make. But this same simplicity means that the account Figgis gives cannot on its own be considered a complete one. For it leaves one very obvious question unanswered. If groups really are persons irrespective of what lawyers and jurists would have us believe, why should it matter *what* lawyers and jurists say on the subject of group personality? The main thrust of Figgis's argument is that life must always take priority over law, facts over theories, reality over artifice. Yet if so, what should groups have to fear from the attention of individualists and fictionists, since group personality, if real in Figgis's sense, should in another sense make group persons untouchable? The answer to these questions is not to be found in the text of the paper Figgis delivered in 1905, nor in the text of the lectures he published two years later. Rather, it lies in the immediate background against which these works were produced. For in the

---

jurisprudence should not be used mistakenly, but nor should they be mistaken for practical proposals.
[25] Figgis, 'The Church and the secular theory of the State', 189.   [26] *Ibid.*, 192.

years between the publication of *The divine right of kings* and the publication of *From Gerson to Grotius* Figgis had not only discovered Gierke; he had also discovered that life and law do sometimes clash, with potentially disastrous consequences.

III

The clash which caused Figgis concern above all others took place in Scotland, and it concerned a church. In 1900 the Assembly of the Free Church of Scotland had elected by 643 votes to 27 to enter into a union with the United Presbyterians. The Free Church itself had been created in 1843 following a split in the established Church of Scotland – then, about a third of the church's members had broken away to form a new body (inevitably by means of a deed of trust), still believing in the principle of establishment but free from state control over its internal affairs, and organised around a strict adherence to the theological tenets of Calvinism. The decision of 1900 altered this, because the United Presbyterians were more liberal in their interpretation of Calvinism than had been the founders of the Free Church; they were also opposed to the principle of church establishment. It was for these reasons that the minority of 27 (who came to be known as 'the Wee Frees') opposed the union, and despite the size of the majority that approved it, they took their case to law, claiming that the decision of the Assembly had been *ultra vires*. The Wee Frees argued that the Free Church could not reconstitute itself in this way, because its very existence was determined by the terms of its original constitution; where these terms were altered, the church must cease to exist; therefore, the church must belong to those, however small in number, who upheld the principles of its founders. These were deep and difficult issues, and eventually the case reached the House of Lords. There, after much deliberation on what were often obscure questions of theology, the Lords decided in favour of the Wee Frees, and awarded them the name of the Free Church, along with the whole of its property and all its buildings. Unsurprisingly, this decision caused a considerable outcry, and it proved to be more or less unworkable in practice.[27] Finally, an act of parliament was

---

[27] One of the lawyers for the new United Church, Taylor Innes, lamented that the judgment of the Lords had 'hurl[ed] itself through the land like a tornado, unroofing manses, emptying Churches, closing Colleges, giving Mission Halls to the moles, and Sunday Schools to the bats' (quoted in K. R. Ross, *Church and creed in Scotland: the Free Church case*

required to sort out the mess, and to redistribute the property of the church in a more equitable manner between the competing parties.[28]

For Figgis, the decision of the House of Lords in the case of the Free Church of Scotland – the ultimate 'legal' decision in the case – was simply wrong. It was not that it was anti-clerical (though Figgis remarked on the incongruity of civil lawyers attempting to interpret Calvinist texts on the church's behalf), nor that it was illiberal (though many called it that), nor even that it was unwise (though it most certainly was); it was untrue. The error lay in the Lords' failure to acknowledge that the church, like any church, had a personality of its own, and could not therefore be identified with the merely artificial personality described in the legal documents drawn up at the time of its formation. By identifying the church with the strict terms of those documents, the law denied to it, or any other church, the capacity to change, develop and grow, on its own terms, in accordance with the life that it chose to lead. That churches, along with most other forms of human association, were capable of such development was to Figgis self-evident. And nearly ten years after the original case, when he came to produce his final work of political theory, *Churches in the modern State*, his indignation at the sheer wrongness of the decision remained. Indeed, it is the Scottish Church case which provides the book with much of its impetus. In it, Figgis asks of any church:

Does [she] exist by some inward living force, with powers of self-development? or is she a mere aggregate, a fortuitous concourse of ecclesiastical atoms, treated it may be as one for the purposes of commonsense, but with no real claim to a mind or will of her own, except so far as the civil power sees good to invest her for the nonce with the portion of unity?[29]

This, for Figgis, was the key question; and it was to provide a clear answer to this question that he attempted in *Churches in the modern State* to produce a coherent *Genossenschaftstheorie* of his own.

But before looking to see what that theory was, it is worth

1900–1904 and its origins (Edinburgh, 1988), p. 1). This may be somewhat melodramatic, but it conveys the immediate effect of the final decision in the case, which was to divide the material life of the church from the lives of most of its members.

[28] This was The Churches (Scotland) Act of 1905, which vested the funds of the Free Church in a Parliamentary Commission, whose job it was to distribute those funds as nearly as possible in accordance with the spirit in which they had been raised.

[29] Figgis, *Churches in the modern State* (London, 1913), p. 40.

considering in more detail the Scottish Church case itself, which was so crucial to the development of Figgis's political thought, and therefore to the development of English political pluralism as a whole. The first point to note is that although Figgis believed that the point at issue was group personality, this did not involve the issue of the group's corporate status understood in any strictly legal sense. No-one believed that the Scottish Church case was to be resolved by deciding whether or not the church was a corporation. It was a trust, and the question was whether or not the original terms of the trust were binding on successive generations of the church's members. In this sense, it was not a case which can be fitted neatly into the heart of Maitland's arguments about group personality, since Maitland believed that the primary purpose of introducing English (and by extension Scottish) lawyers to the concept of the *Genossenschaft* was to enable them to ascribe corporate status to groups with a greater degree of accuracy. Yet for this very reason, the Scottish Church case helps to illuminate the part of Maitland's argument which is least clear – that is, its conclusion, where Maitland moves from non-concessionary fictitious personality to a conception of group personality as something real. The Free Church of Scotland had already addressed itself to the issue of concessionary personality at the time of its formation in 1843 – the break in the established church had occurred precisely because some of its members could not accept the state interfering in its internal affairs as it was used to interfere in the affairs of chartered corporations. Although the dissidents still believed in the broad principles of church establishment, they utilised the general rules of trust law to create a group capable of self-governance, and organised around principles that its members had chosen for themselves. The significance of the case of 1903 was that it seemed to suggest that the ability of a group to make use of these legal facilities was not enough. As a result, it allowed Figgis to give a clear answer to the question of whether there is any need to move from a liberal regime of rule-governed group life to a world in which the governance of groups is determined by the personality that they really possess. For Figgis, no system of rules, however liberal, could suffice on its own, because any system of rules bound the group of individuals that used it to the terms under which they used it, and thereby denied that group the capacity, as a single group, to develop, or grow. The one thing that general rules do not allow for is inherent change. Therefore, groups organised in accordance with general rules must be artificial. Like machines, they may do many of the things that natural men do; but they cannot change as men change, unless someone steps in to change them.

What Figgis gives us is a straight contrast between growth, or life, on the one hand, and rules, or law, on the other. This separating out of life and law might seem like a curious way of approaching what was a problem *in* law, but it is certainly possible to make sense of the Scottish Church case in Figgis's terms. For it was a dispute between those who understood the church as an evolving, and those who saw it as a fixed, entity. The House of Lords, perhaps unsurprisingly, came down on the side of fixity. But because, as Figgis saw it, life is always stronger than law, their decision was unsustainable, even though it was not without cost. The church, starved of material resources, continued to exist in the continuing activities (and protests) of its members, and eventually the law had to recognise this, which meant recognising that the 'legal' version of events had been the wrong one.[30] Nevertheless, it must be pointed out that if the Free Church of Scotland did have an organic personality, it was a personality of a rather peculiar kind. For this was a person that had found it necessary to present itself before the civil courts in order to have decided the nature of its personality, and this had proved necessary because the church had been unable to decide the matter for itself. In all but the rarest cases, there is no analogy here with the persons of the natural world:[31] when a man is unable to decide which of various personalities he is to bear, he may end up before the courts, but it will not be because he has brought himself there; on the whole, a man who wished to take himself to court would be considered insane. In this respect, there seems good reason for saying that the Free Church of Scotland cannot have constituted a single entity, as Figgis would have us believe, for if it had formed such an

---

[30] It was, however, one of the ironies of a case full of ironies that this recognition could only be put into practice by recourse to the traditional tool of concessionary theory, the sovereign 'act'; as the *Scotsman* noted at the time, it might be thought curious, to say the least, that 'the last outcome of the long protest against Erastianism is that the funds and property of the Free Church of Scotland should be vested in a Parliamentary Commission' (quoted in Ross, *Church and creed*, p. 52).

[31] One possible analogy is with a trans-sexual who wishes to change the sex given on his/her birth certificate in order to take advantage of the legal benefits available to one of the sex that they have become (for example, if become a woman, in order to marry a man). But the analogy is still incomplete, because the trans-sexual's case is against those who are responsible for the drawing up of birth certificates (i.e. the state) and not those parts of his/her own person that wish to remain the sex that they were born with.

entity, the case of the church would never have come to court. It is easy to lose sight of this simple fact in the face of what might be described as the Erastian aspects of the case. It is certainly true that the question of church/state relations played an important part in the original dispute. It is also true that the state, in the form of the Lords, sought to decide the form in which the church should continue its existence. But these two facts are essentially unrelated. The state did not set out to impose its will on the church, nor did it insist upon dealing with the theological and other issues that were in question; the church, literally, brought the matter upon itself. And yet this is something which Figgis's own language tends to obscure. He speaks of the church being invested with unity by the civil power 'for the nonce';[32] he states that the case of the Free Church demonstrates that the rights of group persons cannot be guaranteed 'when it comes to the pinch';[33] he declares that any group which behaves as though it possesses powers of self-development is 'liable to be hauled up'[34] before the law. But what brings matters to the pinch, what hauls the whole business up before the law, is the activity taking place inside the church, and not anything that is being done by the state to it. These were arguments about, but not between, church and state. The dispute took place within the church itself.

That the basic moral of the Scottish Church case concerned an association's internal, not its external, relations Figgis was ultimately prepared to accept. He conceded that, at bottom, such cases were about what he called a group's 'powers of exclusion'; that is, they concerned the question of whether an individual should have the right 'to remain in a society pledged to one thing while he himself is pledged to the opposite'.[35] This, though, puts the matter in rather a stark form. An individual need not be opposed to the fundamental purpose of his association, nor, as in the case of the Wee Frees, committed to beliefs which his association no longer wishes to acknowledge, in order for these issues to arise; he may simply object to some of the uses which his association makes of the resources he has put into it. It was a dispute of this kind which provided the point at issue in another of the notorious legal decisions of the period, the so-called Osborne judgment of 1909. In this judgment, by which Figgis was also greatly exercised, it was declared that a trade union could not enforce a political levy contrary to the wishes

[32] Figgis, *Churches in the modern State*, p. 40.   [33] *Ibid.*, p. 39.   [34] *Ibid.*, p. 43.
[35] *Ibid.*, pp. 44–5.

of individual members, however few in number. Again, this was a private case, brought by a group within a group – the Walthamstow branch of the Amalgamated Society of Railway Servants, in the person of its secretary, W. V. Osborne – against the group's governing body, on the grounds that the actions of that body were *ultra vires*. Again, the case eventually required a judgment from the House of Lords. And again, Figgis believed that the conclusion arrived at there in favour of Osborne and his dissenting branch was palpably incorrect. It implied that 'the members of the union are a mere collection of individuals, who are unchanged by their membership of the society, and cannot therefore have the funds subscribed to a purpose to which, even in a minority, they object'.[36] Yet when Figgis writes that this minority was treated as though 'unchanged', it ought to be said that such was self-evident, since had they been so changed the matter would not have come before the courts. The problem was precisely that a small number of members of the union wished to remain members of the specific association that they had individually elected to join (an association that Osborne argued was committed to 'purely Trade Union work'[37]). Figgis was committed to the belief that these individual choices were of less significance than the integrity of the association that each had helped bring into being.

The single most striking feature of both the Scottish Church and Osborne cases is provided by the numbers involved. In each instance a very large association, having decided on a course of action, was seemingly held to ransom by a very small number of its members.[38] It was this sheer incongruity which gave Figgis's argument much of its moral force. But it is possible, as one recent commentator has noted, to think of more 'difficult' instances of a threat to a group's integrity.[39] One such occurred in the United States in 1952. This was the Kedroff case, which concerned the

---

[36] *Ibid.*, p. 65.

[37] See H. V. Emy, *Liberals, radicals and social politics* (Cambridge, 1973), p. 252.

[38] Although it was a matter of considerable controversy within the labour movement at the time as to whether Osborne really did represent the opinion of only a very few. That certainly was the impression given at the Trades Union Congress of 1910, where a motion attacking the judgment in the case was passed by 1.7 million votes to 13,000. But a general ballot of all union members in 1914 told a rather different story: then, the decision to raise a compulsory levy in order to fund Labour party electioneering was approved by a majority of 473,880 to 323,613.

[39] See D. Nicholls, *The pluralist state: the social and political ideas of J. N. Figgis and his contemporaries*, second edn (Basingstoke, 1994), p. 69.

possession of the Russian Orthodox cathedral in New York, and
which has been taken by some to undermine the whole of Figgis's
argument.[40] The case arose following a dispute between Orthodox
Christians living in America and the church's Moscow patriarchate,
concerning the direction in which the patriarchs were taking the
church as a whole. Eventually, a majority of the church's American
members broke from Moscow, and claimed possession of the New
York cathedral on the grounds that they were the church's true
representatives. This decision was recognised in a law passed by
New York State, which had the effect of granting ownership of the
cathedral to the dissident body. However, the Supreme Court found
this statute to be unlawful, and returned the cathedral to the
minority who had remained in communion with Moscow. That
there are parallels between this decision and that in the Scottish
Church case is evident, but there is also one very significant
difference. In the Kedroff case, it was the *majority* of the church's
members that wished to prevent the church from 'changing'. As a
result, it is not at all easy to know on which side Figgis might have
been expected to come down. On the one hand, the moral force of
his argument would seem to ally him with the majority, as the most
striking embodiment of the church's personality, or will. Yet,
crucially, unlike the Free Church of Scotland, the Orthodox Church
was not governed by majority rule; it was governed from Moscow,
by its patriarchs. There is therefore a case to be made here for the
minority, on the grounds that minority decision-making was an
integral part of the church's self-chosen identity. This was the
position adopted in the Supreme Court, where it was argued that
the statute passed by the New York legislature represented an
unwarranted interference in the internal affairs of a religious
society, since it resulted in the effective imposition on that society of
a form of majoritarian rule. Under these circumstances, the advocate of real group personality is caught in something of a bind: a
decision to allow the church to develop on its own terms (i.e. in
accordance with its preferred practices) results in the alienation of
the majority of its members; meanwhile, a decision to let those

---

[40] L. C. Webb, in his essay 'Corporate personality and political pluralism', argues that 'the
Kedroff case made a nonsense of the argument of *Churches in the modern State*' (L. C. Webb
(ed.), *Legal personality and political pluralism* (London, 1974), p. 54). He goes on: 'The lesson of
Kedroff, surely, is that to attribute real personality to groups is to create logical and
practical difficulties of the same order as those that arise when a strictly Austinian
sovereignty is claimed for the State' (*ibid.*).

members speak for the church results in the state coming to choose the church's practices for it. What is more, identifying the voice of the association with the preferences of the majority entails a reversion to the most familiar of all the 'fictions' of corporation theory: the fictitious notion that the many are equivalent to the whole. In the past, this notion had always relied upon the authority of the state to give it force – it was for the state to decide how many would be counted enough to speak for all (in Roman law, the figure was normally two-thirds). In the Kedroff case, the situation would seem to have been no different.

The Kedroff case does not undermine Figgis's whole argument, for the simple reason that Figgis's argument is not just a legal one. He uses legal cases to support his position, but his own case cannot rest on them entirely, precisely because he believed that life is always stronger than law. What the Kedroff case does indicate is that the position Figgis wished to adopt was liable to bring with it a series of hard choices. In particular, it makes it seem likely that the integrity of group personality was itself contingent upon group persons coming to fit a particular mould. This indubitably was the lesson of the Taff Vale case, the last of the great legal judgments to be discussed by Figgis, though the first to occur in time. In 1900 the Taff Vale railway company attempted to sue the Amalgamated Society of Railway Servants (ASRS) for damages following a series of strikes. Up until this point, it had been assumed that trade unions, because unincorporate, were exempt from such claims, and that it was individual members alone who were liable for their actions. This left the common funds of each union more or less untouchable by employers. But in this case the company argued that the technicality of unincorporate status should not prevent the union, which had been behaving in the manner of a corporate body, from being held liable for the actions of its agents. Their claim was rejected by the Court of Appeal, but in 1901 this decision was overturned in the House of Lords, and the ASRS were ordered to pay more than £42,000 in damages. Unsurprisingly, this judgment caused at least as much controversy as the one that was to follow in the case of the Free Church of Scotland. As in that case, the point at issue was the nature of group personality, but in this case the issue was raised in a somewhat different way. First, the arguments in this instance relate directly to the concerns addressed by Maitland in his essays on the subject of unincorporate bodies (one of these was written specifically

in order 'to assign to this Taff Vale case its place in a long story'[41]).
The question was not one of moral or organic, but specifically of
corporate personality. Second, this was one judgment produced by
the House of Lords of which Figgis could approve. By equating the
actions of individuals with the actions of the group, even though the
individuals concerned had not sought to identify themselves with the
group in this way, the judgment ascribed to groups the capacity to
generate a real personality of their own. Corporate status, in this
sense, was no longer to be viewed as a resource made available in
law but as a fact of life which the law is forced to recognise. Third,
though Figgis approved of the judgment, the group in question,
inevitably, did not. For the ASRS the Taff Vale decision was little
short of a disaster. This was the truly distinctive feature of the case –
that, as Figgis admits, corporate personality was ascribed to the
group 'in spite of [its members'] wishes'.[42] Trade unions did not wish
to be liable for damages following a strike, and the result of the Taff
Vale judgment was to make it increasingly difficult for trade unions
to carry out the sorts of activities for which they had come into being
in the first place – in the words of one history of the period, its
immediate effect on the British labour movement was 'frankly
disabling'.[43] But it did ensure that trade unions were treated as
persons.

The Taff Vale case, like the Scottish Church case, can be used to
provide support for the doctrine of real group personality. It is,
however, support provided at a cost. The advantages that group
personality brings with it can be seen to come with constraints all of
their own; and these constraints, like the advantages, depend upon
the state for confirmation. Of course, this does not mean that the
state creates the attributes of group personality; it simply confirms
them. Nor does it mean that groups must always be presenting
themselves before the courts for decisions regarding their personal
affairs. Where groups are free from controversy, either between
members or between the group and the world outside, their personal
affairs will remain their own concern. But for a group to remain free
from controversy its members will have to do their utmost to preserve
the continuous life of the association, and to avoid introducing to
that life extraneous concerns, which is when the trouble begins. The

---

[41] See Maitland, *Collected papers*, vol. III, p. 271.
[42] Figgis, *Churches in the modern State*, p. 179.
[43] See R. C. K. Ensor, *England 1870–1914* (Oxford, 1936), p. 378.

doctrine of real group personality would seem to encourage group members to value the integrity of their association above everything else. And yet it was in this doctrine, Figgis believed, that the key to political freedom lay.

IV

The obvious response to a claim of this kind is to ask why we should consider this to be freedom. But a better question is to ask what sort of group would consider this being free, since it is a point on which Figgis is quite clear. Such a group is one with its own way of life and its own moral standards, which accepts that those standards apply to itself alone, but which believes that where they do apply they apply absolutely. Such a group, in other words, is a sectarian church. Figgis's argument runs as follows: the conventional, or concessionary, theory of group personality implies the thesis that 'no church should have any standard of morals different from those of the State';[44] this denies to churches their defining functions, which involve stipulating particular modes of behaviour for their members, on the basis of self-chosen doctrine and ritual;[45] in so far as they do perform these functions, churches exercise 'real authority over their members';[46] as such, they must be deemed to have real personalities of their own; however, churches cannot claim authority over the life of the state as a whole, as that would involve a return to the authoritarian tendencies of early modern political theory; nor can churches seek to claim authority over the members of other associations, since the conflicts that must result will require the interference of the state if they are to be resolved; instead, 'the business of Christians is with the moral standard of their own society, and with themselves as members';[47] while 'it is the essence of the Church to be different from the world and to proclaim that difference';[48] so, real group personality implies sectarianism.

What is interesting about this argument is not its internal line of inference, which is sound enough, but the use which Figgis makes of its conclusions. For he believed that there was the basis here for a

---

[44] Figgis, *Churches in the modern State*, p. 68.

[45] Figgis uses as an example the invasion of the 'rights' of the church entailed by the 1851 Divorce Act, which allowed the use of churches for the marriage of divorced persons; and Figgis warned of further possible encroachments if the state were to compel clergymen to stand in such ceremonies against their wishes (see *ibid.*, pp. 14–18).

[46] *Ibid.*, p. 224.   [47] *Ibid.*, p. 130.   [48] *Ibid.*, p. 134.

new theory of the state, what he calls 'a true, that is a realistic, political philosophy'.[49] The name he gave to this philosophy was 'multiplied sectarianism',[50] and though the name itself did not catch on, the phrase he used to describe the political condition that it postulates fared rather better. That phrase was 'the *communitas communitatum*', which derived directly from the world of medieval political thought. By it, Figgis understood a society made up of self-formed and self-governing associations, each of which co-existed in a broader framework, itself capable of generating a sense of community. This broader community was the state, but although broader, it did not condition the lives of those lesser groups that it contained. Figgis accepts that the state must possess a degree of coercive power, in order, as he puts it, 'to ensure that [groups] do not overstep the bounds of justice'.[51] But the state was never to use that power to impose its will on the lesser communities within it, and ideally it was never to use that power at all, since the groups within it ought to be concerned with their own affairs alone, leaving the bounds of justice intact. The idea of the *communitas communitatum* encapsulated what Figgis understood by 'realism', and he associated it above all with the writing of Althusius and Gierke. In England it was an idea that was to be associated with Figgis himself, and it was for this, rather than the less wieldy 'multiplied sectarianism', that he came in time to be known.

That Figgis's idea of the *communitas communitatum* is a noble one is hard to dispute. But given the sectarian conception of group life on which it rests, it can still be asked whether it is, as Figgis supposed, a 'realistic' one also. To answer this question, it is necessary to break it down into two parts. The first part concerns the relations of groups within the state to each other; the second concerns the relation of each group to the state itself. In both cases, Figgis postulates a society in which the relations between groups are peaceable because the affairs of any one group are no concern of any other, the state included. But in neither case is this vision sustainable. Where it is a question of the relations between associations other than the state, Figgis anticipates difficulties only when one group attempts to encroach upon the territory of another, at which point, he concedes, the state may have to intervene. It is of course true that group persons, like individual persons, may clash. But it is also true that

---

[49] *Ibid.*, p. 225.   [50] *Ibid.*   [51] *Ibid.*, p. 90.

group persons, unlike individual persons, contain individuals, who may themselves clash with the group. This is an eventuality to which Figgis pays little attention, but it was by far the likelier source of conflict. Moreover, it was the source of conflict in the case of the Free Church of Scotland, which did not result from one association doing battle with another, as individuals might, but instead started when one association sought to merge with another (as individuals cannot), and then attempted to claim a recalcitrant group of individuals as its own. Eventually, the argument did resolve itself into a dispute between two distinct groups (the Wee Frees and the United Free Church) over a single set of property. But its origins lay in the claims made by two distinct groups (the original Free Church and the new United Church) over a particular set of men. Once this is seen, it will also be seen that similar situations may arise, not only when an association chooses to change, but whenever an individual or set of individuals chooses to belong to more than one group. This, of course, is a frequent occurrence – a man may belong to a trade union as well as a church, to a church as well as a political party, to a political party as well as a trade union. It does not follow from its frequency that conflict must also be frequent, nor that these conflicts will always end up in court. It does follow, however, that conflict will always be possible, and that the possibility of conflicts of this kind will only disappear when individuals are protected from the claims and counter-claims of competing associations. This may well happen if the associations to which individuals belong are all self-contained sects. But a society in which individuals are encouraged to join self-contained sects is not one in which their capacity to associate with one another will be exploited to the full.

Figgis's idealised *communitas communitatum* presupposes that men are certain about the associations to which they belong, and that they only belong to one such association. It also presupposes that the life pursued by any one association has no bearing on the life pursued by any other. Here, again, Figgis's case rests on his sectarianism. In allowing that the state is entitled to regulate groups when they come into conflict with one another, Figgis is assuming that groups will not conflict very often. This is because he assumes that groups will on the whole concern themselves with ends which are theirs alone, and which impose demands on their members alone. When conflicts do arise, it will be because separate associations happen to be pursuing similar ends, and therefore wish to make use of the same resources (in the case of the Free Church, this meant the same buildings). By his use of the examples of trade union cases like the Osborne judgment, Figgis means to suggest that this thesis is applicable to group life as a whole. But are all groups, including those with such overtly political ends as trade unions, really characterisable in these terms? Unlike churches, trade unions exist in order to make claims on others – were their ends realisable by their members alone, they would not be the associations that they are. To be told that the state will not become involved in group affairs so long as that group displays no concern with the affairs of the rest of society is an unlikely consolation for any group whose formation was brought about in order to secure some economic or political result requiring at least some changes in behaviour on the part of the rest of society. The associations which most nearly fit Figgis's model are those which may be identified as avowedly non-political – religious societies, institutions of learning or of recreation. And a community made up of lesser communities all of whose concerns are otherworldly, or purely academic, or purely recreational is, at the very least, a somewhat improbable model of a political society.

If we turn now to the question of the relation of any one of these groups to the state, it is clear that similar, if distinct, problems arise. Again, Figgis presupposes that state and group can operate peaceably alongside one another because each will be operating in separate spheres: the state exists simply in order to establish certain bounds of justice, within which groups are free to pursue their self-chosen ends; the state does not pursue such ends itself. In this respect, Figgis envisages something close to Oakeshott's ideal conception of the state, understood as analogous to a *societas*.[52] There, purposive associations are able to flourish within a framework of rules provided for them by the state, the rules guiding, but not controlling, their endeavours. However, Oakeshott recognised that this relation between the state and other groups was conditional on the state being a different sort of association from these other groups – it was a rule-governed *societas*, they were end-governed *universitates*, and this alone ensured that neither posed a threat to the other. Figgis did not make this distinction. His state was precisely the same sort of association as the groups it contained. It was a *communitas communitatum*; it was not a *societas universitatum*. Figgis conceived his state in

---

[52] This is a point made by David Nicholls in the only book-length study of Figgis's political thought (see Nicholls, *The pluralist state*, pp. 80–1).

these terms because of the lesson he learned from Gierke, the same lesson which Oakeshott chose to ignore: that whatever is true of the state also holds for the associations within it, and thus whatever is true of the associations within it also holds for the state. For Figgis, as for Gierke, it was a question not of analogy, but of reciprocity. Having learnt this lesson, however, Figgis cannot escape from its consequences. He cannot claim, as Oakeshott does, that the state is in the business of regulation, while the groups within it pursue set goals. The groups within his state are 'communities', with goals certainly (though not set ones), but also with rules, which regulate the lives that their members choose to lead. They are not simply 'enterprise' projects, to which individuals may or may not become attached during the course of a life-time; they are a way of life in themselves. This is what Figgis understands by real group person-ality, and it follows from it that each of the communities to which men belong will perform many of the tasks that Oakeshott identifies with the state alone, as well as generating that sense of 'loyalty' which Oakeshott identifies with the state alone, such that we can expect each such community to have its own sense of what constitutes the bounds of justice. It also follows that the state will have to perform many of the tasks that Oakeshott identifies with enterprise associations, as it seeks to generate its own sense of community. Overlap is inevitable. And when two or more associations attempt to perform one and the same task, conflict, as Oakeshott knew, can never be far behind.

Figgis alludes to the possibility of such conflict, but only to be able to discount it. As always, his focus is on the position of churches in the state, and he insists that, once churches are granted powers of self-development, 'all other matters between church and State are a question of detail'.[53] Of the terms of this self-development, he writes that a church must be allowed to exercise complete authority over its members, given only 'the requirements of citizenship in a secular culture'.[54] Yet these 'requirements', like the 'detail' to which he refers, are likely to be just what is at issue. Many churches, to say nothing of other forms of community, may find that what the state understands by the requirements of citizenship lies at odds with what they expect of their own members. There are political theories which ascribe to groups and to their individual members the right to resist

---

[53] Figgis, *Churches in the modern State*, p. 99.   [54] *Ibid.*, p. 90.

the authority of the state in such circumstances, when to acquiesce would require the abandonment of strongly held principles. These are the theories which would allow certain sorts of associations to set for their members moral standards which entail acts of civil disobedience. However, these theories operate in just that area which Figgis dismisses as detail – they deal with the difficulty of balancing the socially divisive effects of disobedience against the requirements of the broader community. This difficulty lies at the heart of political theory, which is nothing more that the study of the problems posed by living in large communities. Yet it can only be dealt with if the theorist is prepared to differentiate between different kinds of group activity, which is to acknowledge that not all such activity is of a certain type.[55] Without this acknowledgment, the difficulty, which can hardly be denied, must simply be counted as illusory. There can, then, be a political theory which reinforces a diversity of group life, but Figgis's, because it ignores the political side of the problem, is not it.

v

In the end, Figgis chooses to fall back on history, or the 'facts', as he calls them. These are not the facts which justify political theories, but the facts which reveal all political theories to be contingent – the 'true facts . . . always stronger than abstract theories',[56] which constitute historical reality. Gierke used history, and a sense of national historical identity, to provide the ultimate framework within which the problems of relating the state to other associations might be resolved. Figgis simply uses it to show that there is no legislating for the ways in which people may be associated with one another. By the time he came to write *Churches in the modern State* he no longer wished to construct a theory of history, believing as he by then did that all theory, in whatever form, was liable to stifle diversity. There was to be no more striving for a 'solution', whether historical or not. There were just 'the facts', and the fact that political theorists could

---

[55] Many examples of this sort of theorising were produced in the United States during the 1960s and 1970s, of which perhaps the most celebrated is Michael Walzer's *Obligations: essays in disobedience, war and power* (Cambridge, Mass., 1970). Walzer cites Figgis as a major influence, but in fact goes much further in attempting to set out the grounds for evaluating which sorts of associations, founded on which sorts of beliefs, should be permitted to resist the state's attempts to control their members.

[56] Figgis, *Churches in the modern State*, p. 66.

do nothing to contain them. Having promised us a realistic political philosophy, Figgis has to content himself with reality on the one side, and philosophy on the other.

This sense that theories of the state are chimerical is the one constant theme running through Figgis's work, from *The divine right of kings* to *Churches in the modern State*. Finally, it becomes the dominant theme. At no point did Figgis make the attempt to dispense with the state altogether. But he did become increasingly convinced that any attempt to identify its institutional basis was futile; it was never, in his terms, to be 'reconciled with the facts'.[57] In his earliest work, these doubts had been overcome by his readiness to extract from Austin a theory of toleration, allowing the institutional basis of sovereignty to take second place behind its moral basis in the divine law of utility. Experience, coupled with Gierke, taught him that this was wishful thinking, and by the end Austin was nothing more to him than another 'mere verbal theory'.[58] In his earliest work he had also relied on what he called there 'the laws of historical development', to explain how the condition of toleration had been achieved in England. The reliability of these, too, he came to doubt, but here Gierke, who relied on such laws himself, had no alternative to offer him. This left two possibilities. The first was to embrace the condition, not of toleration, but of its counterpart, a degree of disorder, and this, in public, Figgis could not do. The second was for him to do nothing, and to say nothing more. This is what he chose, and following the publication of *Churches in the modern State* Figgis gave up writing on the subject of political theory, and devoted himself instead to religious topics, on which he became a celebrated lecturer in both England and the United States.[59] By doing so, he allowed himself to be returned to the point from which he had once tried to escape – to a very English reliance on the ability of people to muddle through on their own.

[57] *Ibid.*, p. 84.   [58] *Ibid.*

[59] It was while travelling to America for a lecture tour in January 1918 that Figgis's boat was torpedoed, and though he survived, it was an experience from which he never recovered. He died on Palm Sunday the following year.

CHAPTER 7

Barker and the discredited state

I

By the time Figgis published *Churches in the modern State* in 1913, it formed part of an identifiable movement in English political thought. This was the movement that Ernest Barker was to identify a year later as 'the new federalism', and both Maitland and Figgis were seen by Barker as exponents of this distinct new creed. Of Figgis Barker wrote that he made an 'ally in the religious sphere'[1] for those who were campaigning elsewhere for greater group freedoms, whether on behalf of trade unions, local authorities, or nations within nation-states; and of the work of Figgis and these others Barker himself more or less approved. Indeed, Barker's *Political thought in England*, though giving space to the full range of recent developments in English ideas, makes it quite apparent where the author's own preferences lay. In a choice between, for instance, Herbert Spencer's scientific individualism and Bernard Bosanquet's metaphysical statism, Barker's sympathies are clearly with the latter.[2] Yet as between Bosanquet's stark, and T. H. Green's more emollient view of the place of the state in national life, Barker's chose to side with the less strident of the two. He was, in essence, a mild idealist, philosophically conservative, politically liberal. As such, he found much in the new federalism he could admire – the emphasis on the group as opposed to the individual ('if we are individualists now', Barker wrote, 'we are corporate individualists'[3]), the insistence upon freedom of association, the distrust of centralised power and bureaucracy. But it also meant that he had his misgivings. As a liberal, he

---

[1] E. Barker, *Political thought in England*, p. 182.

[2] In 1927 Barker gave expression to his sense of debt to 'the late Dr Bosanquet's *The philosophical theory of the State* . . . in almost everything I have written on social matters' (E. Barker, *National character and the factors in its formation* (London, 1927), p. 136).

[3] Barker, *Political thought in England*, p. 181.

could not follow those who wished to go down the path of French syndicalism and move outside of the state's domain altogether. The state had to remain as what he called 'a necessary adjusting force',[4] in order to distinguish between, and then decide among, the claims of different groups. The freedoms enjoyed by all groups were of paramount importance, but they were also, Barker knew, incommensurate, and liable to clash. Meanwhile, regarding those like Figgis, whose inspiration was drawn less from France than from Germany, Barker had scruples of a more philosophical kind. He was quite happy to accept that groups under the law were possessed of a juristic personality in their own right. What he could not accept was that this personality must be counted, in some fundamental sense, real. This did not mean that he rejected the case for real group personality out of hand, nor that he discounted the advantages which it had over its most obvious rivals. But he felt that these were deep, and, in England at least, uncharted waters, which were liable to draw political theorists towards the sorts of absolutes which characterised German philosophy, and which caused Barker disquiet throughout his life. 'We must not', he wrote, 'push too far our claims on behalf of group persons'.[5] Yet once given this proviso, and another concerning what he called 'the needs of adjustment', he was ready to acknowledge that 'all the emphasis recently laid on rights of associations suggest lines of thought which are valuable and likely to be fruitful'.[6]

What Barker did not attempt in his 1914 survey was to develop some of these lines of thought himself. In part this was a consequence of the book's format (it was a short history book, almost a text book[7]), and in part a consequence of Barker's uneasiness about metaphysical speculation. Nevertheless, this uneasiness was somewhat different from the kind displayed by Maitland. It was not the result of modesty, real or false, nor of trepidation about what a foray into the world of German idealism might involve. It was something more like a considered opinion. Unlike Maitland, Barker did not think of himself as a mere lawyer, nor merely as a historian, but as a political theorist also. In 1928 he was to become the first holder of the chair in political science at Cambridge. In 1914 he was already the author of a substantial introduction to the political thought of Plato and Aristotle, as well as a work on Bergson. Barker had things of his own to say about the various forms of human association, and about

---

[4] *Ibid.*, p. 183.   [5] *Ibid.*, p. 180.   [6] *Ibid.*

[7] *Political thought in England* appeared under the imprint of the Home University Library.

the particular form of human association known as the state; he simply lacked the place to say them. So, while continuing with his history of political thought from Herbert Spencer onwards, he began to write a separate paper about the state and the place of groups within it, which sought to locate the problem in a broader historical context, and to attempt some sort of resolution of it. He completed this paper in May 1914, though it was not published until February the following year. Its title was 'The discredited State', and in it was contained Barker's personal contribution to the development of the new federalism.

II

The task Barker set himself in 'The discredited State' was to find some sustainable alternative to the theories of group personality that had been set out by Gierke, Maitland and Figgis. Barker was consistently resistant to the idea that some *thing* is created when a group of individuals comes together, and sought instead a formula which could convey a 'oneness without any transcendent one'.[8] The formula he arrived at is that of the 'organising' or 'associating idea': individuals come together in order to further some idea that they share, and it is in the light of that idea that their joint endeavour should be described. Thus, he suggests, groups are best to be understood as 'schemes'.[9] The merit of this approach for Barker is its inherently consequentialist slant, which allows associations to be assessed in terms of what they do rather than what they are. So it becomes possible to distinguish between different sorts of associations – as Barker asks, do we really want to call all associations persons, allowing criminal societies like the mafia to claim the same status as a trade union or a church?[10] The ground Barker seeks to occupy is somewhere between the notion of real, and that of fictitious personality, and he writes: 'Ideas are, and are not, fictions: they have hands and feet; but they are not persons, any more than they are

[8] E. Barker, 'The discredited State', *Political Quarterly*, 5 (1915), 111.
[9] *Ibid.*
[10] *Ibid.*, 113. It is interesting to note that Hobbes was troubled by the same question, and that his distinction between 'private bodies regular, and lawful' (such as the family), and 'private bodies regular, but unlawful', was designed to address this very point. What he understood by the latter were bodies of men that 'unite themselves into one person Representative, without any public Authority at all; such as are the Corporations of Beggars, Theeves and Gipsies, the better to order their trade of begging, and stealing' (see Hobbes, *Leviathan*, p. 163).

fictions.'[11] By emphasising these external, functional parts of the body, Barker is in effect drawing attention to the two key characteristics of group activity as he understands it: the capacity to do, and the capacity to move, or change. His concern is that organising ideas should remain focused on the idea itself, and not become preoccupied with the business of organisation. Against those who would single out the idea of the state as liable to stifle growth and social diversity, Barker writes of all associating ideas: '[They] have their . . . pathology . . . They may become mere bundles of paper swathed in red tape They may become office chairs or organising secretaries.'[12]

What is significant about Barker's account is that it allows him to distinguish between the state and non-state organisations on the grounds of their respective 'ideas'. The state, he writes, is a separate, distinctive organising idea, for it is the scheme or idea of 'law and order'.[13] This idea is among the most important of all possible schemes through which individuals associate with one another, and at one point Barker describes it as 'the idea *par excellence*',[14] thereby setting himself apart from those who would diminish the state regardless of the need that all communities have of a common adherence to the idea of order. Equally, though, by establishing that it is only one idea, not the only one idea, Barker makes clear that other schemes may compete with it in the attempt to secure an equivalent hold over the individual. Indeed, he argues that some associating ideas, particularly those of religious organisations, would seem to embrace a higher purpose than that of the state, whose end he describes at one point as 'the needs of mere ordered life'.[15]

Where Barker's argument runs into familiar difficulties is when he attempts to characterise the relation that subsists between the state and other associations. Of this relation he writes as follows: 'We may conceive of the State as . . . a scheme based on the political idea of law and order; we may conceive it as containing, or at any rate co-existing with, a rich variety of schemes based on a rich variety of ideas.'[16] One obvious problem with this formulation is establishing a sense in which the state can either contain, or co-exist with, the other schemes, and yet remain the organising idea of 'order'. The state's purpose, after all, is exclusively that of *providing* order; but the notions of both co-existence and containment seem to imply that order is a

[11] Barker, 'The discredited State', 113.   [12] *Ibid.*, 112.   [13] *Ibid.*, 113.
[14] *Ibid.*, 118.   [15] *Ibid.*, 120.   [16] *Ibid.*, 113.

given, for order relates here to the relationship *between* the state and other schemes. There is, in truth, a paradox here: if the state co-exists with other schemes, those schemes must be 'other' in the sense of essentially unconcerned with order; if they are unconcerned with order, the state cannot simply co-exist with them, for its existence is defined in terms of the maintenance, or 'organisation', of order. Similarly for the state that contains other schemes: if it contains them by ordering them, their essentially 'other' character is lost; if it does not order them, its character as an organising idea is lost. The state, as the organising idea of order, is in a sense the organising idea of organisation. As such, it is not an organisation which can have its idea or scheme simply compared to other ideas or schemes, for these others, as organising ideas, inevitably undermine its very reason for being. Barker cannot avoid, any more than could Hobbes, the difficulties that arise when the state is given the same formal structure as all other groups, yet also an identity which depends upon all other groups being in some sense structured by the state.

The way Barker attempts to find round this logical difficulty is provided by history. His approach to the question of the relation between the state and the disordered panoply of associational life, in contrast to Hobbes's, is not founded on a timeless logic. Instead, he sets out to describe an evolutionary, or dialectical, relationship in which the requirements of the political idea of law and order are both determined by and determinants of non-political social existence. In this way, he is able to provide a sense in which the state idea and other ideas do co-exist, for they are taken to have a continuous effect on one another just because they are not equivalent. Law and order is an idea which depends upon those other ideas which it has as its purpose to order, since it can only order what exists at any given time, and any order it achieves will be a reflection, or at least a re-fashioning, of the contingent circumstances which face it. Barker expresses this relation as follows: 'The rubrics of law are not reality; they are cases in which to put reality; but the cases may fit reality well or badly, and since reality has a way of growing, they may help or hinder its growth.'[17] He does not stipulate how one is to decide an order of priority between the cases and what they contain, and so it is far from clear what would count as a 'good fit'. All he will say is that it is 'a fascinating problem – how far legal

---

[17] *Ibid.*, 112.

categories are created by the demands of social growth, and how far legal categories create or rather determine social growth itself'.[18] However, Barker has no need to resolve this problem if his concern is merely to establish that law and the subjects of law are inseparably dependent on each other. Given such interdependence, it is at least the case that the operation of the state idea cannot be understood apart from the rich variety of other schemes which have grown up and continue to grow alongside it.

If this historical perspective provides a sense in which the state co-exists with other associations, it does not, however, clarify how we are to understand the needs of the state when compared to the needs of other associations. It does not, in other words, tell us when and on what grounds it is possible to say anything about the role that the state *should* play. Yet Barker does wish to make some general claims about the appropriateness and utility of the political idea of law and order. To do so, he requires what must be called a meta-perspective on the historical dialectic of law and growth, order and change. Having described law as a set of cases to hold reality, he writes that 'the Austinian notion of sovereignty is such a case' and goes on: 'The reality it seeks to contain is the associating and organising idea of law and order.'[19] Austin, therefore, is proposing a case in which to put the 'rubrics of law', which are themselves cases – he is providing a meta-case. In this sense, Austin may be identified with political theory in general (and Barker does identify him in this regard not only with Hobbes but with Hegel as well): he is attempting to contain the idea of order within a further idea, which is the idea of political theory. Here, then, we have a form of 'containment' which is clearly opposed to Barker's wish that the idea of the state should contain a rich variety of schemes, for the point of the Austinian notion of sovereignty is that it pre-ordains the single scheme (or rather, meta-scheme) that holds in relation to the organisation of the organising idea of order. As will perhaps be evident, it is not at all easy to state clearly how we should understand the differences between organising ideas, organising ideas of order (states), and the organisation done by an idea of the organising idea of order (political theory). Barker does not altogether convince that he has thought the complexities of his position through. However, he does postulate a clear parallel between the dialectical relation of political theory to historical

---

[18] *Ibid.*   [19] *Ibid.*, 119.

circumstance and that of law to growth. The Austinian account of sovereignty is necessarily one-sided because it is only one side of a dialectical relation – just as law is tied to the 'reality' of growth, so political theory is tied to the 'reality' of changing historical conceptions of the associating idea of law and order. It is, by Barker's lights, impossible to pre-determine the province of the state's activities, for the state is granted a differing scope for its activities in different eras. Thus as the idea of co-existence can be understood as an aspect of history, so, also, can the idea of containment, giving it a sense directly opposed to the 'containing' ambitions of Austinian theory: our idea of the state idea should contain a rich variety of ideas, for the application of the state idea varies throughout history. Barker offers the contrast between the needs of early modern communities (particularly of the sixteenth century) whose basic social requirement was the establishment of a.strong centre of control, and some modern communities (notably early twentieth-century Britain) in which conceptions of social existence as heterogeneous pointed towards a decentralised vision of political authority. Earlier theories of the state identified it with 'bare, unitary sovereignty';[20] latterly, attempts had been made (by advocates of the real personality of associations, among others) to incorporate within the state idea other pictures of political organisation, thereby offering an alternative to the centralising tendency of theory from a previous, and fundamentally different, age. Austin, by resurrecting the idea of the 'bare' state, suffers because he cannot mould his thought to a different, and equally real, reality. A looser conception of the state is sometimes the case that fits the cases of law best.

It is by means of such an argument that Barker is able to suggest that the state has been 'discredited'. There is more than one sense in which this phrase can be understood. At its most literal, it denotes a historical condition – it refers to periods in history when bare, unitary sovereignty has been superseded by something else. However, there is the further implication that our awareness of these historical facts entails a new understanding of what the state is across time, or at least of what it cannot be. What is discredited here is some entity not just to which things happen, but of which it is possible to speak in general terms of approval and disapproval. Baker's article, after all, is not just a work of history. It also purports

[20] *Ibid.*

to be a work in political theory. What needs to be asked, therefore, is what sort of political theory Barker's argument concerning the organising idea of law and order is capable of sustaining. This may be broken down into three more specific questions. What is the alternative to the bare theory of the state sovereignty? Why should it be approved? How might it be promoted?

III

The first of these is the most difficult to answer. Part of that difficulty derives from Barker's vagueness on the subject of what an alternative conception to Austin's might actually conceive. He calls it 'polyarchism';[21] yet he says no more of its structures – the forms of law-making, of institutions, of democratic procedures given by such a conception – than that it offers the prospect of 'a federal sort of thing'.[22] But the difficulty also arises from the uncertainty of the relation between such a conception of the state, and the state idea itself, the organising idea of law and order. Is Barker's polyarchism something which is contained by the term 'state' – one of its variables – or is it something opposed to the organising idea of law and order, and therefore to the idea of the state itself? In *Political thought in England*, written at the same time as 'The discredited State', Barker announces that 'the State is always with us'.[23] Further, in the section dealing with the thought of T. H. Green, he declares that: 'If we challenge the State, we must challenge it in fear and trembling. The presumption is always against us. The whole system of acknowledged rights is almost certain to claim, and to deserve, a higher allegiance than the most ideal of ideal rights.'[24] The suggestion of these declarations is that 'the State' refers to whatever organising idea of order holds sway for a community. Moreover, it does not seem to be something which can be 'discredited' – its status is determined by the fact that it is acknowledged, and therefore presupposes that the process of ascribing or denying credit has been gone through, for the presumption is *always* against us. This is a position which makes Barker's idealist sympathies readily apparent. But it is also a position which 'The discredited State' necessarily revises. That article, in stark contrast, far from asserting the state's omnipresence, gives voice to the conviction that in the British instance it has never really

---

[21] *Ibid.*, 120. [22] *Ibid.*, 119.
[23] Barker, *Political thought in England*, p. 250. [24] *Ibid.*, p. 60.

existed.[25] The state from which the British have been spared appears here as 'a sovereign and majestic State . . . such as Hegel conceived'.[26] It is the sovereign also of Bodin, Hobbes and Austin.[27] This, then, would suggest that the federal sort of thing that Baker sees as the antidote to Hegelianism and Austinianism is not contained in the idea of the state, but contrasted to it. Barker appears in 1914 to be arguing both that political life is centred on the state, and that political theory can deny that the state exists.

One explanation for this seeming contradiction would be that Barker changed his mind. However, not least because Barker himself gives no indication that this is so, a more satisfactory account would be one which sought to reconcile these two positions. One way this might be done is to re-emphasise the two levels at which the argument of 'The discredited State' operates. On the one hand, the state is an idea which is constitutive of political activity – it is 'the political idea'. On the other, the state is an idea which political theory tries to organise. The change suggested by Barker's position in 'The discredited State' is not one of mind, but of emphasis: he emphasises the different ways in which the political idea of order may itself be organised. It is the contention of 'The discredited State' that the political idea of order plays a fluctuating role in the history of a community, such that any attempt to characterise that role must incorporate a sense of its fluidity. By postulating this further level of thought, Barker hopes to strike a balance between his consciousness as a historian that the state is not a timeless idea, and his consciousness as a political philosopher that the state is an identifiable, and distinct, organising idea. Inevitably, though, this balance is not easy to achieve. There is a tension between these two positions which is unavoidable, and which is an aspect of the paradox outlined above. The state is given as both an entity and as a mode of thought. The entity is a logical construct; the mode of thought is part of a historical process. The logical construct must be fixed and rigid, for logic is the imposition of fixity and rigidity on even recalcitrant material. Further, the fixity of the state construct is the idea of fixity, or order. The historical process, meanwhile, must be fluid, for history places the vagaries of circumstance in the vanguard. The tension arises when a political theorist who embraces both positions seeks to describe what happens to the

---

[25] See Barker, 'The discredited State', 101.   [26] *Ibid.*   [27] See *ibid.*, 108–9.

state idea – the organising idea of order – when ideas of the state are discredited.

Barker demonstrates that he is aware of this tension. At the end of his paper he concedes that 'the discredit of the State is a sign that it has done its work well, and is doing its work well'. And he goes on: 'The State will come into credit again, with a rush, at the double, as soon as it is seen to be doing its work badly.' The paradoxical nature of these statements – the discredited state is creditable, the credited state operates discreditably – can only be understood if there are seen to be two perspectives from which the question of the state's identity can be approached. One is philosophical, and gives us the state as the idea of order. The other is historical, and gives us a variety of different ideas of the state. It is some of these latter ideas that do discredit to the state, for they may seek to discredit the idea that an idea of the state can be in some sense sovereign or supreme. What generates the paradox is that the historical conditions that are conducive to this sort of thinking – the conditions conducive to polyarchism – might themselves be described as the conditions of order, since it is a primary characteristic of polyarchic thought that it takes order as a given. In other words, political theorists who point to the possibility of different groups co-existing outside the framework of the sovereign state do so only when different groups can be seen to order themselves. This seems to presuppose the priority of the state idea, for the state idea is, after all, nothing more than the idea of order. When order is lacking, ideas of the sovereign state achieve prominence, and political theorists become involved in the business of seeking order themselves. But when order is achieved, though ideas of the sovereign state may be undermined, the state idea, by definition, is not. It simply moves to the background. It was as a historian that Barker came to see this. And it was because he was a historian as well as a political philosopher that he was able to describe the state as something that can be discredited, yet is always with us, and when discredited doing its work well.

IV

The position Barker adopts in 'The discredited State' is undeniably a complex one, and it not always clear that Barker himself fully appreciated the difficulties of working through such an argument as he constructs. The purpose of his article was to clarify the status of arguments about the role of the state. However, the variety of approaches to the role of the state which his own argument incorporates does not clarify the issue so much as reinforce its complexity. What Barker's argument does clarify is the constraints that operate upon the general exercise he had undertaken, which was to adopt a standpoint from which the state idea, ideas of the state, and ideas opposed to the bare idea of the state could all be reconciled within a single intellectual perspective. That perspective, it turns out, is the perspective of history. As such, it is not a point of view which offers the political theorist much prospect of being able to express a preference for one or other form of political organisation, nor even of being able to formulate a political theory of his own. There is a sense in which Barker balks against these limitations. At one point he argues that polyarchism is particularly suited to the English way of life. The English, he suggests, are a 'clubbable' people,[28] well able to organise themselves into small groups and associations without need either of the state or of political theory to guide them. Yet this insistence on the clubbability of the English serves only to reinforce the distinction from which Maitland and Figgis had tried, unsuccessfully, to escape: between political theory on the one hand, and the ability of the English to muddle through without it on the other. Moreover, it leaves Barker's argument dependent upon a particular historical condition, the temperamental suitability of a particular nation to the structure of the polyarchic, or discredited, state. There are two problems with this. First, Barker's argument, taken as a whole, embraces a form of historism, which understands all political conditions as impermanent. Second, what is permanent in Barker's argument is the dialectical reading he brings to the impermanencies of history. He regards historical conditions, organising ideas and political theories as all to be understood as dependent upon one another. Given this approach, it is hard to know how the political theorist can intervene in order to champion his preferred idea of the state: it is, after all, the approach of the bystander, and depends upon a sense of distance from what is being viewed. Barker appears to acknowledge this also. When he writes of recent historical developments which have led to the undermining of

---

[28] This notion of clubbability was a theme to which Barker returned throughout his life, up to and beyond the Second World War. For a full account of its place in his political thought see J. Stapleton, 'The national character of Ernest Barker's political science', *Political Studies*, 37 (1989), 171–89.

the 'forced and bare universal' of state sovereignty, he declares, not that we should participate, but that 'we should rejoice in its practical criticism by the logic of fact'.[29] It is 'fact' which criticises an idea such as sovereignty, and it does so 'practically', which is historically. Moreover, fact can also reinforce an idea, however forced and bare it might appear to the onlooker. 'The discredited State' was finally published in 1915 with the following addendum:

This paper was written in May 1914. It has been left as it stood without any but verbal alteration. It is curious to reflect how differently one would have written in January 1915. Germany has shown that the sixteenth century has not been altogether overpast – at any rate in her own case.

And yet the fundamental questions remain and will emerge when the waters abate. Meanwhile, the State is proclaiming, 'It is necessary to live'. We have forgotten we are anything but citizens, and the State is having its high midsummer of credit.[30]

As a historian, Barker was able to recognise the contingency of the claims that were being made on the state's behalf. But as a historian, he also recognised that there was nothing he could do about it.

---

[29] Barker, 'The discredited State', 116. [30] *Ibid.*, 121.

CHAPTER 8

Cole and guild socialism

I

In fact, Barker's prediction that with the advent of war the state would enjoy its high midsummer of credit proved to be only half right. Certainly, the war years did bring with them a vast increase in the scope of the state's activities – in the pursuit of a national, corporate war effort it came to employ more people, levy more taxes and regulate more activities than had ever seemed possible before. In this transformation of the state into a large-scale 'enterprise' association the lesser associational life of its citizens was not swamped altogether. A volunteer army was raised between 1914 and 1916 which contained many battalions whose members were drawn from the same locality, the same profession or industry, and even the same clubs and churches, such that units arose with subtitles like North-East Railway, First Football, Church Lads, First Public Works, Empire, Arts and Crafts, and Forest of Dean Pioneers. These were the so-called 'pals' battalions, and they were designed to draw on the polyarchic structures of British life, tapping the loyalty men felt towards local and private bodies alongside the loyalty they felt towards the nation as a whole. But although the British army could claim to be made up of 'fellows' and their 'fellowships', this plurality-in-unity had little bearing on the national cause itself, and none on the ways in which it was pursued. The sort of war these men found themselves fighting meant that they were given little more than the opportunity to suffer and die for the greater community alongside men they had known before, and the most obvious consequence of the 'pals' movement was that it allowed for small pockets of national life to be decimated, or worse. It was, in a sense, thanks to the 'clubbability' of the English that 1,880 men from the city of Bradford were killed on 1 June 1916, during the first twenty minutes of the battle of the Somme.[1]

But as well as an unspeakable bloodbath managed by the state, the 1914–18 conflict was also, as one contemporary termed it, 'a professors' war'.[2] There are a number of ways in which this phrase can be understood. First, professors were encouraged to make their own contribution to the war effort by explaining, or at least providing a gloss on, what was happening.[3] Second, those who dealt with ideas found that the war had changed the world from which those ideas were drawn and to which they applied. There were few writing in the academic journals who sought to dispute the claim of one contributor to a 1917 symposium of the Aristotelian Society that 'the present is one of the few scenes of the turning points of history, when unsuspected forces come into play, and the changeless logic of the human brain works with changed premises'.[4] This feeling of being present at a moment of historical crisis does not correspond to Barker's depiction of the war as an aspect of the ebb and flow of conceptions of political order. Rather, it was the uniqueness of the moment that was emphasised, and the social possibilities it brought in its wake that were elucidated. A third sense in which the Great War was a professors' war represents a particular view of the sort of historical turning-point that had been reached: for many, the war was a war of ideas. At its simplest, this view accorded an idea to each of the major combatants, and anticipated that the victor would be able to impose on the world the idea on whose behalf war was being

---

[1] The best short account of the significance of the 'pals' movement is given by John Keegan in *The face of battle* (London, 1991). He writes: 'Perhaps no story of the First World War is as poignant as that of the Pals. It is the story of a spontaneous and genuinely popular mass movement which has no counterpart in the modern, English speaking world and perhaps could have none outside its own time and place: a time of intense, almost mystical patriotism, and of the inarticulate elitism of an imperial power's working class; a place of vigorous and buoyant urban life, rich in differences and in a sense of belonging – to work-places, to factories, to unions, to churches, chapels, charitable organizations, benefit clubs, Boy Scouts, Boys' Brigades, Sunday Schools, cricket, football, rugby, skittle clubs, old boys' societies, city offices, municipal departments, craft guilds – to any one of those hundreds of bodies from which the Edwardian Briton drew his security and sense of identity' (Keegan, *The face of battle*, pp. 217–18). What is interesting about this description is that, give or take some of the associations involved, it corresponds unerringly to Gierke's Germanic ideal.

[2] See C. D. Burns, 'When peace breaks out', *International Journal of Ethics*, 26 (1915–16), 91.

[3] Ernest Barker, for example, was a regular commentator on the progress of the war, contributing many letters and articles to the newspapers, most on patriotic or sentimental themes. These were collected in 1917, under the title *Mothers and sons in wartime and other pieces* (London, 1917).

[4] L. P. Jacks, G. B. Shaw, C. D. Burns and H. Oakley, 'Symposium: ethical principles of social reconstruction', *Proceedings of the Aristotelian Society*, 17 (1916–17), 293.

waged. Bosanquet called the war a battle of 'conflicting philosophies of history',[5] and there were certainly many professors on each side who were prepared to line up behind what might be called a national philosophical cause.[6] However, the war of ideas was not seen solely as an extension of what took place on the battlefield. There was a further dispute about the simple fact that supposedly advanced industrial nations were resolving their differences on the battlefield, and about whether ideas might be in part responsible for this. Nor did it escape the attention of many that these nations were, in theory at least, sovereign states. As a staunch patriot and whole-hearted supporter of the war effort, Barker could be satisfied with a perspective which seemed to leave the political theorist powerless to do anything about the hold states exercised over their citizens after August 1914. But others could not. For them, the war was a calamity which was a symptom as well as a cause of the supremacy of the idea of the sovereign state. They did not believe that the sorts of issues raised by Barker in his article could be put to one side while the war continued. Rather, they felt that the continuation of war threw these issues into sharper relief.

Some of the 'professors' who became prominent wartime critics of the idea of the sovereign state – like C. Delisle Burns and A. D. Lindsay – are now more or less forgotten. Others – like Bertrand Russell and L. T. Hobhouse[7] – are not. But for the purposes of this book the most significant champion of polyarchic, or federalistic,

---

[5] B. Bosanquet, 'The function of the State in promoting the unity of mankind', *Proceedings of the Aristotelian Society*, 17 (1915–16), 43.

[6] See, for example, Barker *et al.*, *Why we are at war. Great Britain's cause* (Oxford, 1914), a propaganda pamphlet produced by a group of Oxford historians and containing a chapter on 'the German theory of the State'.

[7] Russell's *The principles of social reconstruction* (London, 1916), drew heavily on polyarchic conceptions of group life, and set great store by what could be achieved by giving more autonomy to professions, trades and other bodies, and less to the state itself. Meanwhile, Hobhouse's *The metaphysical theory of the State: a criticism* (London, 1918), contains perhaps the most celebrated of all attacks on 'the Hegelian theory of the God-State' (by which he meant to include English champions like Bosanquet). Its preface, written during an air-raid in the summer of 1918, draws a direct connection between the destruction being wrought and a book of Hegel's Hobhouse happened to be reading at the time. However, neither Russell nor Hobhouse had much time for questions of group personality. Indeed, Hobhouse went much further than Barker in expressing his reservations about attempts to attribute to groups of individuals a personality of their own, arguing: 'Having reached the conception of a super-personal entity, we are inclined to look for this entity, not in the varied forms of associated life which intersect and cut across one another, but in some particular form of association which includes the rest' (Hobhouse, *The metaphysical theory of the State*, pp. 29–30). This was to be one of the most frequently voiced arguments against the idea of real group personality, and it was one that Barker also came in time to share (see below, pp. 217–18).

political theory during this period was the young guild socialist, G. D. H. Cole. Cole's guild socialism both pre-dated and outlasted the war, albeit in neither case by much. His first book was *The world of labour*, first published in 1913, and in it were set out most of the themes that were to engage him until the end of the decade. Cole was, from the outset, a socialist, and as such he readily accepted the Marxist view of the true value of labour, a value which capitalism, committed to treating labour as a commodity, was unable to recognise. What Cole could not accept, however, was that the remedy for this situation was necessarily collectivist, nor that it led inevitably through the state. Rather, he believed that the solution lay in workers' control, with separate groups of workers exercising personal control over what they produced by their own labour, and with the state, in consequence, reduced to a purely regulatory role. These were the themes of guild socialism, and the advent of war did nothing to dissuade Cole of their relevance. As Margaret Cole writes in her husband's biography, it was, in the slogan of the time, 'Business as usual' for the guild socialists, and the war, 'except in so far as it concerned the individual personally, was an irrelevance, however enormous, to their main objective, the real "war" they were pursuing'.[8] Indeed, the war served, if anything, to accentuate Cole's peacetime concerns. As the conflict progressed, the British state became, to Cole's eyes at least, an ever more inefficient, ever more exploitative, and ever more aggrandising organisation, which is just what was supposed to happen to a capitalist state *in extremis*. In the 1917 preface to a second edition of *The world of labour*, Cole wrote that 'questions which in 1914 seemed to have been shelved till after the war have been with us more than ever'.[9] And he went on, *pace* Barker, to declare: 'We are, I think, entitled to argue from the State at war to the State at peace.'[10]

But although the questions remained the same, the ways in which Cole chose to address them did not. In his earliest work, the analysis provided is essentially economic. He does, it is true, touch on the issue of corporate personality in *The world of labour*, where he announces, approvingly, that 'everywhere we are faced by the uprising of the group . . . everywhere we are witnessing the creation of new individualities within the state'.[11] But this concept of group

---

[8] M. I. Cole, *The life of G. D. H. Cole* (London, 1971), p. 71.
[9] G. D. H. Cole, *The world of labour*, fourth edn (London, 1919), p. xxv.
[10] *Ibid.*, pp. xxvi–xxvii.   [11] *Ibid.*, p. 19.

individuality is not one he chose to explore himself, and his analysis
of the economics of worker-controlled industries is diffused more by
a latent romanticism than it is by any wider philosophic concerns.
The war, however, was hard on romance, and the more grossly was
manifested the hold that the idea of the sovereign state exercised
over the lives of working men, the more Cole turned his attention to
the question of the state's essential nature, and the essential nature of
those other associations which men might choose to form. He gave
his views on these subjects in papers delivered before the Aristotelian
Society in 1915 and 1916, and in the introductory chapters he wrote
for his book-length publications of 1918 and 1920, *Self-government in
industry*, and *Guild socialism re-stated*. But they found fullest expression
in the most abstract of all his works, *Social theory*, which also appeared
two years after the war was over. There he devoted himself
exclusively to what he had previously called the attempt to 'create a
political theory to fit the guild idea'.[12] What this theory was exactly
will be discussed below. But what Cole thought it was is clear. It
represented a furtherance of what had been inspired by Gierke,
begun by Maitland, taken on by Figgis, and precipitately abandoned
by Barker.[13] It was an attempt to construct a sustainable political
theory based around the idea of the life of the group.

II

In order to understand this attempt, and to see whether it was
successful, Cole's work is best divided between his exposition of what
was an essentially negative, and what was an essentially positive,
thesis. The negative thesis represents his case against the state as it
had been portrayed by other political philosophers. It was made in
the articles Cole wrote for the Aristotelian Society, the first of which,
entitled 'Conflicting social obligations', drew a response from one of
its targets, Bernard Bosanquet. The positive thesis elaborates the
view of the state that 'fits' the guild socialist idea, and is to be found
in the books Cole wrote towards the end of the decade. These theses,
and the texts in which they may be found, are not self-contained;
nonetheless, before seeing how they overlap it will be useful to treat
them separately. The philosophical view that Cole sought to oppose

[12] Cole, *Self-government in industry* (London, 1918), p. 15.
[13] Cole gives expression to his debt to the first three of these writers in the introduction to
Social theory (see Cole, *Social theory* (London, 1920), pp. 10–11).

was the claim that the state is an end in itself, and therefore categorically distinct from all other forms of association. To deny this was not, for Cole, to deny that the state is necessary, but merely to deny that it is absolute. Like most of the 'new federalists', Cole was not a syndicalist, and he never attempted to escape from the idea of the state altogether.[14] What he objected to was the arbitrariness of the view that made the state an idea different from all others. Why, he wanted to know, should the state be granted an ultimacy which is denied both to the entities which make up the state, and also to the wider world of which states themselves form only a part? If something greater than the individual is sought in order to make sense of individuality, why should that something greater be the state rather than the great variety of other organisations to which the individual belongs?[15] Moreover, Cole takes this objection to hold even given the presence of a common will within a state, and granting its ability to act as a collective unit. In other words, even a state acting with the uniformity of purpose exhibited by the national communities of Europe in wartime 'does not exhaust either the individuality or the organisable individuality of its citizens'.[16]

Cole uses this argument to press the case for the recognition of the 'many non-governmental forms of international relations in art, religion, science and . . . economics'[17] – just those relations which had been swept aside in August 1914. However, perhaps for this reason, his primary interest is not the greater perspective of world-wide community, but the lesser perspective of the individual, who may find that the demands made on him by the state conflict with the demands made by other associations to which he belongs. Internationalist theory seeks to contain the state within a network of interests which transcend national boundaries; in this way, the interests of the state are shown to be partial. Cole also saw the state as a partial institution, but less because of the greater institutions by which it could be contained, than because of the lesser institutions

---

[14] Though he never went quite as far as his guild socialist colleague S. G. Hobson, who exhorted his readers 'not [to] forget that guildsmen are not syndicalists; that they believe in the State as a great spiritual and intellectual force' (S. G. Hobson, *Guild principles in war and peace* (London, 1917), p. 137). Cole sympathised with many syndicalist aims, and in an appendix to one of his books he attempted to explain the difference between English guild socialism and French syndicalism as simply the result of the different political and economic conditions prevailing in the two countries (see Cole, *Self-government in industry*, pp. 303–21).

[15] See Burns *et al.*, 'Symposium: the nature of the State in view of its external relations', *Proceedings of the Aristotelian Society*, 16 (1915–16), 315.

[16] *Ibid.*   [17] *Ibid.*, 324.

which might also contain the individual citizen. He saw the state as one organisation among many, and he asks whether the state has any grounds for claiming that the individual is pre-eminently obliged to it. His answer, unsurprisingly, is that it does not. The reasons for this are two-fold. First, the state does not oblige the individual in a manner any different from that of other associations, for these also set rules which they expect to be obeyed, such that Cole suggests at one point that 'the laws of other functional associations have the same binding character and social status as those of the State'.[18] Second, the state cannot express every aspect of the individual, with the result that individuals will always form themselves into other kinds of association; and Cole is led to ask: 'Is not the very existence of particular associations a sufficient proof that the State cannot fully express the associative will of man?'[19]

These arguments of Cole's clearly echo those of Figgis. Like Figgis, Cole believed that the attempt to provide an ultimate principle of state sovereignty was misguided, that man's social nature was represented by more than one type of association and that these other associations should not be seen as necessarily subordinate to the state. Further, Cole argued, like Figgis, that it is possible to conceive of non-state groups pursuing their interests in a way which does not necessarily bring them into conflict with other associations, nor with the state. In Cole's eyes, the main culprit in fostering prejudice against associational life was not Hobbes, but Rousseau, whom he saw as putting forward the view that all non-state bodies, including churches and guilds, 'inevitably become political in defence of [their] vested interests', and unless controlled become involved in 'conspiracies against the public'.[20] Against Rousseau, Cole maintained that group activities were not by definition conspiratorial. In this respect, Cole does not differ from Figgis in his response to the suggestion that an obligation to a body other than the state will lead to disorder. Both point out that a flourishing associational life within a political community is compatible with an ordered political community, a response to be distinguished from one which accepts that freedom for associations from state control may militate against order, but regards disorder as a price worth paying for such freedom. Cole, like Figgis, does not detail the

---

[18] Cole, *Social theory*, p. 126.
[19] Cole, 'Conflicting social obligations', *Proceedings of the Aristotelian Society*, 15 (1914–15), 150.
[20] *Ibid.*, 143–4.

grounds on which an individual might be justified in disobeying the state because of another obligation and regardless of the consequences. Instead, he concentrates on the conditions which determine that a non-state association need not attempt to usurp the state's role in the pursuit of its own interests. These conditions, however, are different from those given by Figgis, whose account of associational life was essentially sectarian, and whose model was religious rather than economic. Cole, though he couples trade unions with churches in the context of his general argument,[21] has as his basic model the guild, or trade union, which is by definition an economic association. Because economic, its concerns cannot be divorced from the concerns of those who are not its members. Further, if its concerns are to be reconcilable with the concerns of those who are not its members, then the various economic concerns of a political community must be deemed not merely interdependent, but complementary. Cole achieves this form of interdependence by means of the idea of function.

It is the idea of function that sets Cole apart from writers like Maitland and Figgis, who had no use for the term. It is also the key that links Cole's negative thesis to his positive thesis. Indeed, the basis of his positive thesis is a critique of the notion of the real personality of associations by means of the idea of function. Cole was wary of ascribing to associations a status they did not, in their particularity, merit. He did not wish to promote the view that the state was partial in comparison to other associations, and wrote: 'It is my whole point, not that associative acts are wholly social, but that State acts are not.'[22] Moreover, this partiality set all associations apart from the individual. In the last major work of his guild socialist period, Cole makes it clear that he does not regard associations as real persons. In this sense he is closer to Barker than he is to Figgis, for he has decided that a group of individuals is to be defined according to its 'purpose', and he argues: 'There is no such thing, strictly speaking, as the "will" of an association, only the co-operating wills of its members.'[23] He continues: 'An association is not, and cannot be, in any real sense, a "person", because it is specific and functional, not universal.'[24] Where he goes beyond Barker is just in the notion of function, which means more than specificity of purpose. Something may be called functional in relation

---

[21] See *ibid.*, 158.　　[22] *Ibid.*, 154. He calls this 'the particularisation of the State' (*ibid.*).
[23] Cole, *Social theory*, p. 22.　　[24] *Ibid.*, p. 50.

to other entities if its purpose is adapted to theirs. In other words, associations for Cole do not merely *have* a purpose, as they might for Barker; they *serve* a purpose as well. The importance of this distinction cannot be overstated. If the purposes of an association have a functional relation to the purposes of other associations, then their purposes cannot conflict, any more than the purpose of the axle can conflict with the purpose of the wheel. Three questions are immediately suggested by this reflection. First, what is the function of the state? Second, what determines the function of the state, or of any other association? And third, can a political theory founded as the idea of function be a satisfactory one?

III

Cole's answer to the first of these questions comes in two parts. Writing in the broadest possible terms, he declares that the state's function 'should be the expression of those common purposes which affect all the citizens, roughly speaking, equally and in the same way'.[25] Subsequently, however, he specifies that these purposes are 'appetitive',[26] by which he means related to the consumption rather than the production of goods needed by all. On this account, the modern state was to be condemned for exceeding this function dramatically. It had come to concern itself with 'political and co-ordinating rather than economic activities',[27] activities for which its partiality made it manifestly unsuited. As Cole puts it: 'Just as no man ought to be the judge of his own case, so ought no association. Therefore, co-ordination cannot belong to the function of the State.'[28] Instead, the state is one of many functional associations which must be co-ordinated by a greater body. This body will be 'a combination of associations, a federal body in which some or all of the various functional associations are linked together';[29] and of this body Cole declares that 'the judiciary and the whole paraphernalia of law and the police must be under [its] control'.[30] Cole does not detail exactly how this federal body would operate, nor what sorts of decisions it might be expected to make. His purpose is simply to

[25] Cole, 'Conflicting social obligations', 152. Two years later, he wrote: '[The State] exist[s] for the execution of that very important class of collective actions which affect all members of the community in which they live equally and in the same way' (Cole, *Self-government in industry*, p. 82).

[26] See Cole, *Social theory*, p. 66.   [27] *Ibid.*, p. 86.   [28] *Ibid.*, p. 101.

[29] *Ibid.*, p. 134.   [30] *Ibid.*, p. 137.

establish that the task of reconciling differences between groups cannot fall to any of the groups involved.

Cole's description of the state as functionally appetitive is meant to form a part of his social and political philosophy. It is not simply an aspect of the guild socialist case against the economic and political institutions of British life; rather, it occurs in a work he describes as 'primarily philosophical'.[31] What matters, therefore, is less that the state has a purpose which is economic than that it is, simply, 'purposive' – it is what Oakeshott would term an 'enterprise' association. It is for this reason that Cole cannot allow the state to play the sort of role that Figgis, among others, would seem to demand of it – the role of what Oakeshott would term a 'civil' association. Cole's state cannot merely establish the rules by which purposive associations guide their relations with one another, since it is one such association itself. As a result, Cole's state cannot conceive the task of 'co-ordination' in terms of what Figgis would call the setting up of 'bounds of justice', but must instead regard co-ordination as a matter of conforming the purposes of other associations to its own. Cole did not fall into the trap of believing the state to be the same as other associations (a *communitas communitatum*) yet at the same time different (a *societas universitatum*). But if Cole's state cannot be understood as a *societas*, nor can it be understood as analogous to a *universitas* in Oakeshott's fullest sense. This is because Cole recognised that the purposes which are common to all citizens do not carry the same weight with all citizens, and are therefore of less than universal significance. Because individuals will commonly belong to more than one association, it cannot be assumed that the association to which they all belong is the one that each values most highly. It is, for example, in everyone's interest that goods should be freely available for consumption; but this is of greater interest to those for whom consumption is the primary business of life (those who live off their capital) than it is to those whose lives are bound up with the business of production (those who live off their labour). These latter will inevitably feel that the pursuit of interests common to all must take second place behind the pursuit of interests particular to them, for without proper reward for their particular services they cannot make use of generally available goods. The state that serves the common interest does not serve the interests of all. This is, of course, an

---

[31] See *ibid.*, p. 21.

essentially economic argument. But for Cole it had a clear philosophical significance.

It is, however, an argument that contains one obvious flaw. For
although Cole wishes to deny to the state its traditional tools of 'co-
ordination' (it is to have control of neither the law nor the police), he
does not wish to dispense with these tools altogether. Yet if all
associations are purposive, and therefore unfit for the task of co-
ordination, to whom are these tools to belong? And if not to an
association of human beings, then to what? As we have seen, Cole
suggests that they will belong to a 'federal body'. But he cannot
explain how such a body is to be made up. Indeed, it is the
implication of the rest of his argument that no 'body' can be
entrusted with a co-ordinating role, since all bodies, including the
state, are partial by definition. It could be said that these difficulties
follow from Cole's concerted attempt to combine overt guild socialist
politics with an abstracted overview of political life. But in fact they
are latent in his abstract arguments, irrespective of their guild
socialist application. In 'Conflicting social obligations', Cole defines
his terms as follows: 'the State' means government; 'society' means
all organisations, government and non-government; and 'community' means all social life, whether organised or not.[32] The purpose
of these distinctions is to establish that the state is *only* government –
that is, only *a* government, the body of men who hold the reins of
power at a given time – and is not therefore the determinant of the
whole life of a society, never mind of a community. Indeed, Cole
distinguishes the 'social' from the 'political' in these terms, regarding
the latter as related to mere governmental activity, and of lesser
significance in consequence. For instance, he expands on a familiarly
dialectical view of the history of ideas – 'modern social theory . . . is
throughout both a reflection of existing political conditions and an
attempt to justify various opinions'[33] – to incorporate a clear
distinction *between* social and political thought, arguing: 'The current
political controversies turned social philosophy into political philosophy: thinking always of the State, philosophers sought not the
principle of social obligation, but the principle of political obligation.'[34] The political, therefore, relates to the state, which means
government, which means a partial body of men. As a result, and
despite Cole's suggestions to the contrary, the business of co-

---

[32] See Cole, 'Conflicting social obligations', 144–5.   [33] *Ibid.*, 148.   [34] *Ibid.*

ordination cannot be left in the hands of any political body, however it might be constituted, since it is Cole's conviction that all such bodies, indeed all bodies of men, are partial by definition.

IV

If the life of a community is not to be co-ordinated by any particular body or institution, what then is left to co-ordinate it? The answer, unsurprisingly, is that what is left is what Cole calls 'society', the sum total of all institutions and organisations, taken as a whole. Yet this answer too poses a problem, for it is hard to reconcile with the negative side of Cole's thesis, his case against conventional theories of the state. That case was directed, above all, against idealism, which Cole describes as 'this introspective philosophy' and of which he writes that 'just as it vitiates the study of individual consciousness, it is fatal to political theory, because it shuts up the State in the circle of its own ideas'.[35] Cole believed that Hegelians like Bosanquet had glorified the state at the expense of other forms of association. What is more, he believed that such glorification, as practised in Germany, had led more or less directly to the war that was consuming Europe. This identification of the theory of the metaphysical state with the theory of the German state – Cole describing the former as 'Prussophil philosophy'[36] – was fairly crude, even by the standards of the day. But it also obscured what were in fact far greater similarities between Bosanquet's thought and that of Cole himself.[37] Cole's functionalism was designed to dispense with sovereign institutions, and replace them with the sovereignty of associational life in general. As a result, it has to rest on a holistic conception of social existence,

---

[35] Burns *et al.*, 'The nature of the State', 311.   [36] *Ibid.*, 313.

[37] Which is not to say that Cole and Bosanquet did not have very different opinions about the war and how to fight it. Cole, in the words of his wife Margaret, was 'of course a conscientious objector', though never 'a "pure" pacifist': he believed that there were some things worth fighting for, but that any decisions about whether and when to fight had to be a matter of individual not collective judgment; in particular, he detested the idea of fighting under the auspices of the state, in the guise of one of its soldiers ('his strong anti-authoritarianism . . . caused him to detest militarism, uniforms, rank, chains of command') (see M. I. Cole, *The life of G. D. H. Cole*, p. 72). Bosanquet, meanwhile, believed that decisions of such importance could *only* be a matter of collective not individual judgment, and *had* therefore to be made under the auspices of the state. In a lecture entitled 'Patriotism in the perfect State', he describes the state as 'the ark in which the whole treasure of the individual's head and heart is preserved in a world which may be disorderly and hostile' (Bosanquet, 'Patriotism in the perfect State', *The International Crisis*, 1 (1915), 134). He goes on: 'Looked at this way, our country, the State, is all we have' (*ibid.*).

by which the actions of any institution or body can be understood as functional aspects of the greater whole. And this, as Bosanquet pointed out in the reply he wrote to Cole in 1915, was just what the Hegelian conception of the state was designed to convey also. In this reply Bosanquet characterises the Hegelian state as 'constitutional', and its constitution he describes as follows:

A whole of part and organs, all functional (as Hegel of course perpetually insisted) and all bearing on one another in very various relations and degrees of intimacy. It [the constitution] lies . . . in habits, conditions, recognitions. No plebiscite can express it; but it is the nearest thing to an expression of the community's will.[38]

Bosanquet reinforces the connection between the fact *of* function, and the fact *that* functions are aspects of a greater unity, which he calls the constitution, which Hegel called *Sittlichkeiten*, and of which Cole, though he does not identify it, also has need.

Where Bosanquet differs from Cole is in his assertion that this constitution is revealed in the conventional form of the state: 'It acts as the State, in so far as it solves conflicts by authority, though in a civilised society this is never by bare authority, but always by reason speaking with authority.'[39] He goes on: 'The collective force of the whole, when evoked by emergency, either internal or external, will continue to be very great and capable of drastic operation.'[40] In such statements as these, an obvious ground of difference between Bosanquet and Cole emerges regarding their respective willingness to allow the state to act for the whole community when required. What is not clear, however, is whether this difference is satisfactorily to be described as one between different political philosophies. Bosanquet's argument in reply to Cole is that the state, though it is a manifestation of the whole of society, and thus an aspect of the constitution, is nonetheless distinct from the rest of society, for it is the form the constitution takes when *action* is necessary – when there is conflict, in an emergency. In other words, the state, for Bosanquet, functions politically: it is the general will made manifest, and made capable of imposing order when required. Cole does not dispute that communities should be guided by the general will of their members. What he disputes is that the state always expresses this will. In one sense, this is a consequence of Cole meaning something different from Bosanquet by 'the state', such that their views are inevitably

[38] Bosanquet, 'A note on Mr. Cole's paper', *Proceedings of the Aristotelian Society*, 15 (1914–15), 162.
[39] *Ibid.*   [40] *Ibid.*, 163.

incommensurable. But it is also the case that Cole is unhappy with the idea of the general will functioning politically in any form. He says of it that it is not 'a mechanism' and goes on to argue that 'the general will of the community must suffer some leakage as soon as the attempt is made to confine it',[41] If the general will can never be confined to some institutional form, then it has no bearing on politics at all, nor on the issues of political philosophy. Indeed, Cole's case makes most sense not as argument within political philosophy, but one outside, or against, it. The traditional questions of political philosophy – those concerned with authority, justice, punishment and so on – presuppose conflicts of interest, and their solution the institutional resolution of conflicts; Cole's functionalism presupposes the absence of such conflicts altogether. In Cole's functional society, different groups would have less need of a sovereign political institution because, he announces, 'a division of [functional] spheres would obviate many of the conflicts of today'.[42] Similarly, he declares that a consequence of a properly established functional democracy would be 'a substantial and immediate reduction in the use of co-ercion'.[43] It cannot be the case, however, that such harmony is simply produced by a division of functional spheres; it is in the very nature of functionalism that it can only operate *given* such harmony. Cole does not tell us what generates this harmony. All he does is presume on it, in order to make a case against the exercise of political authority in any of its conventional forms.

In fact, Cole concedes that the 'possibility of conflict can never be avoided altogether'.[44] What he will not accept is that it is his task in exploring the nature of social existence to consider where these conflicts will occur, and how they might be resolved. He writes: 'If a machine representing the will of society can be devised to harmonise the occasional conflicts between the various functional authorities, that is no doubt all to the good. But the devising of such machinery is not philosophy, but science.'[45] And he goes on: 'It remains . . . the philosopher's task to say where sovereignty should lie, and the business of the practical man to find the requisite machinery.'[46] This unwillingness to become involved in the mechanics of sovereignty is perhaps the clearest evidence of Gierke's influence on Cole. But although disdainful of mechanistic conceptions of group life, Cole

---

[41] Cole, 'Conflicting social obligations', 156.   [42] *Ibid.*, 155.
[43] Cole, *Social theory*, p. 139.   [44] Cole, 'Conflicting social obligations', 155.
[45] *Ibid.*, 155.   [46] *Ibid.*, 159.

would not embrace any of the organicist alternatives either. For while being influenced by Germanic political philosophy, he was also deeply distrustful of it, and regretful of its influence on European politics. He could not accept that the social life of a community could be given unified political expression, whether organic or otherwise. Instead, he sought to dispense with politics altogether. As a result, Cole's political philosophy is in fact simply ethical – it addresses itself to the question only of how people should behave, regardless of how they are to be governed. Cole, quite simply, wished that people would behave functionally. Beyond this, his conception of political philosophy left him nothing else to say.

CHAPTER 9

Laski and political pluralism

I

G. D. H. Cole's functionalism marks the final stage in the development of Gierke's ideas in an English setting. Indeed, by the time Cole had finished there was not much of Gierke left – gone was the notion of real group personality, along with the organicism, the Hegelianism, the historical sweep and the intellectual rigour, all to be replaced by very little. Nevertheless, Cole does not mark the end of Gierke's influence on English political thought in general. For while guild socialists, and others, were trying to come to terms with the newly distended condition of the British state in wartime, one of Cole's contemporaries, and fellow functionalists, Harold Laski, was attempting to pursue an academic career in North America. Laski left Oxford in 1914, and having been rejected from the army on medical grounds, moved first to Montreal, then to Harvard, where he remained until 1920. It was during this period that Laski developed the theory which he called political pluralism, and he did so against an intellectual backdrop which differed in two important respects from its English equivalent. First, the American experience of the Great War, though politically charged, did not raise to such an acute degree the themes of national identity and national survival which had polarised political thought in England. Second, the United States were combined in a durable and effective federal structure, such that the expression of a federalistic feeling was less likely to represent a distinctive theoretical standpoint there. Indeed, American life seemed already to incorporate much of what was sought by opponents of state sovereignty in England – flourishing associations (many of them protected by a remarkably liberal law of trusts), strong local political structures, a clear demarcation of governmental powers. In consequence, the American setting provided at once a broader and a narrower context for Laski's work than that available to his contemporaries in England: broader, because his geographical distance from the sovereign states of Europe freed him from the potential submersion of his work in arguments about immediate history; narrower, because the success of federalistic ideas in America required something more than a mere federalistic feeling to convey a critique of the idea of the state in general.[1] Laski's political pluralism seeks a balance between these freedoms and these constraints. It is an advance on the wartime arguments in England surrounding political theory, not least in its terminology, which conveys, more than 'federalistic', 'polyarchic' or even 'functionalist',[2] the impression of a coherent philosophical doctrine. Nonetheless, it is also something of a throwback to the concerns of those who wrote about the idea of the sovereign state before the war, for Laski's pluralism encompasses themes which are as easily identified with Maitland and Figgis as they are with Barker or Cole. Laski in America was at liberty to return to the ideas of pre-war English political thought, and in doing so attempted to create something new.

What was most obviously new about Laski's arguments was his employment of the term 'pluralistic'. In using it, not only did he provide a name for what had been a somewhat heterogeneous body of thought, but he also allied that thought with the American philosophical tradition in which 'pluralism' had a particular resonance. It would, however, be a mistake to assume that what Laski brought to the ideas of Maitland or Figgis was simply a pragmatistic bias. It is certainly true that Laski derived his terminology from William James, whom he quotes approvingly in his earliest work on the subject of sovereignty.[3] He was not, though, a disciple of James, as he made clear during the course of his lengthy correspondence with O. W. Holmes Jnr., where he announced: 'I am not a Jamesian

---

[1] Kramnick and Sheerman, in their recent biography of Laski, describe Laski's first major work, *Studies in the problem of sovereignty*, as 'a pluralist hymn to America' (Kramnick and Sheerman, *Harold Laski*, p. 104). Certainly, Laski did describe American federalism as 'more consonant with the political facts than the unitary theory favoured by so many European observers' (Laski, *Studies in the problem of sovereignty* (New Haven, 1917), p. 270). The work as a whole, though, far from being a hymn to America, is an attempt to construct an account of the state in terms general enough, and radical enough, to be applicable to both the American and European examples.

[2] Laski did in fact employ all these terms at various points in his writing, though 'polyarchic' he only uses once (see Laski, *The foundations of sovereignty* (New York, 1921), p. 169).

[3] See Laski, *Studies in the problem of sovereignty*, pp. 8, 10.

by any means.'[4] 'Pluralistic' was, for Laski, something of a term of convenience, and though much which he brought under its umbrella shared a formal resemblance to the tenets of pragmatism, the resemblance was far stronger to the work of historians like Maitland, whose connection with William James was practically non-existent. It is hardly surprising that a movement in political theory which arose out of historical inquiry and historist precepts should share something with a philosophical creed committed to the view that truth-claims are contingent. But it does not follow that the link is a causal one. Laski's 'pluralism' is in fact best characterised not by its etymology but by its broad, and broadly English, range of sources, which ran as wide as Laski's interests, extending from church history to contemporary labour disputes, and from jurisprudence to eugenics.[5] Laski's work before 1920 sought to bring together the diverse strands in recent English political theory which had marked the attempt to do the idea of the sovereign state some or other form of discredit. His arguments echo Maitland on the law of corporations, Figgis on the Scottish Church, Barker on the history of modern political thought, Cole on functional democracy. Laski was no more of a Hegelian than was Cole, but he did, unlike Cole, find himself engaged in a form of synthesis: he brought together ideas and styles previously dispersed among different authors; he engaged with the politics of the left as well as church politics; he switched between historical, jurisprudential, philosophical and political writing; and he did so in a manner both partisan and aloof.[6] Two questions need to be asked about this synthetic undertaking. First, was anything added to these ideas in the mere fact of their being brought together?

---

[4] H. J. Laski and O. W. Holmes Jnr, *The correspondence of Mr Justice Holmes and Harold J. Laski, 1916–1935*, ed. Mark de Wolfe Howe, 2 vols. (London, 1953), vol. I, p. 71.

[5] Laski, who at the age of seventeen had been Galton's 'prodigy' (see Kramnick and Sheerman, *Harold Laski*, pp. 34–8), did not altogether give up on his early mentor's beliefs. In 1916 he wrote to Holmes: 'It seems to me to be so useless to be confident when again and again we are given proof that only the inbred qualities of men really count, and that you spread these by selecting them for survival, and not by building Polytechnics or starting settlements in the slums' (Laski, *Correspondence*, vol. I, p. 17).

[6] Laski's prose style, which in its later incarnation was to provoke George Orwell, in his famous essay on political language, to accuse him of 'mental vices' which rendered his work technically and politically illiterate (see Orwell, *The Penguin essays of George Orwell* (London, 1984), pp. 355–67), was marked during this period by its almost parodic imitations of the conventions of the time: a tendency to generalisation and aphorism; a self-conscious breeziness alternating with a portentous reverence for learning; an off-hand erudition; wordiness. At the same time, he saw himself, and was often seen by others, as something of a firebrand (he eventually lost his job at Harvard after expressing his support for the Boston police strike of 1919). It proved an uncomfortable combination.

Second, was anything added to them in the fact of their being brought together under the heading 'pluralism'?

II

Laski's starting-point was history. His first published book, *Studies in the problem of sovereignty*, consists of a series of historical essays on nineteenth-century controversies in the relations of church and state. In one of these, he writes:

> It is no answer to assert the theoretical infallibility of the State to us who possess the record of history. To acquiesce in its sin, to judge of it by criteria other than those of individual action is to place authority before truth . . . No dogma can hope for immortality since we live in an age of readjustment and reconstruction.[7]

History, for Laski, fulfilled two roles. First, because its record depicts acts rather than theories, events rather than instances, the worth of institutions like the state was revealed to be, at the very least, contingent. It is for this reason that history undercuts the pretensions of those who would assert timeless dogma. In a separate essay in which Laski describes the recent experiences of associations before the English courts (including the Free Church of Scotland and the ASRS), he writes of each case: 'The sovereignty of theory is reduced by the event to an abstraction that is simply ludicrous.'[8] Elsewhere he draws the familiar distinction between abstracted theory and 'the facts', his main target, equally familiarly, being Austin, whose jurisprudence is deemed not only to lack consonance with 'the political facts', but also describes 'a sovereignty so abstract [as to be] practically without utility'.[9] The connection between such charges, and what Laski refers to as the 'sin' of the state, lies in the annexation of the moral judgment of the individual by timeless political theories, which are thus as authoritarian as the states they liberate from the exigencies of history. Laski announces summarily that 'the Austinian theory of sovereignty, congenial enough in its abstract presentation, would as a fact breed simple servility were it capable of practical application'.[10] And it is as a result of this dual flaw in abstract theorising – the fact that it is both redundant *and* dangerous – that history has a second part to play, as the sole viable means of pursuing the questions with which abstract political theory

---

[7] Laski, *Studies in the problem of sovereignty*, p. 209.   [8] Laski, *The foundations of sovereignty*, p. 166.
[9] Laski, *Studies in the problem of sovereignty*, p. 269.   [10] *Ibid.*, p. 273.

had been traditionally concerned. In one of a number of articles and reviews on this theme in the *New Republic*, Laski declares that 'the historic method, in its fullest sense, seems the only hypothesis of investigation justified by the facts we encounter'.[11] Laski does not tell us exactly what he means by 'the historic method, in its fullest sense', nor does he tell us how the facts which justify the historic method are arrived at. Moreover, the declaration in itself is somewhat ambiguous, for it is not clear whether historical inquiry is being held up in a limiting sense, as all *merely* that can be justified, or in an expansive sense, as that which is *uniquely* justified as a mode of explanation. This ambiguity is not unique to Laski; it echoes the strain running through the work of Maitland, Figgis and Barker as well. Laski, however, more than these others, was willing to explore what might be meant by the 'fullest sense' of history by attempting to incorporate a variety of aspects of the historic method in his work. His is an attempt to establish not only that history is justified, but also the full extent of what can be justified by history.

Laski's essays on nineteenth-century ecclesiastical history constitute a significant part of this exploration of the historic method. Their point is to show that the state may be challenged by religious associations, both in the sense that this has happened and in the sense that it ought to be allowed to happen. The examples Laski uses are the Disruption of the Scottish Church in 1843, the Oxford movement, and the progressive emancipation of Catholics in Britain. In many ways, this form of history resembles Figgis's: Laski provides historical instances of the tractability of conflicts between the state and dissenting groups, and also discusses the arguments of those who sought theoretical ballast for the political positions that were adopted; moreover, Laski's use of the example of the Scottish Church produces obvious parallels with Figgis's work. However, both in that example and in the others, significant differences emerge, the most obvious of which is that while Figgis was concerned with recent disputes among members of the Free Church, Laski writes about its nineteenth-century foundation. Indeed, Figgis's use of the Scottish Church case was as an adjunct to, rather than an aspect of, his historical writing, which explored arguments in medieval and early modern thought in contrast to the disputes of the modern era. Figgis's history told the story of a sea-change in political

---

[11] Laski, 'What is history?', *New Republic*, 15 (13 July 1918), 324.

thought which sets apart the modern era from a time when church and state co-existed in a theoretical framework; Laski, meanwhile, tells the story of the struggles of church and state within the period whose advent Figgis so regrets. Laski is not, therefore, offering the possibility of a return to earlier, more satisfactory political arrangements; rather, he is attempting to draw comfort from the details of recent ecclesiastical experiences at the hands of the state.

A consequence of this is that Laski chooses examples which illustrate the complexities of modern encounters between church and state – after all, he must demonstrate that modern conceptions of the state are not unequivocally Austinian if he is to draw sustenance for the case against the state from within the recent history of these conceptions. A further consequence is that Laski chooses examples in which the battle lines between church and state are fairly well drawn. They are all instances of actual or potential conflict between a religious organisation and the government of the day; they stand in contrast, therefore, to those cases – the Scottish Church case of 1900–4 being the paradigmatic example – in which battle was joined between the members of an association, and the question addressed was what part the state should play in the dispute. The Disruption of the Scottish Church did involve a split within that church, as the name suggests. Nonetheless, it resulted from a dispute between a group within the church, and the state, over the state's role in the appointment of ministers. Similarly, the founders of the Oxford movement, though in conflict with the rest of the Anglican Church, were directly engaged with the state, not as an arbitrator, but as the focus of their concerns, for it was against the constraints of Establishment that their arguments were directed. The fate of Catholicism in Britain raises similar questions, though from a different perspective: what was at issue was whether the state should allow its citizens to be members of a church whose leadership was not bound to the state; what was feared was that allowing as much would in the end bring Catholics not merely into conflict with members of other religious bodies, but into conflict with the state itself. Inevitably, these three examples are not always comparable, and in the case of the Oxford movement it is sometimes hard to separate a dispute within the church from a dispute between ecclesiastical and secular authority. Yet it remains true that the subject matter of Laski's history establishes, more directly than Figgis's, the connection between the challenge to the state as an idea and acts of resistance to the secular power. Laski's is a history of disobedience, and of the state's fear of disobedience.

There is the basis here for Laski to use the history of the churches in the nineteenth century to construct a theory of civil disobedience – a theory of when it is likely to occur, and when it is justified. However, no such theory emerges. Laski prefaces and appends his historical essays with arguments about the state itself, and how it should be conceived, rather than concentrating on the specific activities and beliefs which might justifiably be pursued in contravention of the state's authority. Before looking at these arguments more closely, it is worth considering the ways in which the alternative approach suggested by Laski's historical writing – towards a theory of disobedience – would in fact be shaped, and constrained, by his subject matter, just as Figgis is shaped, and constrained, by his. The most important constraint is one which Figgis would readily have accepted: for this remains, after all, church history. The associations which resist the state in Laski's account are withdrawing from the state, and from the world of secular concerns, because they wish to be free to pursue their own affairs untroubled by outside interference. If anything, the examples Laski chooses reinforce more strongly than anything in Figgis the divide between a worldly politics and an otherworldly sectarianism; and in the case of the Oxford movement there is a direct contrast with Figgis's treatment of the Scottish Church case, in which he championed those who would allow the church to evolve as a person might evolve, against those who would tie it to its past. As Laski writes of Newman and his colleagues: 'The Oxford movement set its face firmly towards the past . . . The identity of the church, in fact, was to be found *not in its life but its tradition*' (my italics).[12] There is not much room for issues of real personality here, and nor is there much scope for discussing the question of an association's relations with other associations, for in this and the Scottish instance the very basis for resistance was a claim to complete self-sufficiency. In the case of the Catholic revival, the result of which was the assimilation of a supposedly alien group into the citizenry, Laski's account makes clear that this was both possible and desirable just because religious beliefs do not necessarily have any bearing on political matters. He quotes with approval Sidney Smith, who wrote that 'as long as they fought and paid taxes, and

---

[12] Laski, *Studies in the problem of sovereignty*, p. 75.

kept clear of the Quarter Sessions and Assizes, what matter how
many fanciful supremacies and frivolous allegiances they choose to
manufacture or accumulate for themselves'.[13] Moreover, Laski
qualifies his arguments about Catholic integration with an aside
which sets 'the Irish difficulty apart'.[14] To dismiss the question of
Ireland, where the problems of religious conflict were most pressing,
and where it was far more difficult to draw a line between the
religious and the secular – where, indeed, *politics* were and are
sectarian – is to dismiss the whole range of difficulties that arise when
it is no longer possible to presuppose that non-state organisations will
only concern themselves with their own affairs.

Laski's interest in church history has been described as 'concern
à clef'.[15] It is assumed that he was really writing about the right of
political and economic organisations – notably, trade unions – to
resist state control of their affairs. However, church history has
sufficient distinctive characteristics to make this a problematic business. Further, history itself is a peculiar vehicle for such an exercise.
As Laski understood them, the point of historical events is that they
are single, and history is the mode of explanation designed to reflect
their singularity. If Laski hoped to draw lessons for trade unions from
church history, these could not be lessons which fit the contours of
that history, for the events described were not merely singular, but
also, for one who seeks to establish the ability of lesser associations to
resist the state, not always helpful, the failure of the Oxford movement to steer a course between the Anglican and Catholic Churches
being a obvious instance of this. For Laski's purposes something
needs to be added to the story to make it work. This something is the
political theory of the events related in it. It is not a political theory
which justifies the story – the political theory of sectarian civil
disobedience. Rather, Laski uncovers the theory which he takes to be
latent in the various struggles between the state and other associations through history, in order to produce what might be called a
historical political theory.

Of course, this phrase is still ambiguous. It may mean that political
theory should be discoverable in history; or it may mean that it
should accord with a sense of history. These two interpretations may
be characterised as historicist and historist respectively: the former
suggesting laws of change which govern political life; the latter that

---

[13] *Ibid.*, p. 127.   [14] *Ibid.*, p. 136.
[15] M. Peretz, 'Laski redivivus', *Journal of Contemporary History*, 1 (1966), 93.

political life should be understood as contingent. Certainly both senses are consistent with Laski's own formulation of the connection between history and theory as set out in a *New Republic* article of 1919, where he writes: 'Historical experience seems to demonstrate the variety of means taken by men to satisfy their best social selves. Our business is to try to make the structural expressions of those selves conform to the variety they require.'[16] Much of what Laski wrote while in America may be said to have been a furtherance of this business. Moreover, he tried to further it in both senses outlined above. On the one hand, Laski suggested that history provided evidence that men have sought to create political structures which can accommodate variety. On the other hand, he put forward a series of arguments for the structural arrangements he believed best suited the historical evidence of social variety. The difference between these two positions can be summarised as follows: one posits that pre-eminent among the social selves that men have sought is the self that believes in variety; the other posits that the variety in men's social selves requires a variegated political community, or what Laski was to refer to as 'a pluralistic state'. This difference raises one simple question regarding Laski's 'historical' political theory. Are we to look to history to provide evidence *of* pluralistic thinking, or are we to look to history to provide evidence *for* pluralistic thinking? In other words, is the pluralistic state something made *by* history, or something to be made *because* of history? But though simple to ask, this was a question Laski found very difficult to answer.

Among the answers he attempted, the one which finds clearest expression in his church histories comes in his account of the Oxford movement, whose proponents are described as putting forward 'an unconscious theory of the State'.[17] It is unconscious because it is broader than the specific claims which constituted tractarianism, and its breadth is precisely its point – it is a theory of the state which is taken to allow non-state associations the right to pursue their claims against the state, irrespective of the content of those claims. As argued above, however, it is far from clear that particular claims to religious freedom do offer a justificatory example to all who have a dispute with the state. Elsewhere, Laski applies the same interpretative premise to trade union disputes with the state, which he views as forms of competition between different theories of the state. Unfortu-

[16] Laski and W. Lippmann, 'Authority in the modern State', *New Republic*, 19 (1919), 150.
[17] Laski, *Studies in the problem of sovereignty*, p. 95.

nately, these theories were not spelt out by the participants, whose goals were narrower. Yet if we ask what conception of the state is implied by the goals of trade unions in their disputes with the state – goals which are essentially economic – it is not a conception of social plurality, but of a pliable state, accommodating the needs of trade unionists.[18] Laski acknowledges as much when he says of this new theory of the state that 'it takes the trade union as the single cell from which an entirely new industrial order is to be evolved'.[19] In this regard, the trade union example is a mirror image of the church disputes: the churches Laski discusses sought an independence for the pursuit of ends which had no bearing on those who were not their members; the trade union, as a quintessentially political organisation, seeks its freedom in order to refashion the economic relations of the whole political community. Both, then, are unlikely champions of political pluralism, for in neither case is it clear that the association in question regarded itself as simply one among a group of associations, each possessing an equal claim on the state.

For the argument to work, Laski has to fall back on historicist assumptions: he has to locate historical disputes within a framework of historical change which serves to elucidate intentions and motives not apparent in the actions and statements of the historical actors themselves. The championing by them of a tolerant, variegated, pluralistic political society can only then truly be deemed 'unconscious'. In truth, such assumptions permeate a great deal of Laski's writing in this period. At some points, he reverts to a classically dialectical, almost Hegelian interpretation of progress. For example, his response to the possibility that a community of autonomous associations would be riven by conflict is to state that 'a community that can not agree is already a community capable of advance',[20] which is to presuppose that there is a superficiality to conflict when viewed in the broader context of historical development. Similar presuppositions underscore Laski's treatment of the question of

---

[18] A stronger version of this point was made by Graham Wallas in an argument directed against guild socialism. Wallas contrasts the narrowness of a trade union outlook with the much broader scope of interest of the modern state, and writes: 'Mr Cole, it seems to me, precisely transposes the actual tendencies of the modern State and modern organised vocations. The great advantage of the present State is its insistence on the "differences" rather than the identity of men . . . "Identity", on the other hand, dominates the whole habit of Trade Union and professional thought' (G. Wallas, *Our social heritage* (London, 1921), p. 114).

[19] Laski, *Authority in the modern State* (New Haven, 1919), p. 87.

[20] Laski, *Studies in the problem of sovereignty*, p. 24.

group personality. The issue was not for Laski, as it had been for Maitland and Figgis, pre-eminent. But nor did he consider it a distraction, as it had come to seem to Barker and Cole. Laski was willing to accept that groups of individuals had a personality distinct from the individual personalities of their members, and that this personality, far from being a mere fiction of law, should be counted as something real. He gave expression to these views in an article he published in the *Harvard Law Review* in 1916 under the title 'The personality of associations'. In truth, this article is little more than a restatement of ideas, and cases, borrowed from Maitland and Figgis, and dressed up a little for an American audience. Nevertheless, it is of interest in its own right for two reasons. First, it contains the earliest use by an English political theorist of the term 'pluralistic' to describe what had previously been called 'polyarchic' or 'federalistic' political structures.[21] And second, it contains a clear, if problematic, statement of what Laski understood to be the condition of a properly functioning pluralistic society. At the close of his discussion of the relation between group personality and state sovereignty, Laski writes as follows: 'We shall then say that the corporation, being a real entity, with a personality that is self-created, must bear responsibility for its actions. Our State may, in the result, be a little less Hegelian, a little less sovereign, in its right of delegation.'[22] What is striking about this statement is that it seems to equate 'responsibility' with a kind of freedom. Laski does not wish associations to be free to do whatever it is they want; he wants them to be free to understand whatever it is that they do. Armed with this knowledge, they are to become, not independent, but interdependent, as they become aware of the responsibilities they have to each other. This is what Laski understood by escaping from the sovereignty of the state. As a conception of group personality, it is perhaps as close as any arrived at by an English theorist to the spirit of Gierke's original. But it is also, for this very reason, distinctly Hegelian, since it was Hegel, better than anyone, who understood freedom as a kind of responsibility. The problem is that Laski does not see this. Instead he treats Hegel as one of the advocates of the sovereign state against whom the conception of a pluralistic society is directed. What is more, he identifies Hegel's conception of the state with that of a theorist for whom freedom was the antithesis of responsibility; that is, he

---

[21] See Laski, *The foundations of sovereignty*, p. 157.   [22] *Ibid.*, p. 152.

identifies Hegel with Hobbes.[23] He does so when alluding to Hobbes's comparison between corporations and worms in the body of the state, from which he concludes that 'we have made our State absorptive in a mystic, Hegelian fashion'.[24] Once two thinkers so different, and so different in ways it was precisely Gierke's purpose to elucidate, are conflated like this, the force of Laski's argument is entirely dissipated. Unlike Cole, Laski believed it was possible to embrace the concept of real group personality in a distinctively English idiom, and use it to construct a distinctively pluralistic political theory. But, like Cole, he could not bring himself to comprehend, never mind to embrace, the Germanic preconceptions on which the concept of real group personality rested. Instead, he set the two up in crude opposition to one another. The result is that, more so even than Cole's, Laski's argument is left with nowhere to go.

In the end, where the argument did go was just down the road that Cole had already mapped out for it. Abandoning the idea of group personality, Laski resorted to the idea of function in order to characterise the conditions pertaining in a pluralistic political society. In a book he published in 1919, Laski argued that political pluralism required 'a division, not of powers, but of power on the basis of function',[25] centred around 'two bodies similar in character to a national legislature',[26] one representing the interests of men as consumers, the other the separate interests of men as producers. Laski does not, any more than did Cole, elaborate on how these institutions would work together. If they are not to be controlled by some higher sovereign body, the assumption must be that their successful co-existence rests on the interdependence of function. Yet Laski will not, indeed cannot, explain what generates this interdependence. He will not countenance the possibility that the state, as an association, is itself possessed of a personality, and therefore capable of development in its own right – that, he understood, was Hegelianism. Instead, he simply provides us with the image of 'a society in which authority is not hierarchical but co-ordinate'.[27] The question of what it is that co-ordinates a political society is just the

---

[23] For Hobbes 'Liberty, or Freedome, signifieth (properly) the absence of . . . Opposition and may be applyed no leese to Irrational, and Inanimate creatures, than to Rationall' (Hobbes, *Leviathan*, p. 145).

[24] Laski, *The foundations of sovereignty*, p. 168.   [25] Laski, *Authority in the modern State*, p. 74.

[26] *Ibid.*, p. 88.   [27] *Ibid.*, p. 74.

point at issue here, as it is in most forms of political thought. To suggest only that it is co-ordinated by the manner in which it is made up is to beg that question entirely.

III

What sets Laski apart from Cole is that his arguments about functional assemblies, like his arguments about corporate personality, are intended to form only one aspect of his case against the concept of state sovereignty. Laski's pluralism was not simply designed to discern in history a political theory to fit the guild, or any other, idea. It was also intended to reflect his views about the status of political ideas in general. For it is not simply the state, nor just society, but the world as a whole which Laski describes as 'pluralistic because it exists in time and space'.[28] This is the historist side of his argument, and it does not just lead to a series of claims about political organisation; it also leads to a set of claims about political theory, and the limits of what can be said in it. These limits follow from the contingency of the existence described as pluralistic, and are conveyed by Laski by means of a quotation from William James – 'However much may be collected, however much may report itself as present at my effective centre of consciousness, something else is self-governed and absent and unreduced to unity'[29] – which he then reduces to the simple thesis that 'there are no essential connections'.[30] Two sets of consequences are taken to flow from this claim. First, political theory itself cannot achieve the determinacy to which it has traditionally aspired. Laski urges that political theory become 'constantly experimentalist' (a phrase he borrowed from John Dewey)[31] and writes of his own pluralism that 'it does not try to work out with tedious elaboration the respective spheres of State or group or individual'.[32] Second, political authority cannot be fixed either. Laski disputes any suggestion that the state has a 'moral pre-eminence' as a result of which 'you must fuse your will into its own'.[33] Rather, the state must earn the obedience of its citizens and its will 'is a will to some extent competing with other wills and, Darwin-wise, surviving only by its ability to cope with its environment'.[34] This invocation of Darwin is reminiscent of Maitland. But where Maitland makes the allusion to natural history in order to ask

---

[28] Laski, 'What is history?', 324.   [29] Laski, *Studies in the problem of sovereignty*, p. 10.
[30] *Ibid.*   [31] *Ibid.*, p. 23.   [32] *Ibid.*   [33] *Ibid.*, p. 13.   [34] *Ibid.*, p. 14.

'whether we are not a little behind the age of Darwin if between the State and all other groups we fix an immeasurable gulf', Laski makes it in order to question whether anything about the state or other groups can be fixed in the first place. His is the strongest statement in the brief tradition to which he belongs of the contingency of all aspects of political existence. If Laski's pluralism is an advance on what preceded it, then the advance must lie here. What needs to be considered is whether Laski's thought, otherwise just an amalgam of the ideas of others, is furthered or completed by his insistence that a non-authoritative, or 'pluralistic', state is demanded by the 'pluralistic' quality of the world as a whole.

The conclusion must be that it is not. With regard to the question of political authority, Laski does shift closer to anarchism than his predecessors.[35] The basis of his argument is similar to that of Cole, in which he equates our experience of the state with our experience of government, and government with a partial economic interest. Laski writes that 'a realistic analysis of the modern State suggests that what we term State-action is, in fact, action by government',[36] and in the same spirit he argues that the state 'is in reality what a dominant group or class in a community believes to be political good'.[37] The route from here leads Cole straight to guild socialism, but for Laski it also leads to the assertion that 'the will of the State obtains pre-eminence over the wills of other groups exactly to the point where it is interpreted with sufficient wisdom to gain general acceptance, and no further'.[38] In other words, the state is only pre-eminent where it is obeyed. Laski's purpose in making such a seemingly circular assertion is to emphasise that it is the content of the state's will, and not its provenance, that is important, and he contends that 'it is a matter of degree, and not of kind, that the State should find for its decrees more usual acceptance than those of any other association'.[39] The problem with this argument is that, just because it stops short of

---

[35] In April 1917 Laski wrote to Holmes: 'I have discovered Proudhon and I want you to share the joy. Really he is immense and has all the virtues . . . His theory of the State satisfies all my anarchist principles' (Laski, *Correspondence*, vol. 1, p. 81). Still, this was only one of a great number of enthusiasms expressed in this correspondence, and whatever Proudhon's influence, Laski's political theory was not an unmodified expression of anarchist principles. If this book underplays the influence of French political theory on Laski and Cole, it is because it is an attempt to describe the ways in which theorists like Laski and Cole tried to use Gierkean ideas to construct an alternative to the anarchistic tendencies of French syndicalism.

[36] Laski, *Authority in the modern State*, p. 30.   [37] *Ibid.*, p. 87.

[38] Laski, *Studies in the problem of sovereignty*, p. 14.   [39] *Ibid.*, p. 17.

anarchism – it has been called 'contingent anarchism'[40] – it really is circular. Laski does not stipulate the grounds on which a decree of the state should be ignored, but merely announces that if it were ignored it would not be a decree. He is, therefore, seeking to have it both ways, retaining the notions of law and of statehood while suggesting the severely limited authority of each. Yet a law which depends on its subjects' agreement in all instances to what it authorises is not a law, and when Laski says 'there is no sanction for law other than the consent of the human mind',[41] what follows is that law is impossible. This does not mean that laws must always be backed by the sanction of the state (i.e. that they must always be commands). But it does mean that even when laws operate in an 'enabling' capacity, they must do so on their own terms, not on the terms of those who live under them. The law that requires a will to be signed by two witnesses does not require the assent of whomever it is making the will. It must, of course, be up to each individual to decide whether they wish to accord with this law, and therefore to make use of the resources that the law has to offer. But even if the offer is declined by everyone, the law itself still stands. Law is only possible if individual actions are judged by formal criteria determined in law, and not by the individuals themselves.

The difficulty with Laski's position is well encapsulated in his complaint that for too long the life of individuals and groups had been left 'unconnected . . . with the construction of those rules of conduct by which that life is governed'.[42] This point is familiar enough, for it echoes Figgis's insistence on 'the facts' becoming the basis of law as well as of life. Laski, perhaps, makes the point with more conviction, but in doing so he merely emphasises how little is said by such a demand. To insist that laws should be 'connected' to life is like telling a map-maker that he should be accurate. If he takes this advice literally, his map will be on a scale of 1:1, and therefore not much of a map. If what he creates is to be useful, then the degree of accuracy required will have to depend upon some other criterion. So it is with rules of conduct, which cannot *be* life, any more than a map can be a landscape, or a grammar a spoken language. 'Connectedness' in law-making, like accuracy in map-making, is of course

---

[40] See B. Zylstra, *From pluralism to collectivism: the development of Harold Laski's political thought* (Assen, 1970), pp. 48–50. 'Contingent anarchism' is in fact an oxymoron, like 'somewhat unique'.
[41] Laski, *Studies in the problem of sovereignty*, p. 14.   [42] Laski, *The foundations of sovereignty*, p. 44.

a virtue, for it is indubitably the case that a law which strikes a chord with those who are governed by it is a good. Equally, the condition of living well enough to do without laws is a self-evidently worthy ideal, as is the condition of being able to see far enough to do without maps. These goods on their own, though, cannot act as guides to political life – the 'political' *refers* to actions which are to some or other degree unconnected in Laski's sense. The problems of politics are the problems of deciding what may justifiably be left unconnected to what, and who to whom, with, when necessary, which sanctions attached.

If Laski does not add anything by the insistence with which he makes his case, he does at least extend it with consistency into the realm of questions about, rather than simply within, political theory. For Laski, the 'facts' should not just determine what states do, but what political theorists do also: they should, Laski declares, 'become inductive-minded' and 'make [their] principles grow out of the facts'.[43] This is Laski's 'experimentalism', an important component of his pluralism, and a clearer statement than any other in the pluralistic tradition that the attack on the state brings with it certain consequences for the way that the political theorist should regard himself. However, this methodological precept is in its way no more helpful than anything previously said in that tradition, nor than anything Laski says about the precepts that should guide law-makers. Laski was not advocating that English political thought embrace what was, and still is, called in America political science. At the time Laski was writing American political science had in fact thrown up its own school of political pluralism, originating in the work of A. F. Bentley, which sought to analyse the American political process by looking at the various groups competing for influence within it.[44] This was, essentially, a sociological exercise, and it depended upon case studies of American pressure-group politics. It did not interest Laski. His allegiance was to a different tradition, as he made clear when he wrote of the teaching of political science in the United States: 'In no country in the world is politics so much taught . . . but it ought to be added that rarely is it so badly taught. The ground is always covered but everywhere the emphasis is on description and not principle.'[45] Laski was writing in a tradition, stretching back to

[43] Laski, *Studies in the problem of sovereignty*, p. 13.
[44] The most prominent recent exponent of this school is R. A. Dahl.
[45] Laski, 'The literature of politics', *New Republic*, 13 (17 November 1917), 6.

Hobbes and beyond, in which the central question is not what makes this or that state work, but how states should work in general. In that tradition, his 'experimentalism' represents the admonition not of a political scientist but of a historian – it conveys his sense, as an historian, that theories are contingent and depend upon the circumstances in which they are formulated. The 'inductive-minded theorist', resistant to *a prioristic* explanations, is simply the open-minded theorist. At the same time, Laski did not wish to denude political theory of all prescriptive force. His arguments, as he himself admitted, were designed to refashion political structures, for as he wrote: 'The implied corollary of our purpose is the widespread distribution of power. It will need a new philosophy of the State to satisfy the institutions that purpose will demand.'[46] The new philosophy, then, must help orchestrate new political conditions. Laski's insistence that theory should be pursued inductive-mindedly is an expression of these convictions – a sense that political theory is contingent (historism), and a sense that political theory should reflect historical developments (historicism). But it does not add anything to them, and nor does it resolve the tension between them. Laski was not simply seeking to describe a dialectical process in which theory reacts on circumstance and vice versa; he was also wishing to participate in it, diminishing certain sorts of theory and bolstering certain kinds of circumstance. In this respect, any difference between himself and Gierke, Maitland, Figgis, Barker or Cole is merely one of degree, not of kind. And in this respect, a difference of degree is no difference at all. For though it may fairly be said that an ability to reason inductively is a pre-condition of successful participation in political life, the injunction to theorise inductive-mindedly, however strongly expressed, does not on its own determine either where the theorist should participate, or how.

IV

In 1920, Harold Laski left the United States and returned to England, where he took up a post at the London School of Economics. With this move began a long, complex and well-documented intellectual journey, one that was to end, following another world war, with Laski chairman of the Labour party, and

---

[46] Laski, *The foundations of sovereignty*, p. 29.

the most famous socialist intellectual in Britain, if not the world. Aspects of this story will be discussed in what follows. But 1920 also marks the end of an intellectual journey of a different kind. This was the journey of pluralistic ideas in general, and Gierke's version of pluralism in particular, across the intellectual landscape of English political thought. Laski gave this movement a name, yet by the time the ideas reached Laski they were more or less exhausted, and they were certainly exhausted by the time he finished with them. He added nothing to these ideas beyond his obvious enthusiasm, which was not enough. What is more, he detracted from them by his inability to distinguish between juristic and metaphysical theories of the state, on which so much of the force of Gierke's arguments depends. Both Laski and Cole, like Barker and Figgis before them, took Gierke's ideas in some unexpected directions. But none of them, and least of all Laski, made them any more convincing by doing so.

Still, in 1920, Laski was very far from being exhausted himself (he was only twenty-seven), and nor had he exhausted the things that he wished to say about groups and the state, individuals and their collective enterprises. What he found, following his return to England, was that he could no longer say them in the familiar language of political pluralism. By 1920 the limits of what could be said in that language had started to make themselves clear, even to Laski. Where, exactly, those limits are to be drawn is the subject of the final part of this book. But before then, we need to examine, if only briefly, the alternative means that Laski, and others, found to divest themselves of their opinions on the subject of the state's essential nature, and the essential nature of the groups within it.

CHAPTER 10

The return of the state

I

The single most striking feature of the pluralist movement in English political thought is the abrupt way in which it ends. During the second decade of this century pluralistic ideas were the dominant influence on political theory in England, and there were few areas of intellectual life that they did not touch in one form or another. Then, in 1920, this influence suddenly ceased. Maitland and Figgis were, of course, by this time dead; but more significantly, neither of them had succeeded in founding a school of like-minded historians to pursue their interest in the question of group personality. This was a fact lamented by Laski, who wrote in 1925 that 'men like Maitland – perhaps the greatest legal genius in England since Bentham – were never able to gather around them disciples to carry on their work'.[1] Yet Laski, once a potential disciple, had long since lost interest in these questions himself. As early as February 1920 he had written to his friend Holmes, with typical modesty:

There is only one moment in history where feelings comparable to mine just now have developed – when the Holy Ghost knew that whatever Joseph did was too late because the incarnation had taken place. In other words, I have begun my new book, and I feel lyrical about it . . . I've decided to call it *A grammar of politics*.[2]

The plan for the book was already mapped out, and Laski was able to announce: 'Chapters on the implications of capitalism, syndicalism, socialism and guild socialism follow – all of them having the honour of being rejected.'[3] This work proved to be the major intellectual project of Laski's life, and the first of its many editions eventually appeared in 1925. By then, Laski had substantially

[1] H. J. Laski, *A grammar of politics*, fourth edn (London, 1938), p. 276.
[2] Laski, *Correspondence*, vol. 1, p. 244.   [3] *Ibid.*

modified, if not quite abandoned, all the basic tenets of his earlier pluralism. Meanwhile, Cole, the driving force behind one of the ideologies that Laski accords the honour of rejection, had begun to lose interest in questions of abstract political theory altogether. In 1920, following a brief internecine struggle, the guild socialist movement in which he had placed his faith suddenly collapsed, and the National Guilds Federation was disbanded. Dispirited, and at something of a loose end, Cole began, in the words of his wife, 'to turn his attention to the collation and collection of *facts* – and to the writing of Labour history'.[4] Only Ernest Barker remained as prolific after the end of the decade as he had been during it. Yet at no time during the 1920s did Barker return to what he had called in January 1915 'the fundamental questions' – the questions that follow from the state's identity as an association. In fact, no-one did. From 1920 onwards there was no-one in England prepared to further the case against the idea of the single unitary state, and its single sovereignty.

This rapid demise in the significance of pluralist ideas has tended to be explained in the light of changing political circumstance, and of particular historical events. Following the conclusion of the First World War, the preoccupation of many theorists, including liberals like Barker, was with preventing a Second, and their attention was directed towards practical developments in the field of international relations. Meanwhile, the end of the war arrived with the British state having greatly increased the scope of its activities, and though trade unions had also strengthened their position during the war, the economic slump that followed weakened their authority without cutting back on that of the state. Furthermore, the idea of the state had had new life injected into it, for those on the left, by the success of the Bolshevik revolution in Russia. During the 1920s, those theorists of the left still seeking a more prominent political role for trade unions and other labour associations, among them Laski and Cole, came to pin their hopes on the minority Labour governments. When, in 1931, these hopes appeared to be dashed, attention was directed not towards the failures of the sovereign state but towards the failures of the Labour party, the failures of democracy and the failures of capitalism. Such themes, quintessentially of the inter-war period, did not leave much room for political pluralism.[5]

---

[4] Cole, *The life of G. D. H. Cole*, p. 132.
[5] For an account of the demise of political pluralism in these terms see Rodney Barker's *Political ideas in modern Britain* (London, 1978), chapters 4–6. Barker goes on to suggest that the

But developments in British political life cannot tell the whole story. The most obvious reason for this is that pluralist ideas can never be said simply to have relied on favourable political conditions – after all, political pluralism was conceived in part as a challenge to the overmighty state, and if pluralistically minded authors found that the state had usurped all authority in the 1920s and 1930s, that was at least as good a reason for pursuing their arguments as for abandoning them. Further, however, as this book has argued, pluralist ideas cannot be understood as standing in any simple relation to historical circumstance. The pluralists were themselves historians, and their theories of political life arose out of a historical understanding of political conditions. For this reason the view that pluralists took of the state as an idea was not just a response to the activities of this or that state; it also rested on a set of arguments about how political theory should be related to the times in which it was promulgated. If it was decided that pluralism no longer seemed an appropriate vehicle for political thought, this represented a comment on the internal workings of the pluralist case as well as on the life of the nation. And this is not simply a philosophical judgment; it has a historical basis of its own. For one of the difficulties with attempting to explain the demise of political pluralism solely in the light of the expanded authority of the British state is that it tends to disregard a substantial part of the historical evidence. This evidence is the considerable volume of criticism to which pluralist ideas were subjected during the 1920s, none of which can plausibly be read as

willingness of theorists like Cole and Laski to seek an accommodation with the newly powerful British state was in some sense culpable – he depicts it as something like a failure of political will. Laski in particular is singled out for criticism for abandoning his early attachment to the engaged polemicism of pluralists like Figgis in order to pursue work Barker describes as 'purely reflective and descriptive' (Barker, *Political ideas*, p. 97). The point of this account is to provide evidence for Barker's thesis that it was such as Laski who, by their retreat into the world of academic political theory, and away from engagement with movements like guild socialism, 'allowed the State to step out of political discourse and to become the great unstudied feature of twentieth century British politics' (*ibid.*, p. 103). It is a very strange argument. Of course it is true to say that the state has often been taken as a given in modern British political life. But to blame this on Laski's retreat to his ivory tower is simply perverse. If anything, Laski's thoughts on these matters move in the opposite direction to that ascribed to them by Barker – towards, not away from, a form of political theory which allowed the political theorist to prescribe specific political arrangements rather than having to describe those arrangements happening to prevail. Certainly, as we shall see, the Laski of the 1920s and 1930s can hardly be contrasted with someone like Figgis on the grounds of the latter's greater willingness to get involved in contemporary argument; and Barker's picture of Laski as an intellectual dilettante, slyly abandoning the brave guild socialists to the hazards of the real world without a much needed ideas-man to help them out, is a wholly unconvincing caricature.

simple apologia for contemporary state practice. Much of this criticism came from America, where it appeared in the pages of the *American Political Science Review*.[6] Yet a small but significant portion of it came from England, and a significant portion of that came from the former pluralists themselves. Laski, Cole and Barker, all of whom eventually returned to the question of the state's true nature, each repudiated the pluralist ideas on which they had previously depended. They did not do this because they believed that pluralist ideas had become old-fashioned. They did so because they no longer believed that political pluralism could be made to work.

Laski, Cole and Barker did not come to repudiate their earlier pluralism for precisely the same reasons, and nor did they do so in the same ways. Indeed, the collapse of the pluralist movement revealed more than anything the very different political perspectives of those who had made it up. Laski and Cole eventually became, in their separate ways, Marxists. Barker, meanwhile, came to embrace a form of constitutionalism, based on what he called 'the sovereignty of law'. Yet although there was a large political gulf between them (one that went back a long way, and expressed itself first in Barker's reluctance to be the dedicatee of Laski's first book), their respective changes of heart exhibit certain features in common. Each of them found in pluralism a limited, and limiting, view of political life. As

---

[6] These articles included E. D. Ellis, 'The pluralistic State', *American Political Science Review*, 14 (1920), 393–409; F. W. Coker, 'The technique of the pluralistic State', *American Political Science Review*, 15 (1921), 186–213; G. H. Sabine, 'Pluralism: a point of view', *American Political Science Review*, 17 (1923), 34–50; E. D. Ellis, 'Guild socialism and pluralism', *American Political Science Review*, 17 (1923), 584–96; and W. Y. Elliott, 'The pragmatic politics of Mr H. J. Laski', *American Political Science Review*, 18 (1924), 251–75. The tone of all these articles was consistently hostile, and their criticism tended to take one of two forms: either to claim that political pluralism was an essentially vacuous theory – Coker argued 'there has never been any political philosopher of any era [among whom he includes Hobbes] who would attempt to deny such facts as those addressed by Laski' (Coker, 'The technique of the pluralistic State', 194); or that it had some unforeseen implications, varying from anarchism (Sabine) to fascism (Elliott).

For historical purposes, however, the most significant criticism of European pluralism by an American came before 1920, in the form of Morris Cohen's article 'Communal ghosts and other perils in social philosophy', *Journal of Philosophy, Psychology and Scientific Method*, 16 (1919), 673–90. This article, which criticised the concept of real group personality, was cited by Laski in 1947 as one of the reasons for his subsequent abandonment of political pluralism – Laski wrote that he had been 'converted by Professor Cohen's power of logical analysis to see the error of my ways' (Laski, 'Morris Cohen's approach to legal philosophy', *University of Chicago Law Review*, 15, (1947–8), 577). It should be said, though, that this was not what he reported at the time. In 1919 he wrote to Holmes that Cohen's paper was 'a brilliant piece of logical criticism; but I thought it showed a pretty complete ignorance of history on the one hand and the psychology of administration on the other' (Laski, *Correspondence*, vol. I, p. 223). The essence of Cohen's critique had been that 'the evils of an absolute State are not cured by a multiplication of absolutes' (Cohen, 'Communal ghosts', 689).

these limits revealed themselves, each of them sought a means of understanding political life which did not constrain them in the judgments that they were able to pass on it. They were not simply trying to move with the times. They were trying to find a form of political theory which allowed them to judge whether they wished to move with the times or not. In other words, each of them came to believe, in the end, and regardless of their own political perspectives, that a pluralistic perspective prevented the political theorist from expressing himself at all. The various routes by which they separately arrived at this conclusion forms the subject of this chapter.

II

The first signs of Laski's impending disenchantment with political pluralism were neither philosophical nor political; they were purely personal. In April 1918 Laski wrote a review of G. D. H. Cole's *Self-government in industry* for the *New Republic*. To this point the two men had seemed to be obvious allies. Laski's review made it clear that things were not quite so simple. For although Laski could not bring himself to disavow Cole's guild socialist thesis altogether – he praises it as 'a genuine attempt to formulate the transition we are now approaching'[7] – the tone of the review is grudging, and it is peppered with contemptuous asides: Cole is accused of 'cheap flippancy',[8] and of his style it is suggested that 'every reader will regret intrusions due either to bad temper or insufficient knowledge'.[9] The personal aspect of these remarks set the general tone for Laski's relationship with Cole, which became increasing hostile after his return to England. The dislike was long-lasting, and it was mutual, as Margaret Cole makes clear in her biography of her husband, where she refers to 'a curious, lifelong antagonism between the two'.[10] This antipathy was not in truth all that curious, since both men were vain and difficult. Its interest for present purposes, though, lies in its possible explanatory significance. It seems to offer a plausible motive for Laski's distancing of himself from those pluralist ideas which seemed to place him in the same camp as Cole. Indeed, Beatrice Webb suggested in her diary that just such an explanation might lie behind Laski's realignment within the politics of the left after 1920, writing that '[Laski] dislikes the Cole set intensely, an antagonism which

---

[7] Laski, 'Industrial self-government', *New Republic*, 14 (27 April 1918), 391–2.
[8] *Ibid.*, 392.   [9] *Ibid.*   [10] Cole, *The life of G. D. H. Cole*, p. 201.

perhaps makes him sympathetic to our standpoint'.[11] But there remain two problems with this version of events. First, it is difficult, if not impossible, to know what would constitute satisfactory evidence for making this claim, given that it presupposes the sublimation of psychological factors in abstract and impersonal arguments. Second, it is the case that Cole was himself in the process of moving away from his guild socialist beginnings. Given as much, some other form of explanation is needed – it is hardly possible to postulate a form of the prisoners' dilemma in which both Laski and Cole were so keen to be seen to be different from one another that they ended up doing the same thing – and an explanation offers itself which is quite consistent with the available evidence: both were coming to think pluralist ideas were unsatisfactory in themselves. Certainly this is something which was also suggested by Beatrice Webb in a comment on Cole's public reticence during the early 1920s, when she described him as 'strangled by stale doctrines, stale not because they are old but because they are not true and cannot be embodied in events'.[12] Of course, Webb's judgments cannot themselves be considered either impersonal or impartial. Nonetheless, since both Cole and Laski were to provide explanations of their development as theorists in terms of their changed view of theory and not of each other, to account for changes on the basis of the latter is more likely to complicate than to clarify.

Unfortunately, if we do turn to Laski's explicit statements of his differences as a theorist with the Cole set, the evidence, though ample, is not always clearcut. The very breadth of Laski's attack on Cole makes it difficult to isolate the root cause of his disaffection. In 1919 he criticised Cole's 'defective terminology' and his 'irritating inability to realise that every concept he handles is in fact a historic category';[13] further, he argued, 'the guild socialists have yet to realise that the materials with which they are to work are largely predetermined'.[14] In 1920, he wrote that guild socialism was unlikely to 'make [its] way' until its proponents could show 'the same accuracy in the facts, the same historical perspective, the same width of knowledge as Mr and Mrs Webb display'.[15] In the same year he accused Cole of '*naïveté*' in assuming that 'every workman will be as

[11] B. Webb, *Diaries*, ed. N. and J. Mackenzie, 4 vols. (London, 1982–5), vol. III, *1905–24*, p. 339.
[12] *Ibid.*, vol. IV, *1924–43*, p. 27.
[13] Laski, 'National guilds', *New Republic*, 18 (22 February 1919), 124.   [14] *Ibid.*, 125.
[15] Laski, 'The history of trade unionism', *New Republic*, 22 (12 May 1920), 359.

interested in the success of his guild as Mr Cole himself is to convince us of the whole scheme's value'.[16] In 1921 he spoke, with particular reference to Cole, of the 'facile psychology'[17] and 'vicious intellectualism'[18] of some of those who sought to attack the concept of state sovereignty. By 1925 he felt able to declare, magisterially: 'In 1920, guild socialism was the fashionable doctrine of its time; its influence is now almost negligible . . . and it is generally agreed that it is not a theory of the State.'[19] Leaving aside the malice that obtrudes, three things can be said about this series of complaints. First, the emphasis remains, as it had done in Laski's overtly pluralistic work, on the merits of 'the facts': Cole needs to be more 'accurate', more 'knowledgeable', more historically conscious, less 'intellectualist'. Second, if this criticism comes from a pluralist perspective, it may be said to be self-refuting, for Laski's own fact-based theory of the state does not achieve any more with the facts than did guild socialism. Third, this criticism is vague enough to be compatible with more than the pluralist conception of experimental political theory. In a technical sense, the injunction to view the categories of political theory as 'historic' and the materials as 'pre-determined' is consistent with, and even suggestive of, historicism rather than historism – with and of Marxism rather than, say, pragmatism. More generally, Laski's charges against Cole may be said to add up to a plea for 'realism' in something like its colloquial sense, a 'pragmatic' willingness to stick to the available facts. In accusing Cole of *naïveté*, Laski would seem to be demanding also a 'realistic' appraisal of human nature, resting on a less sanguine view of what is and is not politically possible. That Laski was most vehement in his attacks on Cole during 1920 and 1921, the period of his own transition from the author who had published *Authority in the modern State* to the author who was preparing *A grammar of politics*, makes it hard to know whether Laski can be accused of a certain hypocrisy (he probably can). Nonetheless, these complaints do not need to be seen either as the exclusive product of personal unpleasantness, nor as evidence of double standards. Laski's political thought did come to emphasise historical progress over historical contingency, and also a certain practicality over wishful thinking, such that his attacks on Cole can plausibly be described as representative of – rather than either determinative of, or incompatible with –

[16] Laski, 'Democracy at the crossroads', *Yale Review*, 9 (1920), 801.
[17] Laski, 'Recent contributions to political science', *Economica*, 1 (1921), 90.   [18] *Ibid.*, 91.
[19] Laski, 'Political science in Great Britain', *American Political Science Review*, 19 (1925), 99.

his change of mind about the merits of political pluralism. Given the complicated motives involved, however, they are not the best source of evidence for Laski's developing ideas. That, not surprisingly, comes in his major publications of the period, which must be assumed to represent the most considered, and least personalised, statements of his views.

The most complete, most considered of all Laski's books is *A grammar of politics*. In it, Laski accepts that there must be an association which 'controls the level at which men are to live as men',[20] and that it is this association which we call 'the State'. This level of jurisdiction is required by an 'identity of men's nature';[21] in all societies there exist certain interests held in common, though this does not entail an identity in the content of individual interests, only in their form, for all individuals share merely a desire that their vision of what is for the best should be accorded an equal potential for fulfilment. Laski resorts to an earlier terminology as he declares that individual (or associational) views of the good life do not themselves 'involve identity . . . what we meet is pluralistic not monistic'.[22] But where he departs from his earlier pluralism is in his consequent and explicit recognition that pluralistic interests do need to be adjudicated between by a body bearing some form of sovereign authority, if we are to grant to those interests the sort of protection which they need. As a result, Laski is prepared to concede that all social organisation must have at its heart 'a single centre of control'[23] so that the members of a society can know exactly what sort of body may exercise political authority over them, and what sort of relation between them and such a body the fact of political authority entails. The significance of this concession is that Laski is now willing to separate out the political from the social, in a way which his earlier pluralism disallowed. Previously, he had sought to argue that the political was just one aspect of the social, one among many such aspects, as the state was one among many forms of social association. In *A grammar of politics*, he comes to accept that the political domain is something distinct from the rest of society – it is a separate sphere in which various social issues have to be decided, and thus it is a sphere which has to be allowed to exist on its own terms.

It does not follow from any of this that what Laski was seeking in *A grammar of politics* was the complete detachment of the life of the state

---

[20] Laski, *A grammar of politics*, p. 70.   [21] *Ibid.*, p. 27.   [22] *Ibid.*, pp. 260–1.
[23] *Ibid.*, p. 69.

from the broader life of the society that surrounds it. The reverse was
true. Having accepted that the political dimension of men's lives
must be kept distinct from the lives that each of them chooses to
lead, Laski devotes the main part of his book to arguing that the two
should nonetheless remain as close as possible. He did not accept
that the separation of the state from the rest of society must lead to
the divorce of the one from the other; instead, he sought to imbue
each with as great an understanding of the other as possible. So,
Laski puts forward the view that even a pluralistic society must be
ready to embrace what he calls 'a corporate sense of responsibility'.[24]
Some of the means by which he hoped to achieve this must be
counted primarily ethical – he commends as for the best a situation
in which 'men will prefer to be known for what they do than for what
they possess'.[25] Others, however, have a recognisable political
dimension, as when he argues that 'distinctions of wealth and status
must be distinctions to which all men attain and they must be
required by the common welfare'.[26] Likewise, Laski's treatment of
what we should recognise as essentially political questions – the
questions of what constitutes good government – is dominated by his
concern that government should remain open to the plurality of
concerns of those who live under it. He proposes a variety of reforms
to help achieve this – stronger local government, a less partisan
press, uniform standards of education, a reformed second
chamber,[27] even a written constitution and bill of rights (since 'ideas
so fundamental as these cannot be left to a chance majority in the
legislature'[28]). All these ideas are designed to ensure that the state,
though possessed of political authority, cannot ignore the extra-
political dimension of the lives of its citizens. As Laski says of his state
and its relation to the various groups organised apart from it: 'It will
be open to the State to deny their will, but it will be the nature of this

---

[24] *Ibid.*, p. 61.   [25] *Ibid.*, p. 438.

[26] *Ibid.*, p. 157. The most striking features of this statement is that it precisely foreshadows the
single most celebrated axiom in recent English-speaking political theory, Rawls' second
principle of justice, which runs as follows: 'Social and economic inequalities are to be
arranged so that they are both (a) reasonably expected to be to everyone's advantage, and
(b) attached to positions and offices open to all' (See J. Rawls, *A theory of justice*, new edn
(Oxford, 1973), p. 60).

[27] In fact, Laski was sufficiently reconciled to 'a single centre of control' that he recommended
the abolition not just of the Lords, but of a second chamber altogether, regarding all forms
of bicameral legislatures as 'an historical accident' (Laski, *A grammar of politics*, p. 328). It was,
he believed, 'the single chamber magnicompetent legislative assembly [which] seems best to
answer the needs of the modern State' (*ibid.*, p. 340).

[28] *Ibid.*, p. 305.

system to make that denial a much more difficult, sometimes even more perilous adventure than it is today.'[29] Just as individuals and groups of individuals cannot live socially without recognising the political responsibilities they all share, so Laski is keen to establish that no political body can exist in ignorance of the social responsibilities it has to the individuals and groups of individuals who constitute it.

In this sense, the theme of Laski's work remains that of 'connectedness'. But what distinguishes *A grammar of politics* from what has gone before is Laski's recognition that 'connectedness' cannot be the sole issue in social and political theory. At any given moment the political will never be equivalent to the social, since it is on the distinction between them that the identity of political authority finally rests. As a result, the question is no longer one of equating the political with the social, but rather one of striking a proper balance between them. This is what Laski attempts. In doing so, he does not give up on his earlier insistence that history is the key to a true understanding of politics. But the emphasis of that claim necessarily changes, from predominantly historist to overtly historicist. As a pluralist, Laski had sought to understand the political life of the state purely in terms of the contingent historical condition of the society that contained it. Now, he explicitly acknowledged that state and society stood in a dialectical relation to one another, each reacting upon the other and shaping the other over time. It was the task of the political theorist to map that relation, in order to decide where a balance might best be struck. No longer, therefore, did Laski think his job was done once he had established that abstract claims to political authority are meaningless in the face of political contingency. Instead, he believed his job was to use history in order to decide where and when claims to political authority might best be allowed. 'The answer we must seek', he now declared, 'is one that intelligently anticipates the future as it reasonably interprets the past'.[30]

Within this historicist framework there is still the scope for two very different approaches to the problems of political theory. On the one hand, the theorist may decide that his task is to describe the institutional machinery which best facilitates the balanced interplay of social and political forces. On the other hand, the theorist may believe that the relation between the social and the political has

---

[29] *Ibid.*, p. 430.   [30] *Ibid.*, p. 24.

ossified, such that the machinery itself must be taken hold of in order to re-establish the fluidity of the relation between them. A decision on these issues will depend on the theorist's sense of history, and his sense of how it is progressing. In *A grammar of politics* Laski inclined towards the former view – he believed that a well-grounded constitutional democracy could sustain both a responsive state and a responsible, though pluralistic, society. However, this conviction, while prevailing, was not absolute. For Laski was aware that the ability of individuals to organise themselves into a plurality of groups was itself contingent upon a certain level of material equality holding for a society as a whole. Where that level had not been reached, there was the likelihood that the state would be responsive to a narrow section of society, and society responsible to a partial and narrow-minded state. In these circumstances, the political and the social cease to adapt to one another, and start to corrupt one another instead. Laski expressed his consciousness of this difficulty as follows: 'There is never likely to be an enlightened State until there is respect for individuality; but also there will be no respect for individuality until there is an enlightened State. It is only the emphasis on equality that will break this vicious circle.'[31] When *A grammar of politics* was first published he remained hopeful that this emphasis might yet be achieved within the framework of the British parliamentary tradition, suitably modified. But by 1931 any lingering optimism he still had on this score finally evaporated. The collapse in that year of the second Labour government convinced Laski that tinkering with the machinery of parliamentary democracy would not produce the social changes on which his own vision of political life ultimately depended. So he decided that it was necessary to take hold of the machine. He became an out-and-out Marxist, and he began to explore the prospects for revolution (albeit without violence, something he called 'revolution by consent').[32] From this point on he ceased to think of democracy and equality as two sides of the

---

[31] *Ibid.*, p. 172.

[32] Explaining exactly what he meant by this was not always easy for Laski, particularly as he never gave up on Labour party politics altogether (although he refused all offers of a safe seat). Matters came to a head in 1945, when Laski found himself the party's chairman for a period that included the general election campaign. Labour's triumph in that year was not Laski's. He was accused in various newspaper reports of having championed violent revolution from a Labour party platform during a meeting in Newark (the banner headline in the *Daily Express* on 20 June read 'New Laski sensation: socialism even if it means violence'). Laski vehemently denied these reports and sued the *Newark Advertiser*, where they had originated, for libel. However he lost the case, and at least one biographer has blamed

same coin; one had come to be seen as the price to be paid for the other. And he gave voice to this conviction in the preface that he wrote to the third edition of *A grammar of politics*, published in 1934, where he declared: 'There cannot, in a word, be democracy unless there is socialism.'[33]

By the time he had arrived at this conclusion it was evident that Laski had moved a long way from his pluralist beginnings. Nevertheless, in the introductory chapter he wrote to a fourth edition of *A grammar of politics* in 1938 it was not the length of this journey but its continuity that he wished to emphasise. There, he describes his earlier pluralism as 'a stage on the road to an acceptance of the Marxian attitude'.[34] He commends it for enabling him to perceive state sovereignty as nothing more than 'a concept of power'.[35] What it had lacked, he now believes, was sufficient emphasis on 'the nature of the State as an expression of class relations'.[36] Classlessness must come first, before the state can assume its true place in relation to the rest of society; but given classlessness, the pluralist and the Marxist can agree that the proper role of the state is to provide the 'truly federal nature of society' with 'institutional expression'.[37] There is something to be said for this account of Laski's intellectual development, and not just that it is Laski's own. But it is not the whole story. For it is simply not true that Laski went from thinking of state sovereignty as the exercise of power to thinking of state sovereignty as the exercise of power by a particular class. Rather, he moves, as one commentator has put it, 'from the view that history shows that no group can be sovereign . . . to the view that one group is as a matter of fact sovereign'.[38] In other words, it was sometime between his career as a pluralist and his career as a Marxist that Laski started to take the power of the state seriously. This is the process that I have attempted to describe above. As a pluralist, Laski had seen the state as one group among many, with no claim to pre-eminence. What he had lacked was any means of describing the relation between the state and other groups, given that what distinguished the state from other groups was just its claim to pre-eminence. Lacking any means of rendering the state subordinate to society, he began to explore the

the financial and other damage done to him for his early death in 1950, at the age of 56: see G. Eastwood, *Harold Laski* (London, 1977), p. 160.
[33] Laski, *A grammar of politics*, preface to third edn.   [34] *Ibid.*, p. xii.
[35] *Ibid.*, p. xi.   [36] *Ibid.*   [37] *Ibid.*, p. xii.
[38] H. M. Magid, *English political pluralism* (New York, 1941), p. 59.

relation between society and the state, which meant acknowledging the categorical distinction between the two. It was from this perspective that he came to see the state as an expression of class relations – that is, as an expression of the interests of a particular class. In a sense, this brought him back towards his original pluralism. Yet his conversion to Marxism was only possible precisely because he had abandoned a pluralistic view of the world. In the end, the Marxist view of history provided Laski with a means of subordinating the state to the rest of society. But it only did so because he had come to appreciate the ways in which the rest of society can be subordinated to the state.

III

Cole's retreat from political pluralism was less spectacular than Laski's, and considerably less public. Nevertheless, it was just as final. During the early 1920s, following the demise of the guild socialist movement, Cole published nothing on the subject of social and political theory, and devoted himself instead to lives of Robert Owen and William Cobbett, and to journalism. However, in 1926 he decided to return to the theme of conflicting social obligations, which had exercised him over a decade earlier. He did so in a paper entitled 'Loyalties', which was delivered, as previously, to the Aristotelian Society. In it, Cole reiterates many of the claims that had characterised his pluralistic conception of society, and he continues to insist that the state is simply 'a practical political instrument', something he felt was still unappreciated by 'mere academicians'.[39] Where he admits to having had a change of heart is on just that point which determines the different titles of his two papers: since the earlier piece, he says, he has come to see the problems of social existence less in terms of obligations than of loyalties. The significance of this change of perspective is two-fold. First, it marks a new, and explicit, insistence on the prospect of social harmony taking precedence over the possibility of political conflict. Cole contrasts the 'common sentiment' and 'living impulse' of loyalties with the legalistic imperatives of obligations, and he suggests that his attention was only ever drawn to the possibility of conflicts between the latter because they were in their nature so artificial.

[39] G. D. H. Cole, 'Loyalties', *Proceedings of the Aristotelian Society*, 29 (1925–6), 152.

Previously he had wished to suggest that it was not his business to decide how specific instances of conflict should be resolved; now he openly admits that it is his task to demonstrate their essential superficiality. In the notion of multiplied loyalties he finds an idea suggestive, albeit vaguely, of such a result. This does not mean that Cole now considers conflict between groups of differently obligated individuals to be impossible. But it is the second consequence of his new understanding that he squarely identifies such conflicts as do occur with material forces. He writes that it is not a diversity of loyalties which engenders conflict but simply 'changes in the material environment of man and in his command over that environment'.[40] Men who are loyal to a variety of causes will be compelled to behave with discretion and judgment; in contrast, men who live under conditions of scarcity and competition will find it 'hard [to] distribute their loyalties'.[41] Of these two states of affairs, the first is of course to be preferred to the second.

What Cole produces in this paper is a bifurcated account of social and political life. As goals he announces two distinct sorts of harmony – men and groups of men with one another, and men and groups of men with material conditions. In consequence, he appears to embrace two very distinct approaches to the problems of political theory. On the one hand, his arguments concerning the harmonious relations of men with one another coincide with the basic tenets of philosophical idealism, as, for example, when he states that 'the association, like the individual, must have some knowledge of its "place" if it is to set up for itself any satisfactory standard of social behaviour'.[42] Cole persists in seeking to mark off his own thoughts from Bosanquet's, but his means of doing so – arguing that 'the rational totality of the Hegelian state is not being but becoming' and that the vital question therefore is 'how to become' – simply echo the thoughts of Bosanquet himself, as expressed in his preface to the third edition of *The philosophical theory of the State*, published in 1919. (There, responding to the criticism directed against him by the pluralists, Bosanquet argues that his conception of the state is 'not unified but unifying', with the result that 'some form of Federalism is

---

[40] *Ibid.*, 168.   [41] *Ibid.*, 169.
[42] *Ibid.*, 162. This statement has strong echoes of F. H. Bradley, whose chapter on 'My station and its duties' in his *Ethical studies*, second edn (Oxford, 1927) was, before Bosanquet, the most forceful and the most notorious example of idealist political thought.

strongly advocated by the author'.[43]) Any difference between Cole and Bosanquet is now purely terminological; both agree that the political sphere – the narrowly legalistic, the merely obligatory – must be transcended by a broader, and broadly evolving, social unity, whatever that unity is called. Yet on the other hand, the business of reconciling men with the world of material conditions would seem to presuppose a substantive distinction between broadly evolving social forces, and narrower, legalistic concerns. Men come into conflict with one another, Cole believed, when material resources are inappropriately distributed, and this occurs when political structures fail to accommodate the material needs of those who live under them. The remedy for this situation was not an idealised vision of social integration. Rather, it was a secure knowledge of the ways in which material resources are produced, the ways in which men attempt to control that production, and the ways in which these two may clash over time. At the time that Cole was writing, the securest knowledge of this kind came from Marx, and it was to Marx that Cole ultimately turned.

'Loyalties', then, may be seen as an attempt to reconcile Cole's lingering belief in the political harmony latent in social heterogeneity with a newfound sense that harmonious relations between men are contingent upon the political control of the material world. It can hardly be called a successful attempt, for what it offers, in essence, are two different dialectical views of the world – dialectical idealism and dialectical materialism, Hegelianism and Marxism, metaphysics and economics – which have on the whole been regarded as opposed. (The fact that one has its roots in the other does not make it any easier to adhere to both simultaneously.) Certainly, Cole gives no compelling reason for their being reconcilable, except that it would be helpful if it were so. Nor did he try to reconcile them for long. Though his published output came in the end to exceed even the prolific Laski's, Cole ceased, after 1926, to concern himself with questions of the state's ideal nature, as conceived by the academicians. He lost interest in Bosanquet; he gave up on multiplied loyalties; and in their place, he concentrated exclusively on the merits of, and appropriate tactics for, socialism. His views on these questions changed over time, though never embraced Marx with quite the enthusiasm that Laski showed (in his own terms he was an

---

[43] Bosanquet, *The philosophical theory of the State*, p. lvii.

'undogmatic Marxian'[44]). Furthermore, his response to the crisis of
1931 was more moderate than Laski's, and he persisted in his belief
that parliamentary action, not revolution, offered the best prospect
for the British working class. Yet despite this moderation, and
notwithstanding a lifelong distaste for overweening bureaucracy,
Cole appreciated, in a way that Laski did not, that his mature
socialism was not simply an extension of his earlier pluralist ideas.
He did not refer often to his early beliefs after he had abandoned
them, but when he did, it was with a clear sense of what had
changed. In 1929, looking back over his past intellectual life, Cole
described guild socialism as 'a politically-minded person's Utopia'.[45]
Like all utopian visions, it had an obvious appeal, but Cole had come
to see it as fatally flawed, because it was, in his words, 'dominated by
the idea of government as moral discipline'.[46] In 1926 he had briefly
tried to rescue this idea. After that, he abandoned it altogether.

Cole's intellectual development, like Laski's, has to be understood
in historical terms. But like Laski, Cole cannot simply be understood
as moving with the times. What changed was not just history, but the
view that pluralists like Laski and Cole chose to take of historical
change. As pluralists, they had emphasised the contingency of
historical conditions, and the fact that there was no legislating for
change. In place of timeless political certainties, they had relied on a
view of society which allowed men and groups of men an innate,
ideal capacity to organise themselves. When, in due course, times did
change, as they did with increasing speed during the inter-war years,
pluralists like Laski and Cole found themselves powerless to do
anything about it. It was this sense of powerlessness, more than
anything, which persuaded them that change had to be legislated for,
and this meant that they had to get involved in the business of the
state. What it did not mean was that either of them fell back on
timeless certainties. Cole, writing in 1934, was still convinced that 'we
need as the basis for both economic and political structures a theory
of history derived from an inductive consideration of the facts and
not one imposed *a priori* on the facts'.[47] But he was also convinced
that this theory must be historicist, not historist – it must result in
some certain knowledge of the way that history was going. So, Cole

---

[44] See Cole, *What Marx really meant* (London, 1934), p. 291.
[45] Cole, *The next ten years in British social and economic policy* (London, 1929), p. 161.
[46] *Ibid.*, p. 160.
[47] Cole, *Some relations between economic and political theory* (London, 1934), p. 83.

concludes, 'the task of men in society is to construct for themselves economic and political systems which will make rational action easy because they square with the developing conditions of social life'.[48] It is on the ability of men and groups of men to make sense of developing conditions, not on the conditional ability of men and groups of men to develop, that Cole's view of society came to rest. Of course, everything depends on what the conditions of historical development are actually taken to be. Cole, like Laski, believed that the most convincing account of historical development was Marx's. This belief, certainly, has to be understood as a response to the times through which they were living. But it should also be understood as something of a last resort. Cole, like Laski, turned to Marx only when he had been persuaded that to be a political theorist it is necessary, in the end, to take politics seriously – that is, to take seriously the ways in which men and groups of men seek to control history by seeking to take control of the state.

IV

So we come to Barker, and through Barker back to Gierke. Cole and Laski lost interest in Gierke as soon as they lost faith in their own particular version of the new federalism. But Barker never lost interest in Gierke, despite, or perhaps because of, the fact that among the pluralists his expectations of what could be made of Gierke had always been the most modest. Barker kept faith with this modest pluralism long after Cole and Laski had abandoned theirs. Yet he, too, felt the need to distance himself from it in the end. There is much evidence of this changed perspective in the introduction Barker wrote to his translation of Gierke in 1933, to which we will turn shortly. But the best evidence comes from what is an essentially private source. The Seeley historical library in Cambridge contains a number of books from Barker's personal collection, one of which, R. M. MacIver's *The modern State*,[49] is heavily annotated in

---

[48] *Ibid.*, p. 92.

[49] R. M. MacIver (1882–1970) was a sociologist and political scientist, born in Scotland, but who spent the majority of his working life in Canada and the United States. *The modern State* (Oxford, 1926) was the most abstract, and in that sense most European, of all his works, being concerned with the ideal relation of state and society. MacIver himself, who wrote the book while teaching political science in Toronto, described it as 'a break from the routine' (see MacIver, *As a tale that is told* (Chicago, 1968), p. 88). For an account of MacIver's political ideas in general, see D. Spitz, 'Robert M. MacIver's contributions to political

Barker's own hand. It is clear from these notes that this was a book that Barker read more than once, and in its margins he records the moment at which his own conception of the modern state came finally to be altered.

MacIver's book is of interest in its own right. First published in 1926, it was, after Laski's *A grammar of politics*, among the most widely read works of political theory written in English during that decade. Like *A grammar of politics*, its emphasis is on the constitutional under-pinnings of government, though unlike Laski, MacIver's primary concern is with social psychology, not economics (in this respect, MacIver is closer to Bosanquet than he is to either Laski or Cole). But for present purposes, what is most interesting about *The modern State* is its treatment of group life. In Barker's words: 'MacIver is an associationist, but not a pluralist.'[50] What this means is that MacIver, though insisting on the importance of associations within the state, does not seek to place all associations on the same footing as the state, and nor does he concern himself with what might happen when the state and other associations clash. For MacIver, the state was an association of a categorically different kind from any other. He attempted to convey his sense of this difference as follows: 'The State is, as it were, the paved highway of social life, bordered by fields and cities. It is the common way which serves them all.'[51] What is significant about this image is the sense it gives of the state as a conduit to, rather than an expression of, the good life. That life is found in the associations that men form among themselves; it is there, as it were, that men live and find nourishment. The state simply enables them to move from one version of the good life to another, and it allows different versions of the good life to co-exist in a common setting and in awareness of one another. In this sense, MacIver's image captures exactly the spirit of Oakeshott's *civitas*. For Oakeshott, a state of this kind conditions but does not control the ways in which groups of individuals choose to live, and exists precisely in order to generate a mutual consciousness of the differences between them. The same may be said of MacIver's 'paved highway', which is, in Oakeshott's terms, nothing more than a set of

---

theory', in M. Berger, T. Abel and C. H. Page (eds.), *Freedom and control in modern society* (New York, 1954), pp. 297–312.

[50] Barker, *MacIver*, p. 484. (Notes in this form refer to the page in Barker's copy of *The modern State* on which particular annotations can be found.)

[51] MacIver, *The modern State*, p. 482.

rules governing conduct (for MacIver it is simply 'law'). As a road, the state maps out for its citizens how they are to get from A to B; what it cannot do is tell them that they must go from A to B, and nor can it decide whether it is to A or to B that each of them wishes to go. MacIver, unlike Oakeshott, does talk of the state as an expression of the general will. Yet the terms in which he does so – 'not so much the will *of* the State as the will *for* the State . . . not so much the will of the citizens as the will of each person to be a citizen'[52] – are those of which Oakeshott, whose *cives* are bound not by common interests but by a common loyalty, would undoubtedly approve.

Barker, though he does not exactly disapprove of MacIver's associationism, does make it clear that, on a first reading at least, he did not consider it to go far enough. Barker remained convinced that the state was an association like other associations, and was therefore liable to clash with other associations whenever its purpose conflicted with theirs. When this happened, Barker still did not believe that the state should be allowed to triumph on the basis of any claim to universality or pre-eminence. As such, he remained a pluralist. He could not accept that the state, even understood as law, was categorically distinct from other associations, which were simply purposive; thus he could not accept that the state was sovereign. Of MacIver, he notes: 'He limits sovereignty – but not law. But in keeping sovereignty of law he keeps sovereignty as something universal and coercive.'[53] Barker still wished to contain the state in the world of groups in general, not to contain groups in general within the world of the state. He summarised his position in a remark he appends to the last page of MacIver's book:

I believe in a limited State. But I think it is limited by persons and the sovereign rights of persons individual or associated. I do not involve a community distinct from the State or a law superior to it: I only involve persons and their rights.[54]

That, at least, was his view in 1926. For underneath this comment he subsequently added the following: 'I have altered my view since [1931] to allow law as sovereign.'[55] Barker does not tell us what it was that caused him to change his mind. But the introduction he wrote to Gierke two years later represents the clearest possible attempt to give this change of mind public expression.

Barker's introduction to his translation of Gierke's *Natural law and*

---

[52] *Ibid.*, p. 11.   [53] Barker, *MacIver*, p. 18.   [54] *Ibid.*, p. 488.   [55] *Ibid.*

the theory of society was designed both to complement and to offset Maitland's earlier introduction to *Political theories of the middle age*. Like Maitland, Barker set out to sketch the historical background to the ideas with which Gierke's work deals, although in this case the emphasis was on early modern not medieval thought, and on natural rather than Roman law. Like Maitland, Barker indicates the ways in which Gierke's treatment of these ideas has a bearing on the fundamental questions of political philosophy. Unlike Maitland, however, Barker is quite willing to address these questions himself. Indeed, he uses his introduction to Gierke to set out what has by now become his own political philosophy. This philosophy is not complicated, and it is summarised by Barker in a single sentence: 'The State', he declares, 'is essentially law, and law is the essence of the State.'[56] What this amounts to is the doctrine of the sovereignty of law, for Barker insists that the state is simply a society turned into a legal association 'by virtue of a legal act or deed called constitution, which henceforth is the norm or standard, and therefore sovereign'.[57] As such, it is a doctrine that stands in obvious contrast to Austinianism, which announces that law, far from *being* sovereign, is whatever the sovereign declares it to be. This contrast, and the echoes in his language of the idea of the *Rechtsstaat* (where, in Maitland's words, law and state exist 'in, for and by the other'), give to Barker's philosophy something of a Gierkean flavour. Yet it would be quite wrong to suppose that the doctrine of the sovereignty of law is included by Barker in his introduction to Gierke in order to explicate Gierke's own thought. The reverse is true. Barker arrives at the doctrine of the sovereignty of law in the course of his introduction to Gierke as part of a critique of the idea on which Gierke's whole doctrine, including his particular conception of the *Rechtsstaat*, ultimately depends. That idea is the idea of real group personality.

Barker bases his critique of the notion of real group persons upon the distinction he draws between three different types of personality. The first of these he calls 'psychological personality', by which he understands 'the power or capacity of self-consciousness which belongs to a sentient being aware of its own sensations'.[58] Barker is clear that the only possible bearers of psychological personality are individual human beings. The second type of personality Barker distinguishes is 'moral personality', which is, in his words, 'built upon

---

[56] Gierke, *Natural law*, p. xxvii.   [57] *Ibid.*, p. xxiii.   [58] *Ibid.*, pp. lxii–lxiii.

psychological personality but transcends that on which it is built'.[59] Moral persons are psychological persons who have come to recognise that their personality is not unique, and who thereby come to share 'a common life and common rules of life'.[60] (In these terms, the condition of moral personality equates to what Oakeshott would call the condition of 'civility'.) Because moral personality is built on psychological personality, it too can only belong to individual human beings. Finally, there is 'legal personality', which is 'a power or capacity for legal action – a capacity recognised by law (and only existing when recognised by law) for originating such action as belongs to the scheme of law'.[61] Legal personality has a narrower scope than either psychological or moral personality because it can only exist within the confines of the state. (Unlike Oakeshott, Barker does not assume that moral personality, or civility, is contingent upon the existence of the *civitas*.) In another sense, however, legal personality has a broader application, for it alone can belong to groups as well as to individuals. Groups, like individuals, are capable of playing the part of persons under the law. And this is the image that Barker employs – 'personation' or 'the playing of parts'. He compares legal persons to the *dramatis personae* of the theatre, and the state to the stage on which their legal dramas are enacted. The origins and broader implications of this image will be explored in the final part of this book. For now, what matters is the connection it enables Barker to establish between individuals and groups of individuals. Groups are indeed capable of bearing the same sort of personality as individuals, but only because individuals have their own parts to play within the life of the state.

If groups are *capable* of bearing legal personality, the next question to be asked is what sorts of groups *should* bear legal personality. To answer this question Barker reverts to the account of group life he had already given in 'The discredited State', where groups were described as 'schemes'; now, employing slightly different language, he argues that groups must be understood in terms of their 'purposes', and judged accordingly. He reiterates his earlier point that one of the reasons for denying that groups are necessarily legal persons (in the way that individual human beings are necessarily psychological persons) is that it allows us to distinguish between those groups which are, and those which are not, deserving of legal status.

[59] *Ibid.*, p. lxiii.   [60] *Ibid.*   [61] *Ibid.*

(And Barker makes the further point that individual human beings
are not necessarily legal persons either – some may be denied legal
status for reasons of custom or prejudice; others may forfeit it as the
result of some criminal act.) What is more, Barker continues to insist
that the state, as a group or association, must also be understood in
terms of its own particular purpose. That purpose is what he had
previously called 'law and order', and now refers to simply as 'Law'.
What has changed, however, is his understanding of the relation
between this purpose and the purposes of other groups. For Barker
now accepts that the purpose of the state cannot be compared to the
purposes of other associations. The state exists in order to provide
the legal framework within which other purposes co-exist, be these
the purposes of individuals or of other groups. The state's purpose,
therefore, is to order purposes other than its own. This does not
mean that it creates them. Barker is adamant that legal personality,
though it depends on the state, does not originate in the state, but in
the life that exists independently of it (the 'moral' life). He accepts
that legal persons, like the characters in a play, are the products of
artifice. But in another sense, he claims, they must still be counted as
real, for they reflect the reality of the world in which men live, and
they have an enduring existence only in so far as they reflect that
world accurately. Legal persons, like the players in a drama, have a
life of their own – what Barker calls 'a permanent being'[62] – only
when they are well drawn; the state, like the stage, must 'hold up a
mirror to nature'.[63] Thus Barker is far from advocating a return to
the 'concessionary' views against which Gierke's work was a reaction.
But he is insisting that the world of the state, like the world of the
stage, be recognised for what it is, a world distinct from the world in
which men live, a world created by men to help them make sense of
the world in which they live, a world which exists on its own terms.
Barker will not allow the dramas of individual lives – the psychological and moral dramas which generate individual personalities – to
be confused with the particular drama that is created for legal
persons by the state. Nor will he allow the drama of the state – with
all its pomp and all its circumstance – to be confused with the lives
that individuals, singly or in groups, pursue for themselves. The state
has its own part to play, that of providing the world of psychological
and moral persons with a definite structure where it is needed. No

---

[62] *Ibid.*, p. lxxvi.   [63] *Ibid.*, p. lxx.

other group can do this, and it can only be done through law. It is in this sense, and this sense alone, that Barker understands law, and therefore the state, to be sovereign.

It might be said that this alteration in Barker's views amounts to little more than a change of emphasis. He was always, as we have seen, doubtful about the value of ascribing a necessary, or real, personality to groups. He was also enduringly aware, even before the Great War, that the state had its own necessity, and was in that sense itself a permanent being. But even if only a change of emphasis, Barker's doctrine of the sovereignty of law has a particular historical significance. In his introduction to Gierke, Barker reiterates the concern he had expressed nearly twenty years earlier, that one of the dangers of the doctrine of real group personality was its tendency to slide into syndicalism. He knew very well that Gierke was not a syndicalist, but he believed that the interpretation of Gierke's thought in England had been drawn in that direction, and he cites as evidence Figgis's *Churches in the modern State* (he had by this time made public Figgis's confession to him in the grounds of Mirfield). However, syndicalism was no longer his overriding concern. The theory of the real personality of associations may also, he wrote, 'keep other company'; that is, 'it may trend towards that very doctrine of the absolute State from which it is supposed to be our rescue'.[64] Barker had come to believe that where groups are taken to be real persons, reality itself may be seen as belonging not to a plurality of groups, but to one group that transcends all the rest. This is impossible so long as the state is understood as a merely legal association, existing to provide a framework for the co-existence of merely legal persons. But it is possible, and even probable, where the state is conceived as a real person in its own right, with a mind, and a will, of its own. In Germany, in 1933, the state was being conceived in just these terms, though the actual term most often used was not 'a person' but 'a People', or *Volk*. Gierke was a theorist of the *Volk*. That in itself, Barker knew, did not make him a fascist (his was, in Barker's words, a 'rarefied and qualified doctrine'[65]); but it did leave the doctrine itself open to abuse by those who were. This is just what was to happen in Germany. It was what had already happened in Italy. There, Mussolini's 'Corporative State', while paying lip-service to the idea of the *communitas communitatum*, had soon evolved into the

[64] *Ibid.*, p. lxxxiv.   [65] *Ibid.*, p. lxxxiii.

single *personalità superiore* of the Italian nation-state itself. This, Barker believed, was what was liable to happen whenever the attempt was made to translate the idea of the *communitas communitatum* into practice.[66] Among the English pluralists, the idea of the *communitas communitatum* was in fact most closely associated with the 'syndicalist' Figgis. This does not make Figgis in reality a fascist,[67] any more than it does Althusius, to whom Barker, like Gierke, attributes the idea in its purest form. But it does reveal by how fine a thread the integrity of Gierke's rarefied and qualified doctrine finally hangs.

Barker believed that the job of political philosophy was to describe the means of escape from what he called 'the wilderness and the chaos' of social existence.[68] Chaos is simply anarchy, or the condition of lawlessness. Wilderness, though related to chaos, is something else. It is the condition of excessive legality, when law comes to stifle and eventually to destroy the life that surrounds it. This may happen if the state is especially parsimonious with its grants of legal personality, and the freely formed purposes of men are denied the security of legal recognition. But it may also happen where the legal personality of groups is recognised as something more than it really is, and becomes confused with life itself. Under these circumstances, the way of life of the group – the supreme, transcendent group – swamps and then destroys all other forms of purposive activity. As a pluralist Barker knew that the way of life of the group could never be more that the way of life of one particular group, which as one group among many was nothing more than a contingent expression of the purposes of its members; and as a pluralist Barker had used this knowledge to challenge the idea of state sovereignty. Now he saw the need to challenge the idea of group sovereignty, and the tendency of that idea to make the contingent interests of particular groups politically supreme. The only way of doing this was to rescue the state from the world of contingent interests, and to set it up as the

---

[66] See *ibid.*, p. lxxxv.

[67] Barker does not call Figgis a fascist, but nor does he stop very far short of it. One of the footnotes to his introduction to Gierke reads as follows: 'It will be noticed that Dr Figgis . . . speaks of the theory of real Group-personality as "the essence of what is true in modern nationalism, and in the claims for the rights of Churches and of Trade Unions". Perhaps he was thinking of the claims of national minorities when he used the phrase "modern nationalism". But the phrase may equally apply to the claims of a national majority to control the whole of life' (*ibid.*, p. lxxxiv). It should also be borne in mind that Mussolini, as Barker would have been aware, was quite happy to describe himself as a syndicalist in his youth.

[68] *Ibid.*, p. lxxx.

merely legal arbiter of those interests, with a purpose that, in Barker's own words, 'exists beyond space and time'.[69] In 1914 Barker had wished to work with history against the state. In 1933 the task was to work with the state against history. That, better than anything, tells the story of English political thought during the first third of this century.

[69] *Ibid.*, p. 1.

PART III

The personality of the state

CHAPTER II

The mask of personality

The English political pluralists did not have any especial interest in the work of Thomas Hobbes. They were, of course, aware of him as a theorist of the state, and they were as alarmed by his vision of the state as they were by any. But they did not make any attempt to establish what was distinctive about Hobbes's view of the state, and nor did they recognise that his theory of the state was a theory of group personality also. Instead, they tended to equate his ideas with those of other theorists of state sovereignty, and in doing so to gloss over the ways in which Hobbes's ideas were unique. So Maitland identified Hobbes's conception of the state with the cruder picture provided by Henry VIII, allowing the sovereign of each to be understood simply as the life-giving head of a body politic. Figgis, as a former Austinian, placed Hobbes alongside Bodin, as one of 'the creators of the modern world',[1] though as a former Austinian he preferred not to dwell on this fact; Barker, meanwhile, bracketed Hobbes with Austin himself, seeing each as advocates of what he called the 'bare' theory of state sovereignty. Cole preferred to discount Hobbes altogether, concentrating instead on Rousseau as the likeliest enemy of corporate freedom. And Laski made the clumsiest equation of all, choosing to identify Hobbes's view of freedom with the one produced by Hegel. Among English writers of this period, only Bosanquet came close to Gierke's understanding of what made Hobbes different. But Bosanquet was not a pluralist.

This inability, or unwillingness, to recognise the distinctiveness of Hobbes's theory of the state extends to Barker's introduction to Gierke. There, Barker describes Hobbes as a representative of the 'dual' contract theory of government – 'the first ninety-nine contract, by one sort of contract, with one another; and then they contract, by

---

[1] Figgis, *Gerson to Grotius*, p. 12.

another sort, with a hundredth person'[2] – so failing to acknowledge that it was precisely this sort of double contract that Hobbes's account of persons and things personated was designed to avoid. Hobbes's ninety-nine contract only with one another, not with their sovereign, nor with the Leviathan that their sovereign represents, and when Barker says that 'Leviathan is himself, after all, included in a contractual bracket',[3] he is simply wrong. Nevertheless, there is one sense in which Barker does manage in his introduction to Gierke to engage with Hobbes in a way that none of his fellow pluralists managed. This is in his use of the 'mask' as a metaphor for legal personality. It was pointed out earlier in this book that Hobbes's conception of 'fictions', and indeed of 'authors', has something in common with the more usual literary sense of these terms. But Hobbes would not have thought of literary fictions in the novelistic terms to which we are now accustomed. He would have thought of the theatre. Moreover, it is to the image of the theatre that the third player in Hobbes's account of persons and things personated inevitably points; for alongside the author and the fiction, there is, of course, the 'actor'. Yet it would be wrong to suggest that the theatre simply provides an appropriate metaphor for Hobbes's arguments concerning persons and their representatives. As Barker points out in his introduction to Gierke, the concept of personality does not simply bring to mind the theatre; it actually originated there. The English 'person' comes from the Latin *'persona'*, and the Latin evolved from the Greek, where 'person' originally signified a mask, worn by an actor upon the stage. Thus personality itself was once the metaphor, and its application to what we should now think of as the world of 'personal' affairs depended upon the congruence of that world with the world of the theatre. Individual human beings, and things other than individual human beings, were once only to be understood as persons in so far as their actions might be compared to the action that takes place upon a stage. Barker knew this, and he would have known that Hobbes knew it as well.

We know that Hobbes knew it because he tells us. As he explains in chapter XVI of *Leviathan*:

The word Person is latine: instead whereof the Greeks have πρόσωπον, which signifies the *Face*, as *Persona* in latine signifies the *disguise*, or *outward appearance* of a man, counterfeited on the Stage; and sometimes more

---

[2] Gierke, *Natural law*, p. lxvi.   [3] *Ibid.*

particularly that part of it, which disguiseth the face, as a Mask or Visard: And from the Stage, hath been translated to any Representer of speech and action, as well in Tribunalls, as Theaters. So that a *Person*, is the same that an *Actor* is, both on the Stage and in common Conversation; and to *Personate*, is to *Act*, or *Represent* himself, or an other; and he that acteth another, is said to bear his Person, or act in his name.[4]

The man who did the most to translate the idea of personality from the theatre to the tribunal, and thence to everyday speech, was Cicero,[5] and Hobbes acknowledges this by quoting directly from Cicero to make his point: it is acting, or the playing of parts, that Cicero has in mind, 'where he saies, *Unus sustineo tres Personas; Mei, Adversarii, & Judicis*, I beare three Persons, my own, my Adversaries, and the Judges'.[6] These three persons correspond to the three different types of person that Hobbes has already sought to distinguish: when I act in my own name, I am acting as a natural person; when I act in the name of my adversary, I am acting as an artificial person; and when I act in the name of a judge, I am acting as a fictitious person, for I do not represent one particular man, but all men, or the state. In each case, the performance of an action is equivalent to an act of personation; and whenever I perform an act of personation, what I am doing is putting on a mask.[7]

Barker does not refer to Cicero in his discussion of the theatrical origins of the concept of personality, and nor does he refer to

---

[4] Hobbes, *Leviathan*, p. 112.

[5] In fact, Cicero employed the idea of the *persona* in a variety of different ways when it was taken outside of a strictly legal context. G. W. Allport identifies four in his *Personality, a psychological interpretation* (London, 1938): first, to describe the way that one appears to others (but not how one really is); second, to describe the part that one plays in life; third, to describe an assemblage of personal qualities that fit a man for work; and fourth, to describe a form of distinction or dignity (for example, in a style of speech or writing).

[6] Hobbes, *Leviathan*, p. 112.

[7] Pitkin points out that the source of the quotation that Hobbes uses here makes it somewhat inappropriate. It comes from Cicero's 'On the character of the orator', and it refers to the moment when the orator tries to imagine himself into the various parts that are played out in a legal setting, in order to forearm himself against the arguments he might encounter there. In this sense, Pitkin suggests, there is no representative performance taking place in the Hobbesian sense (i.e. no acting in another's name before an audience), only an imaginative performance inside the orator's head (see H. Pitkin, *The concept of representation* (Berkeley, 1967), pp. 24–5). Pitkin goes on to argue that Hobbes's conception of representation is not, in fact, best understood in theatrical terms. There is something to be said for this view, as we shall see, with regard to the representation by natural persons of artificial persons. However, Pitkin neglects the other sort of representation for which Hobbes allows – the representation by artificial persons of fictitious persons – and in this regard, her account is incomplete. As we shall also see, the representation of fictitious persons by actors does fit the terms of the stage.

Hobbes by name. But in invoking the idea of legal personality as a kind of mask, it is clear that Barker is seeking to reintroduce to the question of group personality the clearcut distinctions which mark its origins, and which were deployed both by Cicero and by Hobbes. In particular, by moving back from the tribunal to the theatre, Barker hopes to raise the two questions on which he believes the whole issue of group personality must turn. First, *to* whom or what does the mask of group personality attach? Second, *by* whom or what is the attaching done? Just how clearcut are the answers that Barker gives to these questions we have already seen: the mask is attached to 'purposes'; the mask is attached by 'law'. Barker's own purpose in giving these answers was to escape from the metaphysical uncertainties of the doctrine of real group personality by emphasising the artifice involved in the attaching of masks, while yet continuing to emphasise that artifice does not entail arbitrariness. The point about masks, for Barker, was that they could be well or poorly drawn, and well or poorly chosen, as a play can be well or poorly written, and well or poorly cast.

Unfortunately, however, these issues are not quite so clearcut as Barker supposed. The two questions that he asks each contain a certain ambiguity, and this ambiguity is brought out if we make explicit the connection that Barker chose not to make, between his account of mask-wearing and mask-giving, and that provided by Hobbes. Barker supposes that the relation between a mask and the 'bearer' of that mask is a relatively simple one, allowing us to seek to identify the particular men or things to which particular masks attach. But Hobbes knew it was more complicated than that, since he knew that a mask may attach to some one or thing in two different ways. On the one hand, a mask may be said to attach to the actor who wears it, and whose words and actions bring the mask to life; on the other hand, it may be said to attach to the particular part that an actor takes himself to be playing, and which the mask itself symbolises. This distinction can be illustrated by means of a simple theatrical example. An actor playing King Lear may feel that the part requires him to wear a crown upon the stage. This crown will have neither the actor's nor the king's name on it, and will in all likelihood have been worn by other actors playing the part of other kings. To whom, in this instance, do we wish to say that the crown is attached? Is it worn by the actor, who provides it with actions, or by Lear, who provides it with a character of its own? Probably, we should want to say both, but we cannot by definition say that it is 'worn' by both in the same way. It is this distinction which gives rise to Hobbes's distinction between artificial and fictitious persons, and between the different sorts of authority required in each case. On the simplest Hobbesian model, an actor wears the mask of a natural person, who is then author. In these circumstances, the author *is* the mask, which then attaches to the actor alone. (The actor may himself be the author, if he speaks in his own name, but this does not alter the basic nature of the relation.) However, on the more complicated model of fictitious personality, the actor wears a mask which has been drawn up by an author in order to allow for the representation of some 'character' – an incapable man, an inanimate thing, a figment – incapable of representing itself. Here, the mask is quite separate from the author, and is attached by the author both to whatever requires representation (the fiction) and to whomever is to do the representing (the actor). It is this form of authority which bears comparison with 'authorship' in the theatre – the dramatist creates the mask which creates the part that the actor is to play. This need not be a mask in any literal sense: the lines an actor is given to speak, just as much as the costume he has to wear, constitute a formal representation of the character it is his task to represent. Thus when an actor delivers a line as Lear, just as when he wears a crown as Lear, we may legitimately ask to whom the words, or crown, are attached. Is the author giving them to the actor, or is he giving them to the part? This is by no means an unanswerable question, but the fact that it is a question to which there is more than one answer is something that Barker chooses to ignore.

The ambiguity contained in Barker's second question – by whom or what are the masks attached? – is of a different kind. As well as supposing that the business of attaching masks is an inherently simple one, Barker also supposes that there is no overlap between the business of attaching masks and the business of wearing them. Yet he accepts that masks, which are attached to associations in so far as they constitute 'purposes', are themselves attached by an association – 'the legal association' – which has its own purpose – 'law'. As a result, it is at least possible to ask whether this association might not require a mask of its own. The answer Hobbes gave to this question was quite clear. His legal association, or commonwealth, does not attach fictitious personality to other associations, for the simple reason that it does not itself do anything; it is, like all associations,

incapable of action in its own right. It is, in other words, nothing but
a mask, which is worn by the actor known as sovereign. The difficulty
with Hobbes's position, as we have seen, is that it is hard to know
how this mask is authorised, since Hobbes insists that the fictitious
personality of associations can only be authorised by the sovereign,
who must already wear the mask of the commonwealth. If Barker's
legal association is itself to be understood as a person, he too must
explain how that personality is to be attained, given the dependence
of legal personality on the prior existence of the state. Of course, he
could choose to deny that his state is itself a person. But if so, he will
then have to explain how it, as an association, is capable of attaching
personality to others. For he has already insisted that associations,
lacking psychological and moral personality, are only capable of
acting in their own right when possessed of legal personality. If the
state lacks such personality, how can it be capable of the action
required to attach personality elsewhere? Barker tells us that the
state is an association, that associations act as legal persons, and that
legal personality is attached to associations by the state. He has
therefore either to tell us what attaches legal personality to the state,
or to tell us what allows the state to act in the absence of such
personality. This he fails to do.

By disregarding these more complex issues in his introduction to
Gierke, Barker effectively discounts the history of English political
thought over the previous thirty-three years. Indeed, it is reasonable
to suggest that if matters had been as clearcut as Barker imagines,
most of the problems which engaged the English pluralists (including
Barker himself) need never have arisen. In fact, English pluralism
arose out of a perceived need to address precisely those questions
which Barker preferred to ignore. The pluralists wished to know
whether groups were capable of producing their own legal personality (i.e. their own masks), and they wished to know whether the
state was also in need of its own legal personality (i.e. a mask of its
own). It is true that their answers to these questions were no more
satisfactory than the answers Barker gives to his. It is also true that by
returning the language of legal personality to its theatrical origins
Barker provides a consistent means of understanding these questions.
But it is not true that the particular use Barker makes of the idea of
the legal drama enables us to make sense of the dilemmas encountered by the pluralists. His approach is too simplistic. Instead, something closer to the complexity of Hobbes's account is required. Only

with the aid of such an account is it possible to make sense of the failure of political pluralism in its own terms.

To move from Barker back to Hobbes is not intended to suggest that Hobbes's solution to the problem of group personality was after all the right one. Rather, it is to suggest that an examination of the gap between Hobbes's solution and Barker's might help explain why the problem proved so intractable. This is what will be attempted in the final part of this book. The theatrical concepts deployed by Barker do open the way for a philosophical overview of the history that has gone before. They only do so, however, if they are used in a more expansive manner than Barker allows. It is necessary to get away from the particular questions posed by Barker – to what is the mask attached? by whom is the mask attached? – and instead to pose two which make better sense in Hobbes's terms. What, we need to know first, does it mean for a group of human beings 'to play a part'? And second, what is the part that is played by the group known as the state?

CHAPTER 12

The mask of the group

I

What do we mean when we speak of an actor playing a part? On the stage, it means that an actor puts on the costume, or utters the words, appropriate to a particular role. But do we want to say that the 'playing' follows from the manner in which the actor moves in his costume, or speaks his words, or do we want to say that it follows from the particular words and the particular movements that the actor is required to perform? Do we, in other words, wish to think of the player taking charge of the part, or of the part taking charge of the player? This is the ambiguity that lies at the heart of the theatrical concept of the *persona*, and it has its roots in the etymology of the term. As both Hobbes and Barker point out, the word *persona*, which originally denoted just the mask worn on stage, soon came, by what Barker calls 'natural transference',[1] to refer also to the actor who wore it. The possession of a *persona*, therefore, might denote one of two conditions: it might refer to the capacity of an actor to perform, or interpret, certain roles; alternatively, it might refer to the particular role it is given to an actor to perform. In the first instance, we recognise the presence of the *persona* on stage in the freedom enjoyed by an actor to interpret a part as he sees fit. In the second instance, we recognise it in the constraints that act upon the actor, binding him to the performance of certain actions. Thus we may say of personality, as of authority, that its possession has no necessary connection with freedom of action. That depends upon the conditions under which it is assumed, and the terms on which it is given.

This uncertainty as to what is involved in the possession of a *persona*, or personality, has come through to contemporary usage.

---

[1] Gierke, *Natural law*, p. lxx.

Though we no longer make the explicit connection between the *persona* and the mask, we continue to use the term 'personality' to conjure up the superficial trappings of public performance – those who live their lives in the public eye are frequently described as 'personalities', and expected to behave in the theatrical manner befitting that term. At the same time, however, we persist in using the idea of the person to provide a contrast to this sense of superficiality. So, for example, the behaviour of a 'personality' may be contrasted with that of 'a real person', and of a particular individual the public personality may be set against 'the person inside'. When it is applied outside of the purely public domain, the term 'personality' is more often used to refer to what is essential in our natures than to what is external – in this regard, it makes perfect sense to speak of our 'personalities' making each of us what we are. Yet even here, in the psychological sphere, an inherent ambivalence remains. Personality, which is commonly used to denote the essence of individuality, may also be used to denote the face that an individual presents to the world. It may still, therefore, be seen as a mask, as it was by Jung, who understood personality to be 'the mask that hides individuality'.[2] For this reason, it remains possible to conceive the relation between psychological personality and an individual's true nature in two entirely different ways: on the one hand, it could be said that an individual's personality is what lies behind his public mask; on the other, it might be argued that it is only by stripping away the mask of personality that we discover the individual within. This double meaning is a reflection of the double meaning that the idea of the *persona* once enjoyed in the theatre, where it described both the mask and the man behind the mask. And it is because of this double meaning that the notion of group personality cannot be explained simply by equating it to the notion of the playing of a part. First of all, we need to decide what we mean when we use that phrase. Are we talking about the part or are we talking about the player?

II

Barker, though he appears not to notice it, ends up talking about both. When he introduces his analogy between the state and the stage, he describes the former as 'a place of legal actors, all of whom

---

[2] Quoted in G. W. Allport, *Personality: a psychological interpretation*, p. 40.

play a role, and each of whom may be called a *dramatis persona*';[3] here, personality belongs to the actor. Later, though, he describes legal personality as 'a mask . . . which is created by an agency, and attached by that agency to an object';[4] here, personality belongs to the mask. It is true that on Hobbes's account there are circumstances in which the same person can be simultaneously mask and actor: this occurs whenever a natural person acts in his own name, thereby ensuring that the person of the representative (the actor) and the person of the represented (the mask) are one and the same. But Barker's account of mask-wearing and mask-giving was intended to distinguish between legal personality and those forms of natural personality (psychological and moral) which belong to the individual alone. He cannot, therefore, equate the actor with the mask, since it was his whole point that legal personality does not belong to the individual, but is attached to individuals and groups by some external agency. Hobbes's actors are persons who wear the mask appropriate to the situation they find themselves in, a mask belonging either to themselves or to another. Barker's actors, meanwhile, are persons only in so far as they are provided with the appropriate mask.

If we look closely at what Barker is saying, it quickly becomes clear that he is saying something very different from Hobbes. Indeed, Barker's account of persons and things personated can be said effectively to reverse the account given in chapter XVI of *Leviathan*. For Barker, legal personality is not something that comes in a series of masks worn by a series of actors. Rather, it is itself *a* mask, or *modus*, which being attached to an actor allows that actor to speak and act in the manner of a legal person. Hobbes's masks allow actors to speak and act in the name of others, which requires that these others be in possession of names; if they are fictions, they must be given names by an author, so that we know on whose behalf the representative acts. But Barker's mask simply enables actors to speak and act in the name of legal personality itself. It is the difference between an actor who wears a crown in order to play the part of King Lear, and an actor who wears a crown simply to play the part of a king. In the first instance, the crown helps us pick out a particular character; in the second, it helps us pick out a particular type of character. So it is with Hobbes's and Barker's masks. For

---

[3] Gierke, *Natural law*, p. lxx.   [4] *Ibid.*, p. lxxi.

Hobbes, the mask binds an actor to the particular person whose words and actions the actor then performs; for Barker, the mask binds the actor to behave as though a person, with the rights and duties appropriate to that role. As a result, the two men arrive at diametrically opposed views of what is entailed by the concept of group personality. Hobbes understands groups to become persons when an artificial person (an actor) puts on the mask of the group. Barker understands groups to become persons when the group (the actor) puts on the mask of artificial personality.

In his introduction to Gierke, Barker uses this definition of group personality to construct an account of corporate freedom. To begin with, he distinguishes between states which are chary in their grant of the mask of legal personality, and those that seek to make it as widely available as possible. Among these latter he would include the English state, which made the mask of legal personality freely available in the 1862 Companies Act, in contrast to those states, like Germany, which remained wedded to the principles of the concession theory. Barker then goes on to distinguish between states which provide only what he calls 'the mask of full corporate personality' for groups, and those that offer to groups a choice of masks or *personae*.[5] Again, the intended contrast is between England, which alongside the mask of the *universitas* could also offer the mask of the trust, and Germany, where, in Barker's words, 'the State was less richly equipped'.[6] Barker's message here is that freedom for groups depends, first of all, on their being able to take part in the legal drama, and second, on there being more than one part available in that drama, as an actor's freedom of expression depends, first of all, on there being parts for him to play, and second, on his being given the part that suits him best.

The trouble with this argument is that the second half of it – the part concerned with varieties of masks – makes no sense in Barker's own terms. Barker's fundamental point is that legal personality is a mask; that is, it is the mask that groups must wear if they are to become *dramatis personae*. How then can it be possible for groups to

---

[5] *Ibid.*, p. lxxii.

[6] *Ibid.* Barker does not mean to suggest that either German language or German law were less richly equipped in their stock of terms to describe the group *per se*. German is notoriously replete with words which signify groups and associations, including *Anstalt, Gemeinschaft, Gesellschaft, Verbinding, Vereinigung, Verband* and so on. Barker's point is that German law, under Roman influence, lacked a variety of means to provide groups with the specific appearance of group persons, and this, of course, was Gierke's feeling as well.

acquire a *persona* by adopting a mask other than that of *the persona*, the mask of legal personality? The answer must be that it cannot, unless we are prepared to confuse, as Barker appears to, the *persona* given by the mask with the *persona* of the actor who wears it. Groups can only wear a variety of masks if they are assumed already to possess the *persona* of an actor, thereby rendering them capable of playing more than one role. Yet Barker insists that groups only become actors in the legal drama when they wear the mask of the legal person. Legal personality is either one of the masks that groups wear on stage, or it is the one mask they wear whenever they appear on stage. It cannot be both.

We can illustrate this point if we return to the example of the actor, the king and the crown. If an actor must (say for convention's sake) wear a crown when he is to play a king, he cannot play a king if he is wearing something other than a crown. Of course, this does not mean that it is impossible for a king to appear on stage wearing any other sort of costume (Lear can still appear in rags, for example). But this will only be possible if we already know that he is a king. It is the same for Barker's groups. If they must wear the mask of personality in order to be persons, then no other mask will do. If they are to wear other masks, it must be because we already know them to be persons. Yet Barker tells us of no way to recognise groups as persons unless we see them in the mask of legal personality. What results, unsurprisingly, is a thoroughly confused argument, something that is best illustrated with the aid of Barker's own example, that of the trust. A trust, as Maitland knew only too well, did not turn a group into a person. Indeed, it was the whole point of trusteeship that groups were considered incapable of acting in the manner of persons, which is what required the appointment of trustees to act in their interests. It is therefore impossible to see how a group might be said to adopt the *persona* of a trust, since the ability to adopt any such *persona* would negate the very need for trusteeship. It is, instead, a separate group of individuals who separately adopt the *persona* of trustees, and they are able to do so precisely because each is already a person in his own right. Barker tries to tie the idea of the trust into his general conception of masks by invoking Maitland's celebrated remark that the trust is a form of 'screen',[7] behind which all manner of group activities can take place. But all he achieves by doing so is to

---

[7] See *ibid.*

reveal how careful one has to be in the use of this sort of language. For while it is true that a screen is a form of mask, it is not a mask in anything like the sense that Barker has been using the term. A screen masks merely by concealing what is behind it; it does not mask by providing representation for the actor who stands behind it. Both the costumes that actors wear in the course of a drama, and the curtain that comes down at the end, may be said to provide 'masks' for the action. But whereas one helps us to understand what is taking place on stage, the other tells us that what is taking place on stage is no longer our business. It was as an aid to concealment, not as an aid to comprehension, that Maitland understood the trust to operate.

If we wish to use the theatrical origins of the concept of the person to make sense of the arguments of Maitland, and others, we need to get away from Barker's view that legal personality is itself a mask, and return instead to Hobbes's view that legal persons are separate masks, separately worn by the artificial persons who represent them. Once seen in these terms, it becomes clear, as it was to Hobbes, that the important questions about group personality are neither which mask, nor how many masks, but rather where the masks are drawn up, and how. And this becomes even clearer if we use Hobbes's account of mask-wearing and mask-giving, rather than Barker's, to attempt to distinguish between the freedoms enjoyed by groups in various kinds of states.

The three kinds of state we need to distinguish are the concessionary state (seen by Barker as the state with one, infrequently dispensed mask), the liberal state (seen by Barker as the state with one, frequently dispensed mask), and the state that also makes provision for trusts (seen by Barker as the state with more than one mask). In Hobbes's terms, the concessionary state is one in which masks are only provided for groups by one, particular author. In theatrical terms, we may say it is comparable to a stage on which a single dramatist puts on his own plays. This implies no necessary limit as to the number of parts that may be drawn up; but it does suggest that no part will be drawn up unless the dramatist considers it appropriate to the drama he wishes to produce. In a liberal state, meanwhile, masks can be drawn up as and when there is a demand. The theatrical analogy for this would be a stage on which the drama is put together by all those involved in the drama, and who wish to see particular parts being performed. Again, this does not tell us anything about the number of parts that may be played (many people may decide that they have no interest in the production); but it does tell us that the drama itself will be entirely conditioned by the wishes of those who expect to be involved, whether on stage, back stage or simply in the audience. The liberal state might not provide for the most compelling theatre. But this will be compensated for by the sense of involvement shared by all those who choose to participate.

The case of the state which allows groups to be organised around a deed of trust is somewhat different. Because groups represented by trustees are not persons, there is no place for trusts in Hobbes's account of persons and things personated. Nevertheless, it is still possible to find a theatrical analogy for what is involved. Actors performing on the stage do not always need to represent a particular character in order to be seen to act. When a drama is wholly improvised, the actors may give the impression of acting out a part merely by dint of the actions they perform. So it is with trustees, who do not represent any one or thing in particular, but are able to give the impression that they do simply by performing their own actions in a particular manner. In improvised drama, unlike in dramas of a more conventional kind, everything depends upon the act itself, such that we can know nothing about the characters in the drama until we have seen it being performed. Similarly, we can only say something about the personality of a trust's beneficiary once we have seen the manner in which the trustees act. Of course, trustees, like improvising actors, cannot be allowed to do anything they like, and if their performance is to be convincing it will have to be adapted to the expectations of the audience that witnesses it. But trustees can create the part that they are playing – the mask that they seem to represent – as they go along. A state that includes trusts as well as corporations is like a stage that allows for the production of unscripted dramas alongside the production of scripted ones.

What these analogies demonstrate is that a coherent account of the various freedoms enjoyed by groups cannot concern itself simply with varieties of masks – a great many masks do not necessarily equate with a great amount of freedom, since it is possible to have a large number of corporations within what remains a concessionary state. Nor, *pace* Barker, can a coherent account seek to identify one particular agency with whom the distribution of masks rests, and on whom all freedom is taken to depend. The sorts of freedoms Barker wishes to distinguish do not depend on one author, but on whether the drama has only one author, more than one author, or possibly even no author at all. It is this that determines the nature and availability of legal personality. Thus what matters for groups is not the distribution of masks as such. What matters is the type of drama in which they are going to appear.

III

Barker's attempt to equate the liberality of states with the availability of the mask of legal personality makes little enough sense on its own terms. It makes even less sense if we remember that Barker intended it to form part of an introduction to the ideas of a theorist who believed group personality to be real. Barker's account of groups and their *personae* makes it impossible to understand why Gierke, or anyone else, should have bothered themselves with the issue of real group personality, since Barker's account makes it clear that un-limited freedom is quite compatible with the distribution of masks, or fictitious personality. If a group can acquire legal personality simply by donning the relevant mask, what complaint can a champion of group freedom and group identity have against a state that makes this mask available to any group that wants it? Yet, as we have seen, this was precisely the point at issue for Gierke and for his English followers. They did not accept that a state which offered legal personality to all groups was an adequate substitute for a state in which all group personality was understood to be something real. It was this insistence on something more than mere accessibility which made their thought distinctive, but nothing Barker says in his introduction to Gierke explains why they should have felt the need to insist on it at all.

We can explain it, though, if we revert to the account of groups and their *personae* borrowed from Hobbes. On that account, group freedom can be seen to depend not just on the accessibility of masks but on the type of drama in which those masks were to play a part. Different dramas are capable of generating different kinds of freedom, yet it remains true that in each case the freedom enjoyed by any particular group can never be said to depend upon the group itself. In Hobbes's preferred state – the concessionary state – all freedoms inevitably rest with the author of the drama, who is sovereign. But even in a liberal state, where groups acquire masks as and when desired, it is not the groups themselves who do the acquiring; rather, it is done for them by those individuals who have decided to provide the group with a personality of its own. Nor does the group wear the mask itself; it is worn for it by an actor, its appointed representative. The group itself does nothing, which is what makes it a fiction, and depends for everything on the natural persons (its members) who give it a mask and the artificial person (its representative) who wears it. In a state, meanwhile, which allows a group's interests to be handled by trustees, everything comes to depend upon the actors alone. Where they are skilled, they may create a very clear impression of the group in whose interests they act; but as in an improvised drama, if the acting is bad, the spell may soon be broken, leaving nothing behind but the exposed persons of the actors themselves. And it was this that provided Maitland with his complaint against the trust – not that it was illiberal, or inaccessible, or impractical, but that it was an *ad hoc*, or haphazard, business, depending too heavily in each instance on both the standards of the actors and the tolerance of the audience. Likewise, Maitland's objections to the kind of liberal legislation exemplified by the 1862 Companies Act did not turn on the issue of group freedom *per se*, but on the question of the people in whom it was vested: he could hardly complain that the 1862 Act was limiting in its effect on corporate life; but he could complain that it left the crucial decisions in the wrong hands, relying on the individuals who made up a particular group to invent for it a corporate personality, rather than relying for such personality on the group itself. As Maitland had discovered, inviting people to incorporate their associative activities in the formal drama of the state was not the same as ensuring that everyone and everything is represented there. The doctrine of real group personality was designed to ensure that groups would be freed from their dependence on authors and actors, however liberally disposed those authors and actors might be. It was designed to ensure all groups a place on the stage in their own right.

The doctrine of real group personality was also designed, as we know, to take issue with Hobbes's doctrine of persons and their representatives. Hobbes was quite clear that groups could only be secured of their own personality if other persons – natural or artificial – were prepared to secure it for them. Maitland, like Gierke, was adamant that groups, *qua* groups, must secure it for themselves. Thus where Hobbes saw group personality as a mask, with a separate author and actor, Gierke and Maitland saw the group person, or mask, as author and actor in its own right. In historical terms, this meant a departure from Hobbesian, or Roman, views of group personality, and it was hardly surprising that Gierke and those who followed him chose to abandon the notion of personality as a mask altogether. In conceptual terms, however, it does nonetheless remain possible to make sense of the doctrine of real group personality in Hobbesian terms – that is, in the language of 'authors', 'actors' and 'masks'. For it is important to remember that Hobbes did allow for masks to be their own authors and their own actors, if only when they are worn by the natural person that they represent. A natural person is, as a person, a mask, but is also, as a natural person, author and actor of the words and actions performed in that mask. We may therefore say of real group persons that if they are to be both the mask, and the author of, and actor in, the mask, they must possess their masks in the manner that natural persons possess theirs. Once seen in these terms, it becomes clear that the central question is precisely the question that Barker's account of mask-wearing and mask-giving begs. How can a group, whose personality is given in a mask, also be the person responsible for what is done in that mask? And it also becomes clear that the answer to this question depends on the answer to another. How can a natural person, whose personality is given in a mask, also be the person who is responsible for what is done in that mask? In other words, if natural persons are masks, where do the masks of natural personality come from?

The answer is that they come from life: the masks of natural persons are described in the lives that they lead. When a man speaks for himself, he speaks for the person who chooses what is said, such that the mask that he wears is indistinguishable from the words and actions that he performs. If we wish to recognise the mask, we can look only to the words and actions performed in it. This is not to suggest that the masks of natural persons are improvised – improvisation involves the attempt by an actor to create the impression of a separate *persona* distinct from his own. The masks of natural persons create no impression beyond the impression created by the actions of the actor himself. Of course, on Hobbes's account, natural persons can be represented by artificial persons, in which case the actor will be wearing a natural mask which is not his own. But even here, we will only be able to identify the mask if we have some awareness of the actions performed – the life lived – by the natural person to whom it belongs. If one man threatens another in the name of a third, the threat will be understood to belong not just to a name, but to a person we associate with certain actions (that is how we make sense of the threat). If the ownership of a threat is understood without reference to the actions of the author, it will be because it has been issued on behalf of something that is just a name – a fictitious person rather than a natural one. And a threat will only be issued on behalf of a person that cannot act if some other person or persons have established the terms on which actions can be performed for them. The difference between natural personality and fictitious personality is that the masks of natural persons are described in their actions, while the masks of fictitious persons are described in the constraints that act on the persons who represent them.

A number of things follow from this distinction. First, it is only the natural person concerned who can truly know what is represented by the mask of their own natural personality. That mask will be set out over the course of a life-time, and it is only those who have seen it described over the course of a life-time who can recognise it with certainty. For natural persons, it is life itself that is the drama, and the drama of each life will be different. Many others will receive many different glimpses of each life, but none can be sure of what the mask represents unless they have seen it all. Where there is doubt about what is represented by the mask of a fictitious person, certainty can be achieved by referring to the 'letters' or 'laws' by which that personality is authorised. But where there is doubt about what is represented by the mask of a natural person, certainty can only be achieved by referring to the life that that person has led. Second, natural personality, in this sense, can only belong to individuals who are capable of perceiving their lives as a kind of dramatic unity. If the actions of an individual are essentially disconnected – if they are instinctive rather than intended, sequential rather than consequential – it will prove impossible for anyone to describe accurately what is being represented by the mask of natural personality. Behind the mask there will be nothing but a fragmentary or disjointed *persona*. Natural personality requires purposive actions to be related to a sense of personal identity, and it was for this reason that Hobbes did not consider children, madmen or fools to be natural persons.[8] Thus what Hobbes calls natural persons must be what Barker calls 'moral' ones. Finally, if groups are to be possessed of masks, or *personae*,

[8] This is, of course, an argument relating only to responsibility for actions. It has no bearing on the question of the rights of children, madmen or fools – Hobbes allowed that these might be turned into fictitious persons precisely so that they could be afforded rights under the law.

comparable to the masks, or *personae*, of natural persons, it must be because they too are capable of generating personality out of the actions that they perform. Groups can only be persons as individuals can be persons if they are capable of acting out their own, personal dramas.

The question of whether a group can act out a drama of its own making must be distinguished from the question that asks simply whether a group can act. Even Hobbes allowed that groups could act, since he accepted that assemblies could be artificial persons, acting on behalf of others. In the same way, there can be no doubt that groups of individuals are capable of playing a single part on the stage – the chorus in classical theatre constitutes a single role despite the fact that it is played by a group of actors. However, what the Hobbesian assembly and the classical chorus have in common is a strict reliance on the conventions of representation in order to be able to act – the actors who play the chorus must speak in unison, and though the members of an assembly need not literally do likewise, they will have to fall back on the convention of majority voting if they are to be able to speak with a single voice. The doctrine of real group personality demands something more than this. It demands that groups act for themselves. For it is the whole point of the doctrine of real group personality that groups should not be forced to rely on formally constituted representatives, be those representatives individuals or assemblies, but should instead be represented by the things that they do. It is true that Hobbes allows for the same group of individuals to be both representer and represented, as when a corporation is represented by an assembly made up of all its members. What he does not allow is that these two groups should be considered the same – one is artificial, built out of the conventions of majority decision-making, the other fictitious, described in letters whose authority comes from elsewhere. The doctrine of real group personality insists that they really are the same, that it is the represented group that is responsible for representing itself. And if this is to be so, then the represented group must be able to act independently of the actions of its authorised representatives, with a life, and character, all of its own.

In the case of the *personae* of the theatre, the idea that they may have a life of their own, apart from the life that is given to them by author and actor, is not uncommon. We can, and often do, think of the characters in Shakespearean drama existing outside of the plays in which they appear.[9] So, for example, it is possible to imagine King Lear as a person existing apart from formal acts of representation, and therefore to imagine him capable of various forms of action in his own right. But can we imagine King Lear capable of the specific action demanded of natural persons, which is the act of representation itself? Can we, in other words, imagine King Lear playing the part of King Lear, as natural persons play their own parts in the course of their natural lives? It is the distinctive attribute of natural persons that they can assume responsibility for the actions performed in their name by performing those actions themselves. Yet it makes no more sense to think of King Lear assuming responsibility for the playing of King Lear than it does to think of King Lear taking over the role of Hamlet. The one part cannot play the other, because every part must be played itself. This is how we recognise the part to be a fiction. So, when we imagine Lear to have a life of his own, what we are doing is nothing more than constructing our own representation of Lear. We know it is nothing more than a representation because it is impossible to imagine how our imagined Lear would take over the part, or any other part, for himself.

What is true of King Lear would seem to be true of groups also. We can imagine groups leading lives of their own, but it is very hard to imagine a group taking charge of its own life. What we are imagining is simply a representation of the group, and we know it is a representation because it is impossible to imagine the group representing anything else. Thus what we are doing when we picture, say, a church leading a life of its own is in fact to picture a life *for* that church. We cannot imagine how the church might take control of that life because we cannot imagine what the church is without the picture we have painted of it. This is in direct contrast to what happens when we picture the life of a natural person: then, the natural person may prove by their actions that the picture is the wrong one. A church cannot do this – however hard its representatives may try – because without the picture we have of the church we cannot recognise what it is for the church to act. So, for example, when the Free Church of Scotland became divided about what

<hr />

[9] 'Much has been written during the past two hundred years about the 'characters' of Shakespeare, and the persons of his plays, the *dramatis personae*, have been considered as though they had a life of their own, could exist outside the play, with a life before the play begins and after it ends' (G. Williams, *Person and persona: studies in Shakespeare* (Cardiff, 1981), p. 1).

constituted the life of that church, it was not a dispute that the church could resolve by some action of its own. What constituted such action was precisely the ground of dispute, and it could only be resolved by some outside authority deciding between the different representations of the church provided by the competing parties. The church itself was no more capable of taking a decision of this kind than Lear himself might be capable of deciding between the competing claims of two actors trying to represent him. That is what makes the personality of the church a fiction.

It is this, then, that constitutes the fallacy of the doctrine of real group personality, that it confuses our ability to imagine groups having their own personality with the ability of groups to decide that personality for themselves. Were we willing to attribute the ability to make such decisions to the products of our imagination, the fallacy would disappear. A willingness to do just that – to attribute self-consciousness to the products of our consciousness – is one of the characteristics of the highest forms of idealism. It is therefore only the highest forms of idealism that can save the doctrine of real group personality. Only if we are prepared to attribute a sense of personal identity not just to individuals like ourselves, but to the individuals imagined by individuals like ourselves (or, alternatively, to accept that all individuals like ourselves are merely imagined by ourselves, a variant on the highest forms of idealism), will it be possible to conceive of groups acting in their own name. If we think in these terms, it will also be possible to conceive of King Lear acting in his own name – Lear playing the part of Lear – and also to conceive of Lear acting in another's name – Lear playing the part of Hamlet. However, it must be said that once we are prepared to accept that Shakespeare's Lear is capable of playing the part of Shakespeare's Hamlet, we will be prepared to accept anything.

IV

There remains one further aspect of Barker's argument to be considered. In describing legal personality as a mask, Barker points out that it is a mask worn by individuals as well as by groups. Because it is a mask, it may be counted a kind of fiction – Barker concedes that 'the term *persona ficta* is not altogether wrong'[10] – yet if

---

[10] Gierke, *Natural law*, p. lxii.

we wish to call it a fiction, we must be prepared to render fictitious the legal personality of individuals as well as groups. Barker is prepared to do this, and he cites as evidence the large numbers of individuals, including all slaves, who have at one time or another been denied legal personality by their states to support his contention that even the legal personalities of individual citizens are 'judicial creations, or artifices, or fictions'.[11] However, he did not make this point in order to show up the ephemeral quality of the legal status enjoyed by individual men and women (particularly, one might say, women). He made it in order to show that although in some sense a fiction, the legal personality of groups was just as substantial, just as tangible, as the legal personality of individuals – that it was, in another sense, just as real. This was not a point that Barker chose to press, concerned as he was to maintain his distance from the doctrine of real group personality in all its forms. Nevertheless, it is an important one, for it suggests that it might yet be possible to construct a modified case for the doctrine of real group personality on the basis of our understanding of the legal personality of individuals. If we think that personality sufficiently tangible to count as something more than a fiction, then we will have to think the same of the personality of groups.

A case of just this kind is alluded to by Barker, and discussed by Gierke, in the pages of *Natural law and the theory of society*. This was the argument put forward by the German jurist Samuel Pufendorf (1632–94), who contended that although natural personality (in a narrow, physical sense) could only belong to the natural man, moral personality could belong both to individuals and to groups. Pufendorf understood moral personality to be a *modus*, or form of mask, yet he was also clear that it did not constitute a *persona ficta*, since that term applied only when a mask was attached to some wholly inappropriate object. (Barker gives as an example of a *persona ficta* in Pufendorf's sense the *modus* that was granted by Caligula to one of his horses when he made it senator.[12]) True – which is to say 'real' – moral personality comes into being whenever the appropriate mask is ascribed to some object capable of being accommodated in a rational scheme of understanding. The ideal scheme of understanding, for Pufendorf, was a legal system, and within a legal system could be accommodated both the *persona moralis simplex* (the individual) and the *persona moralis*

---

[11] *Ibid.*   [12] See *ibid.*, p. 119.

composita (the group). In so far, therefore, as the law is able to think of groups acting in the manner of moral persons, we should be able to think of their personality as something real.

However, Pufendorf's argument is far more complex and far more subtle than any brief summary here can convey. It borrowed from both the Germanic tradition championed by Gierke and the Roman tradition exemplified by Hobbes (for which reason Gierke remained unconvinced by it[13]), and thereby arrived at a conception of personality which cannot easily be assimilated to any other. For present purposes, a simpler and more serviceable instance of this sort of argument is the one given in Patrick Duff's *Personality in Roman private law*, which was published five years after Barker published his edition of Gierke. Though Duff's book is concerned only with the theory of the person produced by the Romans – the author concluding that there was no theory, only a series of practical applications – it does attempt, like Barker's, to set out the background to some more recent English arguments concerning the personality of associations. Like Barker, Duff is reluctant to come down on the side of one or other of the competing theories, preferring to suggest that the whole truth of group personality was no more to be contained by a single English theory than it was by a single Roman one. Nevertheless, he was prepared to make one substantive claim regarding the vexed question of whether or not group persons might be thought of as 'real'. English followers of Gierke, from Maitland onwards, had presupposed that although the fiction theory need not imply the concession theory, the concession theory necessarily implies the fiction theory. Duff entirely reverses this line of reasoning. He suggests that although 'a Fictionist must believe in the need of Concession to insist on Concession . . . does not imply a belief in Fictionism'.[14] The first of these contentions, for which Duff offers no evidence, is in fact false, since it is quite possible, as we have seen, to regard the 1862 Companies Act as an instance of fictionism while still regarding it as making a break with the

---

[13] Gierke argued that the *persona moralis composita* could not be strictly equivalent to the *persona moralis simplex*, since Pufendorf insisted that the former still had to be built out of the latter – that is, it had to be built out of individuals, by means of contracts. Gierke's judgment on Pufendorf is essentially the same as his judgment on the other great Germanist of natural law theory, Althusius, and he suggests that 'the individualistic basis of [Pufendorf's] thought prevents him from achieving anything more than a purely formal assimilation of the group-person to the individual' (*ibid.*, p. 120).

[14] P. W. Duff, *Personality in Roman private law* (Cambridge, 1938), p. 235.

concession theory. In support of the second, however, Duff writes as follows:

To a student of Roman law it must be obvious that legal Personality can be at once real and conceded; for he has a clear example plainly before his eyes. The State could confer 'legal' personality on a slave; in early Rome all manumission was controlled by the State, but there was nothing fictitious about a freedman's personality. All Personality at Rome was created, and created by the State, except that of a *civis Romanus ingenuus*, but no-one could deny that a freedman was a real Person.[15]

What is true of individuals, Duff implies, can be true of groups as well.

This argument is one that clearly fits the model outlined by Barker. Legal personality is effectively understood by Duff as a mask – as a 'character' or 'mode' – which is given out by the state to such individual objects as it sees fit. These objects must be real, it is implied, because the state will only attach the mask of personality to such objects as it understands to be real. It is the reality of the man who wears the mask – the freed slave – who makes for the reality of the personality that is given by it. Certainly, this is an argument that makes better sense in Barker's terms than it does in Hobbes's. The citizens in Hobbes's commonwealth do not have the mask of personality granted to them by their sovereign, acting in the name of the state; rather, they grant their own personalities to the sovereign in order that he might act in the name of the state. The individuals who do have their personality granted to them by the sovereign (children, madmen, fools) are in receipt of this concession precisely because they have no real personality of their own – their personality is a fiction. Here, the concession theory certainly implies the fiction theory. All other individuals within Hobbes's state already possess their own personality, which when represented by the sovereign commits them to act in accordance with the sovereign's commands. As a result, there can be no distinction in a Hobbesian commonwealth between freedmen and slaves, since there are no persons within the commonwealth who may be said to lack a legal personality. The children, madmen and so on who depend upon the state for legal personality are not slaves, because they are not persons in the first place – it is meaningless to think of them being deprived of something they cannot by definition possess for themselves. No other individual can be counted a slave, because all other individuals are in

[15] *Ibid.*, pp. 235–6.

the same legal position, committed where required to act in accordance with the actions of their sovereign, and where not, free to do as they please. Moreover, as Hobbes makes quite clear, when required by the sovereign to perform some action which will result in the loss of personality (for example, to submit oneself to death in battle), the individual is at liberty to resist. It is this that makes Hobbes, despite everything, a liberal, at least so far as individuals are concerned.

Duff's argument holds for slaves. The fact that it holds for slaves, however, does not in itself tell us that it holds for groups as well. Indeed, Duff's argument only holds for slaves because we are willing to think of slaves as persons who have been denied their personality. If it is to hold for groups it must be because we are also willing to think of groups as persons denied their personality. Yet this is the very point at issue, and it is at issue because, as Hobbes demonstrates, it is possible to think of groups in quite different terms, as being something other than persons, and as having a personality not given to, but invented for them. Duff fails to address this point, and because he fails to address it, he fails to provide any reason for supposing that what is true of slaves is true of groups. That would require something more, some concrete evidence that groups, like slaves, are to be understood as persons-in-waiting, rather than being understood, like children, madmen and fools, as persons only by a fiction of law.

The truth is that Duff, like Barker, has failed to recognise that there is more than one way of understanding the business of mask-wearing and mask-giving, and that therefore there is more than one way of understanding the act of concession. On the one hand, concession can be seen as the business of granting to some one or thing permission to act in the manner of a person. Here, the concession is to the actor, whom we must understand to be real if the mask of personality is to be worn at all. On the other hand, concession can be seen as the business of granting to some one or thing the pretence of their own personality, thereby enabling an actor to act for them. Here, the concession is to whomever or whatever the actor represents, and we must understand it as a fiction, if only to explain the need for an actor to represent it. In the first instance, the state has to decide whether or not it wants a particular actor to wear the mask of personality. In the second instance, the state has to decide whether or not it wants the mask of a particular person to be worn at all. It is the difference between allowing an actor to play the part of a king, and looking for an actor to play the part of King Lear. It is also, in theory at least, the difference between conceding personality to slaves and conceding personality to groups.

Both these means of granting personality are examples of concession because in each case it is left to the state to decide how many persons there should be within the state. The significance of the difference between them becomes more apparent if we look to see what happens when the state renounces its ability to make this decision. On Duff's model, it must be supposed that when the state ceases to concede personality, it allows the mask of personality to be attached automatically to all who are capable of wearing it. Certainly this is what happens when a state abolishes slavery. Of course, decisions will still have to be made concerning the nature of legal personality – the rights and duties of legal persons vary from state to state (Roman freedmen do not bear the same legal personality as British citizens) – and decisions will still have to be made about those individuals (children and so on) who are incapable of bearing the rights and duties of legal persons. But the state will no longer be in the business of creating legal persons where once there were none. On the Hobbesian model, however, the state that renounces concessionary activity continues to be involved in the business of creating persons. This is because, on the Hobbesian model, there are no persons-in-waiting to whom legal personality can automatically be ascribed. When the state renounces its ability to concede personality it simply renounces its right to determine (in letters) when fictitious persons are invented. It has still to answer the question of how they are to be invented; in other words, it has still to decide how legal persons are to be recognised (in laws). When the mask of legal personality is understood to belong to all actors in the state, we can recognise all actors as persons before we know what is represented by the mask of legal personality. But when all actors in the state are understood to wear the mask of particular persons, we cannot recognise those persons until we know what the masks represent. Therefore, even when the Hobbesian state decides not to draw up any masks itself, a decision still has to be made about the persons that the masks represent. And this is why it is possible to have a fiction theory which is not also a theory of concession. A state may decide, as the British state decided in 1862, that it no longer wishes to set limits to the number of groups that can become persons in law.

After 1862, any group could become a corporation. But this did not mean that the mask of corporate personality could simply be attached to any group. The state still had to create an identity for groups that would be represented as corporations – a name, an address and so on – and it still had to insist that an identity of this kind would only be given to those groups that accorded with the principles of group activity laid down by the state ('seven persons associated for any lawful purpose'). The 1862 Act did not present groups with corporate personality; it showed them what they would have to do if they wanted to invent one.

It could be said that the state – any state – does exactly the same for individuals, insisting on a name, an address, a formal identity in law. But in so far as states do create the identity of individuals, what they are creating are fictions. Duff cannot argue that the personality of the Roman freedman is real if it is also true that that personality belongs simply to a name. The personality of the freedman is real only because it, like his name, attaches to something real, something that we can identify apart from the mask. If Duff's argument is to apply to groups, therefore, it must be because the identity of the group is similarly clear. However, if we look to the arguments that have surrounded the idea of group personality, we can see that it is the question of group identity that causes the most problems. For example, the Scottish Church case of 1900–4, to fit with Duff's model, would have to turn on the issue of whether or not a particular group was to be recognised as a person. It did not. It turned on the question of which of two groups was to be recognised as a particular person – the person of the Free Church of Scotland. The state had to decide with which of these groups that person was to be identified. The incident in the history of the Church of Scotland which appears better to fit Duff's model is the Disruption of 1843, when a group within the church sought to break away as a group in its own right. But though the group succeeded, it did not succeed on Duff's terms. The Free Church of Scotland was not a group seeking the legal status of a person (it did not at all wish to become a corporation); it was a group seeking personal legal identity, and it was granted that identity by the state, in law. We know it was granted by the state, in law, because it was to the state that the competing parties went sixty years later in order to have the question of that identity resolved. Of course, it could be argued, as it was at the time, that the church should have been provided with an identity which allowed it to decide its identity for itself. But as the Kedroff case demonstrated, even an identity of that kind – even the most open-ended of all identities – is simply another kind of invention.

Duff's argument does not work as it stands. Groups are not obviously comparable to freedmen and slaves. Were they to be, it would have to be demonstrated that a group has a real identity comparable to that of the individual man. There are two ways this could be done. It might be argued that groups are capable of having their identities determined apart from the law, and of coming before the law as potential persons in their own right. There is some truth in this. We are all capable of ascribing an identity to a group – a family, a football club, a church, a nation – without the help of the state. The difficulty is that there is no reason to suppose that without the help of the state the identity we ascribe to any group will be the same. The alternative is to argue that even the real identity of individuals is determined by the personality given them by the state. In this way it could be claimed that the freedman, though real enough in his own right, nevertheless has no identity apart from the *persona* that is given to him by the state. It would then be possible to argue that groups, constituted as they are by real things – real human beings, real buildings, real activities – have their real identities determined by the *persona* that is jointly attached to those things by the state. So, for example, the identity of a group would be fixed by the fact that it is a corporation, as the identity of a man might be fixed by the fact that he is a citizen. The difficulty with this argument is that it requires that legal personality will have to do more than simply condition how individuals act. It will have to determine who they are. To be a citizen, as to be a corporation, will not simply be to be provided with a mode of action; it will be to be told what actions to perform, what to say, what to do, what to be. The part will have to take over the player, so that the player can have no existence apart from the part, and law will become the whole of life. In this respect, Barker was quite correct. Even in modified form, the prospects offered by the doctrine of real group personality are still those of chaos or wilderness.

CHAPTER 13

The mask of the state

I

We have dealt with what Barker calls the 'objects' to which masks attach. What, then, of what he calls 'the attaching agency', the state? Initially, Barker is happy to describe all the state as a stage, just as he is to describe all the persons within it as actors treading across its boards. The literal image of the stage, however, is rather too passive to convey that sense of agency on which Barker's idea of the state depends. So he extends his analogy to take in those agents – the dramatist and the producer – with whom responsibility for the staging of any drama rests, and he compares the tasks that are faced by these two with the tasks faced in the production of legal performances by the legislator and the judge respectively.[1] In this sense, Barker attempts to identify the state not just with the site of the legal drama but with the business of staging it. There is, though, a further extension of this theatrical imagery for which Barker has to allow. Although he chooses not to dwell on this point, he notes that there are occasions on which the state has itself to appear in the guise of a legal person. This will happen whenever there is the need to hold the state responsible in law for the performance of particular actions, whether in the private sphere (say, the repayment of debts) or in the public (say, the punishment of criminals). What Barker does not explain is how this can happen. How can the state be provided with a mask of its own? On Barker's own account, the state is responsible not in law but for it, for the staging of the drama rather than for the playing of a particular part in the play. It is this that allows him to call the state a stage, since it is the role of the state to make it possible for others to act out the parts that are assigned to

[1] See Gierke, *Natural law*, p. lxxi.

them. Yet if the state is to be a legal person, the stage has somehow to rise up and walk across its own boards. The state, which is a stage, has to play a part on the stage that is the state.

In the theatre, almost anything is possible. Actors can appear on stage disguised as parts of the scenery, only to come to life when the action requires. The individuals responsible for the drama – the dramatist, the producer, the stage manager and so on – can also take part as actors, assuming any and every role as they see fit. Alternatively, a drama may contain within it parts entitled 'dramatist', 'producer' etc., each to be played by a different, or even the same, actor – there is absolutely no reason why a stage should not have performed on it a representation of the production of a play. One thing, however, is not possible. The person or persons who are responsible for a drama can never appear on stage in the guise in which they are responsible for it. If a playwright takes part in one of his own plays, we do not see him on stage as the playwright, but rather in whatever role within the drama he has chosen to adopt. If an actor appears on stage in the role of 'playwright', we do not see him performing in the role of the playwright who was responsible for the drama in which the role appears. This is true even if the role is taken by the playwright himself. No character can appear on stage to take responsibility for the drama in which that character is involved; were this to happen, the drama would collapse. For it is, as we have seen, impossible to imagine a character in a drama in the act of drawing up his own part, just as it is impossible to imagine one character in a drama coming to play the part of another. Once we are shown on stage the means by which the drama has been brought to the stage – the mechanics of the production, the artifice behind the fiction – what we are witnessing is no longer the drama itself, simply an explanation of it.

Therefore, if the part of dramatist is to be included within the drama, it will have to follow that the dramatist is not responsible for the drama in which he appears. If we see the part of 'playwright' being performed on stage, and the character in the act of writing parts for a play, it must be assumed that he is writing parts for another play, and that what we are witnessing is the creation of a drama within the drama. Once this is established, then absolutely anything is possible – it will even be possible for King Lear to play the part of Hamlet, if the production of the one play comes somehow to include within it a portrayal of the production of the other.[2] But this will only be possible because the play within the play is simply part of a wider drama, and it is those who are responsible for the wider drama who are ultimately responsible for the secondary one as well. This is the difficulty with any attempt to portray the state as a legal person in Barker's terms. If the state is to have a part in the legal drama, it must follow that there is a wider drama than the one produced by the state. Yet it is the state, and the state alone, which Barker understands to be responsible for the legal drama as a whole. The dilemma is clear. If the legal drama is simply a play within a play, something needs to be said about where ultimate responsibility for the drama lies. Yet without ultimate responsibility for the legal drama, it is no longer clear what role is left for the state. After all, once the scenery starts to move, it ceases to be scenery; that role is taken on by whatever forms the backdrop to the movements that follow.

This dilemma is by no means unique to Barker. The best illustration of it is provided by Hobbes. Within the Hobbesian commonwealth, the sovereign is unquestioned author of whatever legal drama takes place there. No legal persons can come into being except on the authority of the sovereign, with the result that all performances undertaken in the name of such persons must ultimately depend on the authority of the sovereign. This is the condition of juristic order: no part will be represented on stage unless the sovereign has decided it belongs there. What this ensures is that the legal drama will, if nothing else, be orderly – there will be no confusion about who is responsible for it, nor about what can and cannot be seen on stage. What juristic order cannot ensure, however, is that the drama will be a good one. It may be, of course: a good author will seek to have portrayed on stage parts that are both well drawn and well matched, flexible enough to suit their actors and

---

[2] The idea of the play within the play is of course a familiar one in Shakespearean drama, not just because plays are put on within plays (*A midsummer night's dream*, *Hamlet*), but also because characters are frequently to be seen 'playing a part' during the course of a play. The best example of this is probably *Henry IV, Parts I and II*, along with *Henry V*, in which the acting out of roles by the *dramatis personae* is the dominant theme (Hal acts out the role of wastrel, as he is later to act out the role of king). Characters in Shakespearean drama can also act out each other's parts, and not solely for the comedic purposes of impersonation. In *Henry IV, Part I*, Act 2, Scene 4, Falstaff takes on the role of Hal, and Hal takes on the role of his father, the king, in a foreshadowing of the more serious business that is to follow. However, this is possible precisely because what we are shown is a play within the play, orchestrated by the author of the drama as a whole. The one thing Shakespearean characters can never be seen to do is to step out of one drama and into another.

familiar enough to suit their audience. But all that juristic order ensures is that there will be an author, and only one author, and that the drama will be whatever that author wishes it to be. Hobbes can offer advice as to how an author should proceed with his task (as he does in chapter XXX of *Leviathan*); but he cannot do the author's work for him. It is possible, therefore, that this work will be badly done, and that what is authorised will seem arbitrary, unconvincing, even nonsensical, stultifying for actors and audience alike. If this happens, both actors and audience must either make the best of what they are given, or attempt to avoid the legal stage altogether. Under the terms of juristic order, there is no alternative.

As well as being author, however, Hobbes's sovereign is also an actor. In one sense, this makes little difference to the above. Most of the acting done by the sovereign takes place in the name of those natural persons who have covenanted to treat the words and actions of the sovereign as their own. When this happens, the sovereign simply puts on the mask of the natural person to whom he speaks, compelling that person to treat his words as commands and his actions as binding. There is no dramatic dimension to this performance. The sovereign is under no obligation to provide a convincing, or accurate, or even consistent representation of the person represented by the mask. All that is required is that the individual who provides the audience for the words and actions being performed should recognise the mask as his own. He may find what is being done in that mask confusing, or arbitrary, or even nonsensical, but having agreed to let the sovereign wear the mask he has no choice but to recognise the performance as his own, and to endure it.

This, though, is not the only form of acting undertaken by the sovereign. Hobbes also states that the sovereign should act in the person of the commonwealth, and in this regard it is quite possible to speak of a dramatic dimension to the sovereign's performance. The person of the commonwealth is a fiction, and as such has an identity apart from both actor and audience; it is, after all, a mask which none will be able to recognise as their own. Because it is a fiction, actor and audience – sovereign and subjects – must share some common understanding of what is being represented. In this instance, therefore, the possibility of representation depends upon the sovereign being seen to act in a manner which befits the mask that he wears. Where the sovereign disregards the mask, the person of the commonwealth disappears. But where the sovereign chooses to recognise the mask as it is recognised by the audience, the person of the commonwealth may come to life, and the audience come to understand that sovereignty is simply the acting out of a particular role.

This is the condition of moral order. It enables sovereignty to become something more than the arbitrary exercise of power, for it requires that the sovereign condition his actions to accord with the expectations placed on the role that he performs. To represent the person of the commonwealth, the sovereign has not merely to act, but to put on an act, and it is this that makes it possible to think of sovereignty, in Hobbes's preferred terms, as an 'office'. However, as we saw in chapter 2, the condition of moral order raises a particular difficulty for Hobbes. The difficulty is that it is not compatible with the condition of juristic order, which requires that the sovereign be author of all fictitious persons, rather than playing the part of one himself. Of course, it is quite possible for the sovereign to invent a part for himself in the legal drama, as it is for a playwright to cast himself in his own play. But we cannot arrive at moral order by allowing the sovereign to authorise the person of the commonwealth, since moral order depends upon our ability to recognise the person of the commonwealth in any act performed by the sovereign, including any act of authorisation.[3] To arrive at moral order the acts of authorisation undertaken by the sovereign must themselves form part of a wider drama. An author can only be represented on stage if the parts that he is seen to create belong to a drama within the drama in which he appears. Therefore, moral order must render the legal drama given by juristic order – the drama authorised by the sovereign – nothing more than a play within a play. And if so, ultimate responsibility for the legal drama must be seen to lie elsewhere than with the sovereign.

[3] Hobbes allowed that the sovereign might appear before the civil courts if a case could be made on the basis of laws drawn up by the sovereign himself: 'If a Subject have a controversie with his Soveraigne, of debt, or of possession of land or goods, or concerning any service required at his hands, or concerning any penalty, corporall, or pecuniary, grounded on a precedent Law; he hath the same Liberty to sue for his right, as if it were against a Subject; and before such Judges, as are appointed by the Soveraign. For seeing the Soveraign demandeth by force of a former Law, and not by vertue of his Power; he declareth thereby, that he requireth no more, than shall appear to be due by that Law' (Hobbes, *Leviathan*, pp. 152–3). This is comparable to a situation in which the author of a play, having cast himself in one of the roles, can be required to speak the lines that he has written for that role. What Hobbes could not possibly accept was the sovereign appearing before the courts to answer a case made against the laws themselves; and this would be the analogy required if the author of a play had to appear on stage in order to act out the role of author.

The result is a series of choices. Juristic order can only be guaranteed by the single authority of a single sovereign, which will ensure that the legal drama of the state proceeds without interruption, but can provide no assurances that it will proceed in a convincing or coherent fashion. Moral order binds the legal drama into a broader drama, thereby ensuring that it must meet the broader demands that come to be placed on it. It only achieves this, however, by transcending the single authority of the single sovereign. Who then is responsible for the broader drama in which the sovereign author plays a part? One obvious answer is to suggest that it must be the responsibility of another author of another kind, possibly of the kind exemplified by Hobbes himself. But this simply reintroduces the problem of arbitrary authority at one remove, as Hobbes himself would have recognised. What guarantee is there that the drama scripted by a political philosopher will be more convincing than the one that might be scripted by a sovereign, if the only demand placed on the philosopher is that the moral life of the state should be his responsibility alone? Moral order requires that the characters portrayed on the stage of the state emerge out of the shared concerns and shared beliefs of all those who participate in the life of the state, whether sovereign or subject. This is perfectly possible – where the members of a commonwealth have a shared belief in the personality of the commonwealth, the role played by the sovereign may be bound into the moral life of the state as a whole. But what it cannot be is certain. As Hobbes was all too aware, the beliefs which people share, though powerful, are by no means uniform, such that any drama which depends upon shared beliefs may quickly degenerate into a series of conflicting claims to authority, and ultimately into chaos. And this is true, as Hobbes was also aware, wherever the ultimate drama is played out, whether among actors, whether among lawyers, whether among philosophers. The only certain guarantee of uniform belief is the arbitrary authority of a single author, be it exercised in a narrowly legal or a broadly moral setting. The only means of evading that authority is to risk the breakdown of order altogether.

II

This was the problem faced by the English pluralists in their various attempts to circumscribe the role of the sovereign state. The one constant theme running through the work of the pluralists was a distrust of arbitrary sovereign authority. But though reluctant to allow one sovereign body the right to authorise the life of the political community as a whole, they did not wish to dispense with the structures of the state altogether. None of them was willing to countenance disorder. Instead, they sought to locate the exercise of juristic authority within a broader moral setting, so rendering the body responsible for it part of a drama for which the ultimate responsibility lay elsewhere. The problem was deciding where responsibility for this broader drama did in fact lie. If the sovereign state is simply one association among many, it is perfectly possible that every other association will have a different idea of the part that ought to be played by the state. To prevent this, some formal structure must be provided within which the role of the state can be identified. Yet if this structure exists simply to provide groups like the state with a formal identity of their own, there is nothing to prevent it from being as arbitrary as the juristic structures it is designed to transcend. Certainly this is not prevented by the mere fact of the broader structures being assembled by political philosophers, who can be quite as arbitrary as the sovereigns about whom they write. To move from an ostensibly juristic to an ostensibly moral setting for the dramas of political life means nothing, so long as the moral setting seems designed specifically to order the juristic life of the state.

This problem manifests itself in the very nature of the idea that the pluralists sought to transcend – the idea of the sovereign state. The concept of sovereignty, as borrowed from Hobbes and pared down by Austin, was a narrowly juristic one, and to the pluralists it seemed highly arbitrary. It also seemed arbitrary to Bernard Bosanquet, whose political philosophy was designed to transcend legalistic notions of authority and to set them against the broader moral authority generated by the political community as a whole. Yet Bosanquet's political philosophy seemed arbitrary to the pluralists as well. Ignoring the setting, and seeing only the claim to authority, the pluralists came to identify Bosanquet with Austin, and to regard his conception of the state too as something that needed to be trans-cended. Both Austin and Bosanquet were felt to be making excessive claims on behalf of what was simply one body among many, even though for Austin that body was a 'portion' of society, whereas for Bosanquet it was society in its entirety. What was needed instead was a conception of authority which would be, in Laski's terms, 'co-ordinate' rather than 'hierarchical', with a broader source than any single body could give it. This, though, was precisely what Bosanquet had sought to achieve by taking ultimate political authority away from the sovereign portion and dispersing it across society as a whole; it was simply that he had continued to refer to his final co-ordinate authority as 'the State'. If Bosanquet's theory of the state was merely to be transcended as he had sought to transcend Austin's, then the result must be a regress. For any conception of authority, whether hierarchical or co-ordinate, constitutes a claim made on behalf of whoever or whatever is to do the authorising; and whatever that person, group of persons, or group of groups is called, and however it is described, the act of authorisation itself will seem arbitrary to those who remain determined to see the role of author as part of a wider drama.

A way out of this difficulty is suggested by Gierke, through his idealised conception of the *Rechtsstaat*. In the *Rechtsstaat* there is no need to isolate a single source of authority, since authority derives from every act that every member of the state performs, up to and including the person of the state itself. As a result, it is possible to identify the mask of the state with the actions performed by the state, as it will be possible to identify the mask of any other group or person with the actions that they perform – there is no need to identify the author, because where all persons are real, all masks authorise themselves. What we are left with is a setting in which life itself becomes the drama, with the parts that are played emerging from the lives that are led. However, the ideal concept of the *Rechtsstaat* depends on a willingness to accept that everything done by every individual and every group makes sense in dramatic terms. The English pluralists could not, or would not, accept this. They saw that where there is no distinction between what takes place on stage and what takes place off – between authorised and unauthorised actions – the results cannot be other than arbitrary. Ideally, of course, every aspect of every life may cohere in such a way as to appear the work of a single author. But in reality, it is just as possible that the lives of different individuals and different groups will make no sense to each other; or alternatively, that their lives will start to revolve around the life of the individual or group whose performance seems the most compelling, whose voice is clearest, whose actions are most visible, whose demands are most strident, the individual or group around whom all performances will come in the end to be ordered. And because the formal structures of authority have been dispensed with, there will be nothing that anyone can do about it.

Unmoved by transcendent idealism, the English pluralists were forced to look towards history to provide the framework within which all claims to authority might be transcended. Through history, all immutable claims were revealed to be contingent, each one just one aspect of a broader drama. This was as true of Bosanquet's theory of the state as it was of Austin's theory of sovereignty – both seemed meaningless apart from the historical conditions which determined the role that a claim to authority might play. In this way, history was able to provide a setting in which the authority of any given state, in whatever form it took, remained 'chimerical', an illusion which it was left to history to sustain or to explode. However, just because ultimate responsibility for the part to be played by the state resided with history, it was impossible to be certain what part the state might be expected to play. As Ernest Barker discovered, history could be as arbitrary as any other sovereign, and the role of the state might be transformed by it overnight, sometimes literally, as happened in Prussia between 14 and 15 July 1870, and in Britain between 3 and 4 August 1914. There was nothing to guarantee that the spectacle presented by history would be a coherent one, so long as all authority was seen to rest with history, and nothing to exercise authority over it.

It was this, then, that necessitated the move from historism to historicism. If the pluralists were to contain the state within the framework of history, they had somehow to order history so as to provide the state with a coherent role, and to begin with, they lacked the means to do so. Maitland, Figgis and Barker fell back on variants on the theme of national character, by which they were able to point up the ability of the English to put the state in its place, but not to establish what that place was. As a result, everything depended on the contingent arrangements that were made within groups and between groups to secure for the state its limited role; everything depended on the ability of the English to improvise group life among themselves. This was the theme of 'clubbability', or more broadly, 'trust'. The sort of history set out by Maitland, Figgis and Barker suggested that the English had been particularly adept at this kind of improvisation. But so long as it remained improvisation, the historian could do no more than sit back and admire the performance, in the hope that it would continue; and the part played by the state could never be quite secure from one moment to the next. Meanwhile, Cole and Laski lacked even this rudimentary faith in the ability of their countrymen to arrange matters for themselves. They wished simply to use history to point up the need for 'inductive-minded' thinking, whereby all claims to authority might be seen to depend upon the circumstances under which they are made. In this way, it was hoped that the state might be provided with a role which tied it to the lives of those who were to experience it. Yet this insistence amounts to little more than a wish to see the state given a role that is other than arbitrary, something which is very different from deciding on the role that the state should play. To tell a political theorist to think 'inductive-mindedly' is like telling an author that he must take account of his audience – and while it may be true that a willingness to take account of one's audience is a pre-condition of successful authorship, the injunction to do so does not tell the author what he is to say, or how he is to say it.

Cole and Laski came to recognise this, and in due course they came round to a different view of history, which was the view provided by Marx. In so doing, they were able to imbue history with a plot, and to provide the state with a clearly demarcated role. Ultimately, the drama was to culminate in the disappearance of the state from the stage of history altogether. But to reach that point, it was necessary to ensure that the role mapped out for the state was properly acted out, and this meant that the drama had to be carefully staged. The state could only assume its proper role if authority could be restored to the producers of the drama, and the producers of this drama were the Marxists themselves. History could provide the broader setting that was needed, therefore, but only on the basis of an unambiguous hierarchy of authority, which is, after all, the hallmark of every Marxist state. For those convinced by a Marxist reading of history, this authority will ultimately produce a genuinely uniform moral order, and thereby put an end to the prospect of a regress. But for those who remain unconvinced, it will, inevitably, seem as arbitrary as anything that has gone before.

Among these last was Barker, for whom the attractions of Marxism were never very great. In the end, Barker managed to resist the pull of historicism in all its forms, and he came to recognise that it was the search for a uniform moral order that was the illusion. The moral perspective, as he insisted in his introduction to Gierke, belongs only to individuals, and individuals, necessarily, differ. If that perspective is to be uniform, it can only be because a form of juristic order has been imposed on the moral life of individuals, rendering it as arbitrary as the narrow juristic existence it is designed to transcend. Therefore, the preservation of the moral life depends upon some distance being maintained between it and the juristic structures that provide it with order. This was the position at which Barker had arrived in 1933. The state, he argued, has to be freed from the exigencies of the moral life, and from the historical back-drop against which that life is played out; it has to create a separate, narrow, potentially even an arbitrary world of its own. Barker still hoped to diminish the potential for arbitrariness, by providing the state with a place in the world that it had created, as a person on the legal stage in its own right. But though he hoped for it, he could not explain how it might be done. So he found himself, in 1933, in a position that had first been set out by Thomas Hobbes, in his *Leviathan*.

CHAPTER 14

Conclusion

Many of the arguments with which this book has been concerned belong to a past age. We no longer hear much about, or seem much to care, whether churches are or are not persons in their own right. We do still, of course, hear a great deal about the legal status of trade unions, but we do not hear the question of that status addressed in the language of legal personality.[1] In fact, most of the clearcut distinctions on which the concept of legal personality depends have been lost under the welter of legislation that marks this century, all of it necessarily designed with what Maitland would call 'convenience' in mind. There have, for example, been many companies acts since the act of 1862, and each one has been concerned with practical issues over and above any abstract ones. As a result, we now have trusts that can incorporate corporations (many charities are now limited companies) and corporations that can incorporate trusts (in the form of pension funds and so on), while the questions of corporate identity and corporate liability, though more pressing than ever, have also become ever more complex. Amidst all this legislation, much has happened to enhance the freedoms enjoyed by groups within the state, and much (notably the trade union reforms of the 1980s) to diminish it. What has not happened is anything that might help to clarify what these freedoms are in abstract or philosophical terms. And what is true of groups within the state is also true of the state itself. The last half century has seen enormous

[1] A fact that Ernest Barker himself seemed to acknowledge in a series of lectures he published in 1951, based on a course he had delivered in Cambridge in the latter half of the 1930s. In the published version he writes: 'The real question, in any discussion of the relation of trade unions to the State, is not the question of whether they are persons, of whatever sort or character . . . The "being" of the group (person or not-person? and, if a person, which sort of person, the moral or the legal?) is irrelevant to that question: the one thing relevant is what the group does, what its activity is, and whether that activity can, and should, be regulated by law' (Barker, *Principles of social and political theory* (Oxford, 1951), p. 75).

changes in the scope of the state's activities, the number and variety of agencies through which it acts, and the manner and likelihood of their appearance before the courts. No-one now doubts, or even considers, whether or not the state can have a legal identity. Instead, we look to the specific identity of specific agencies, as and when they come under the jurisdiction of particular courts and particular laws. If we wish now to address the sorts of questions that were addressed by Maitland, we should have to accept that the abstract concept of group personality is of little or no help; the answers lie in the details.

Nevertheless, it is also true that among the more general concerns voiced by the English pluralists, many have acquired a contemporary resonance. Though English-speaking political theorists no longer concern themselves with the difference between natural and artificial personality, or the difference between fictitious and real, they do show an increasing interest in the question of the state's proper role, and the role that might be played by voluntary associations alongside it. In recent years, this has led to a number of attempts to revive interest in the work of the English pluralists, whose ideas are seen as having been unjustly neglected.[2] This book has not sought to put forward an argument of this kind. The movement that has been described here did not disappear through culpable neglect, but because of the very real limitations of the ideas themselves, limitations which became clear to their proponents as well as to their critics. The history of political pluralism is the history of a series of unsatisfactory solutions to a set of intractable problems, and this book has been an attempt to explain why this should have been so. If it has been successful in that attempt, it will be apparent that there is little to be gained from seeking to reinstate pluralist ideas in a contemporary setting. Early twentieth-century political pluralism did not succeed on its own terms, never mind on ours. But this does not mean that the history of political pluralism has no bearing on contemporary disputes in political theory. There are, in particular, two conclusions which can be drawn from the history that has been set out here.

The first concerns current attempts by political theorists to diminish the part played by the state in each of our lives. Many of the arguments that are put forward in this regard, whether broadly

---

[2] See especially D. Nicholls, *The pluralist state: the social and political ideas of J. N. Figgis and his contemporaries*, second edn (Basingstoke, 1994), and P. Q. Hirst, *The pluralist theory of the state: selected writings* (London, 1989).

philosophical (communitarianism) or more narrowly political (new Labour), have a puzzling quality. The puzzle is that the attempt to diminish the role of the state in certain areas of our lives seems only to necessitate its increase in others. So, for example, the greater the emphasis placed on voluntary associations (such as the family, for communitarians; or voluntary pension schemes, for new Labour), the greater the constraints that come to be placed on the ways in which these associations can operate. This is a theme that has recurred throughout this book. As we have seen, the attempt to enhance the role of voluntary associations does not result in a diminution of the authority of the state; it merely relocates it. The only way in which the part played by the state can be diminished is by marking off an area of social existence into which the authority of the state does not run. And if we do this, we shall have to accept that we can have no control over what goes on there. This does not mean that disorder will inevitably follow – individuals and groups of individuals may be perfectly capable of improvising a kind of order among themselves. But what that order is we will only discover after the event, as a historical truth; there can be no prior, logistical guarantees. The only guarantees come about when some one or thing is prepared to do the work of the state for it. And in these circumstances, though the actors may change, and the names may change, the nature of the role itself – the role of author – necessarily remains the same. This in turn does not mean that it makes no difference where and how political authority is exercised; finding reliable authors and convincing settings for the exercise of authority is the very stuff of politics. But it does mean that the relocation of the drama from a narrowly 'statist' to a more broadly moral, or communitarian, setting does not in itself alter the terms of the drama, or its potential for arbitrariness. It is by the potential for arbitrariness that we recognise someone, or something, acting in the role of the state.

The second conclusion concerns attempts by some historians of ideas to decide whether such a thing as 'the state' exists at all. These arguments, which go back as far as Collingwood,[3] are addressed to the question of whether there are any perennial problems in the history of ideas. Using the idea of 'the state' as an example, it has

[3] See R. G. Collingwood, *An autobiography* (Oxford, 1939), especially pp. 61–3. The more recent range of arguments on this topic are contained in J. Tully (ed.), *Meaning and context: Quentin Skinner and his critics* (Cambridge, 1988) (for a specific discussion of Hobbes and 'the state' see pp. 37–41).

been argued that different theorists at different periods have meant such different things by this idea that it is meaningless to speak of it in uniform terms (what is the state? what is the role of the state?); instead we should look to see what individual theorists might have meant by it (what did Hobbes mean by 'the state'? what did Laski mean by 'the state'?). The history set out in this book offers much that supports this thesis. The different theorists discussed here did have very different ideas of what was meant by 'the state', and it was often this that provided the main ground of difference between them (as for example between the pluralists and Bosanquet). Moreover, as historians themselves, the English pluralists recognised the futility of trying to populate the landscape of political thought with 'immutable' ideas, and it was their sense of the contingency of such ideas that provided their own arguments with much of their momentum. Yet it is also true that the English pluralists, in seeking to move away from the timeless concepts of 'state' and 'sovereignty', found themselves having to face a familiar problem – the problem of authority, as set out by Hobbes. In their attempts to transcend conventional notions of political authority, the pluralists revealed the variety of different settings into which the idea of the state might be transplanted. But though the settings might vary, the problem remained the same. We cannot know how any particular theorist felt about the problem of authority unless we are able to recognise the setting in which he sought to address it, thereby enabling us to understand what he meant by the idea of the state. Equally, though, we have to recognise that the problem is a persistent one, and that it is because of its persistence that different theorists have sought to address it in different ways. In political theory, almost anything is possible, and authority can be claimed by almost anyone, from historians to lawyers, from philosophers to politicians. Because it can be claimed by almost anyone, we can never be certain in advance what anyone means by the idea of the state. But because we cannot be certain what is meant by an idea, it does not follow that there are no perennial problems in the history of ideas. Political theorists mean different things by the idea of the state because they recognise the claims of other theorists to be arbitrary; they seem arbitrary because they do not appear to solve the problem. The truly perennial problems, after all, are the insoluble ones. That, in a sense, is how political theory works.

Bibliography

BOOKS

Allport, G. W., *Personality: a psychological interpretation*. London, 1938

Aubrey, J., *Brief lives*, ed. A. Clark. Oxford, 1898

Austin, J., *Lectures on jurisprudence, or the philosophy of positive law*, ed. R. Campbell, third edn, 2 vols. London, 1869

The province of jurisprudence determined, ed. W. E. Rumble. Cambridge, 1995

Barker, E., *Political thought in England from Herbert Spencer to the present day, 1848–1914*. London, 1915

Mother and sons in wartime and other pieces. London, 1917

National character and the factors in its formation. London, 1927

Church, State and study. London, 1930

Principles of social and political theory. Oxford, 1951

Barker, E. et al., *Why we are at war. Great Britain's cause*. Oxford, 1914

Barker, R., *Political ideas in modern Britain*. London, 1978

Political legitimacy and the state. Oxford, 1990

Bedau, H. A. (ed.), *Civil disobedience: theory and practice*. New York, 1969

Belloc, H., *The servile State*, third edn. London, 1927

Bentham, J., *A fragment on government*, ed. J. H. Burns and H. L. A. Hart. Cambridge, 1988

Bentley, A. F., *The process of government*, new edn. Cambridge, Mass., 1967

Bentley, M., *The liberal mind, 1914–29*. Cambridge, 1977

Black, A., *Guilds and civil society in European political thought from the twelfth century to the present*. London, 1984

Bosanquet, B., *Logic*, 2 vols. Oxford, 1911

The philosophical theory of the State, fourth edn. London, 1923

Letters from Bernard Bosanquet and his friends, ed. J. H. Muirhead. London, 1935

Bradley, F. H., *Ethical studies*, second edn. Oxford, 1927

Burns, C. D., *The morality of nations: an essay on the theory of politics*. London, 1915

Burrow, J. W., *Whigs and liberals: continuity and change in English political thought*. Oxford, 1988

Carpenter, L. P., *G. D. H. Cole: an intellectual biography*. Cambridge, 1973

266

Carr, W., *The origins of the German wars of unification*. London, 1991
Clarke, P., *Liberals and social democrats*. Cambridge, 1978
Cole, G. D. H., *Self-government in industry*. London, 1918
  The world of labour, fourth edn. London, 1919
  Guild socialism restated. London, 1920
  Social theory. London, 1920
  The next ten years in British social and economic policy. London, 1929
  Some relations between political and economic theory. London, 1934
  What Marx really meant. London, 1934
Cole, M. I., *The life of G. D. H. Cole*. London, 1971
Collingwood, R. G., *An autobiography*. Oxford, 1939
  The new Leviathan. Oxford, 1942
  The idea of history. Oxford, 1946
Collini, S., *Liberalism and sociology: L. T. Hobhouse and political argument in modern Britain*. Cambridge, 1979
  Public moralists: political thought and intellectual life in Britain, 1850–1930. Oxford, 1991
Dahl, R. A., *A preface to democratic theory*. Chicago, 1956
Deane, H. A., *The political ideas of Harold J. Laski*. New York, 1955
Dewey, J., *The public and its problems*. London, 1926
Duff, P. W., *Personality in Roman private law*. Cambridge, 1938
Duguit, L., *Law in the modern State*, trans. F. and H. Laski. London, 1921
Dunn, J., *Political obligation in its historical context*. Cambridge, 1980
Eastwood, G., *Harold Laski*. London, 1977
Elliott, W. Y., *The pragmatic revolt in politics: syndicalism, fascism, and the constitutional State*. New York, 1928
Emy, H. V., *Liberals, radicals and social politics*. Cambridge, 1973
Ensor, R. C. K., *England, 1870–1914*. Oxford, 1936
Figgis, J. N., *The divine right of kings*. London, 1896
  Studies of political thought from Gerson to Grotius, 1414–1625. London, 1907
  Churches in the modern State. London, 1913
Fisher, H. A. L., *Frederick William Maitland. A biographical sketch*. Cambridge, 1910
Follett, M. P., *The new State: group organisation the solution of popular government*. New York, 1918
Gierke, O. von, *Das deutsche Genossenschaftsrecht*, 4 vols. Berlin, 1968–1913
  Political theories of the middle age, trans. F. W. Maitland. Cambridge, 1900
  Natural law and the theory of society, 1500–1800, trans. E. Barker. Cambridge, 1934
  Community in historical perspective, ed. A. Black. Cambridge, 1990
Green, S. J. D. and Whiting, R. C. (eds.), *The boundaries of the state in modern Britain*. Cambridge, 1996
Green, T. H., *Lectures on the principles of political obligation*, new edn. London, 1907
Hart, H. L. A., *The concept of law*. Oxford, 1961

Hegel, G. W. F., *The philosophy of right*, trans. T. M. Knox. Oxford, 1967
Lectures on the philosophy of world history: introduction, trans. H. B. Nisbett. Cambridge, 1975
Hinton, J. *Labour and socialism: a history of the British Labour movement, 1867– 1974*. Brighton, 1983
Hirst, P. Q., *The pluralist theory of the state: selected writings*. London, 1989
Associative democracy: new forms of economic and social governance. Cambridge and Oxford, 1994
Hobbes, T., *Opera philosophica*, ed. W. Molesworth, 5 vols. London, 1839–45
Leviathan, ed. R. Tuck. Cambridge, 1991
Hobhouse, L. T., *The metaphysical theory of the State: a criticism.* London, 1918
Hobson, S. G., *Guild principles in war and peace.* London, 1917
Houseman, G. L., *G. D. H. Cole.* Boston, 1979
Hsiao, K. C., *Political pluralism: a study in contemporary political thought.* London, 1927
Hume, D., *A treatise of human nature*, ed. E. C. Mosser. London, 1969
James, W., *Pragmatism. A new name for some old ways of thinking.* London, 1907
A pluralistic universe. London, 1909
Joad, C. E. M., *Modern political theory.* Oxford, 1924
John, M., *Politics and law in late nineteenth century Germany: the origins of the civil code.* Oxford, 1989
Keegan, J., *The face of battle.* London, 1991
Krabbe, H., *The modern idea of the State*, trans. G. H. Sabine and W. J. Shepard. New York, 1922
Kramnick, I. and Sheerman, B., *Harold Laski. A life on the left.* London, 1993
Laski, H. J., *Studies in the problem of sovereignty.* New Haven, 1917
Authority in the modern State. New Haven, 1919
The foundations of sovereignty. New York, 1921
On the study of politics. Oxford, 1926
The dangers of obedience and other essays. New York, 1930
Studies in law and politics. London, 1932
A grammar of politics, fourth edn. London, 1938
Laski, H. J. and Holmes O. W. Jnr., *The correspondence of Mr Justice Holmes and Harold J. Laski, 1916–1935*, ed. Mark de Wolfe Howe, 2 vols. London, 1953
Lewis, J. D., *The Genossenschaft-theory of Otto von Gierke.* Madison, 1935
Lustig, R. J., *Corporate liberalism: the origins of modern American political theory, 1890–1920.* Berkeley, 1982
MacIver, R. M., *Community: a sociological study.* London, 1917
The modern State. Oxford, 1926
As a tale that is told. Chicago, 1968
Mack Smith, D., *Mussolini.* London, 1981
Magid, H. M., *English political pluralism.* New York, 1941
Maitland, F. W., *The collected papers of F. W. Maitland*, ed. H. A. L. Fisher, 3 vols. Cambridge, 1911

Martin K., *Harold Laski, 1893–1950. A biographical memoir*. London, 1953

Meinecke, F., *Historism. The rise of a new philosophical outlook*, trans. J. E. Anderson. London, 1972

Mogi, S., *Otto von Gierke. His political teaching and jurisprudence*. London, 1932

Morison, W. L., *John Austin*. London, 1982

Nettleship, R. L., *Philosophical lectures and remains*, ed. A. C. Bradley, 2 vols. London, 1897

Nicholls, D., *Three varieties of pluralism*. London, 1974

Deity and domination: images of God and the state in the nineteenth and twentieth centuries. London, 1989

The pluralist state: the social and political ideas of J. N. Figgis and his contemporaries, second edn. Basingstoke, 1994

Nozick, R., *Anarchy, state and utopia*. New York, 1974

Oakeshott, M., *Experience and its modes*. Cambridge, 1933

Hobbes on civil association. Oxford, 1975

On human conduct. Oxford, 1975

Orwell, G. *The Penguin essays of George Orwell*. London, 1984

Pitkin, H., *The concept of representation*. Berkeley, 1967

Plant, R. and Vincent, A., *Philosophy, politics and citizenship: the life and thought of the British Idealists*. Oxford, 1984

Popper, K., *The poverty of historicism*. London, 1957

Pound, R., *Interpretations of legal history*. Cambridge, 1923

Rawls, J., *A theory of justice*, new edn. Oxford, 1973

Rockow, L., *Contemporary political thought in England*. London, 1925

Ross, K. R., *Church and creed in Scotland: the Free Church case, 1900–1904 and its origins*. Edinburgh, 1988

Rousseau, J.-J., *The social contract*, trans. M. Cranston. Harmondsworth, 1968

Russell, B., *The principles of social reconstruction*. London, 1916

The autobiography of Bertrand Russell, 3 vols. London, 1971

Scruton, R. (ed.), *Conservative texts*. Basingstoke, 1991

Spencer, H., *The man versus the State*, ed. D. MacRae. Harmondsworth, 1968

Stapleton, J., *Englishness and the study of politics: the social and political thought of Ernest Barker*. Cambridge, 1994

Stocks, J. L., *Patriotism and the super-State*. London, 1920

Tawney, R. H., *Equality*. London, 1931

Tierney, B., *Religion, law and the growth of constitutional thought, 1150–1650*. Cambridge, 1982

Tuchman, B., *August 1914*. London, 1962

Tuck, R., *Philosophy and government, 1572–1651*. Cambridge, 1993

Tucker, M. G., *John Neville Figgis*. London, 1950

Tully, J. (ed.), *Meaning and context: Quentin Skinner and his critics*. Cambridge, 1988

Unwin, G., *The guilds and companies of London*. London, 1908

Studies in economic history: the collected papers of George Unwin, ed. R. H. Tawney. London, 1927

Vincent, A., *Theories of the state*. Oxford, 1987
Wallas, G., *The great society: a phychological analysis*. London, 1914
Human nature in politics, third edn. London, 1920
Our social heritage. London, 1921
Ward, P. W., *Sovereignty: a study of a contemporary political notion*. London, 1928
Walzer, M., *Obligations: essays on disobedience, war and power*. Cambridge, Mass., 1970
Webb, B., *Diaries*, ed. N. and J. Mackenzie, 4 vols. London, 1982–5
Webb, L. C. (ed.), *Legal personality and political pluralism*. London, 1974
Webb, S. and B., *A constitution for the socialist commonwealth of Great Britain*, new edn. Cambridge, 1975
White, H., *Meta-history: the historical imagination in nineteenth century Europe*. Baltimore, 1973
Williams, G., *Person and persona: studies in Shakespeare*. Cardiff, 1981
Winter, J. M., *Socialism and the challenge of war: ideas and politics in Britain, 1912– 1918*. London, 1974
Wolff, R. P., *In defence of anarchism*, new edn. New York, 1973
Wright, A. W., *G. D. H. Cole and socialist democracy*. Oxford, 1979
British socialism: a history of the British Labour movement from the 1880s to the 1960s. London, 1983
R. H. Tawney. Manchester, 1987
Zylstra, B., *From pluralism to collectivism: the development of Harold Laski's political thought*. Assen, 1970

ARTICLES

Barker, E., 'The discredited State', *Political Quarterly*, 5 (1915), 101–21
'Nationality', *History*, 14 (1919), 135–45
Barker, R., 'Guild socialism revisited?', *Journal of Contemporary History*, 9 (1974), 165–80
Beloff, M., 'The age of Laski', *Fortnightly*, 167 (1950), 379–84
Bosanquet, B., 'A note on Mr. Cole's paper', *Proceedings of the Aristotelian Society*, 15 (1914–15), 160–3
'Patriotism in the perfect State', *The International Crisis*, 1 (1915), 132–51
'The function of the State in promoting the unity of mankind', *Proceedings of the Aristotelian Society*, 17 (1915–16), 28–57
Bradley, A. C., 'International morality: the United States of Europe', *The International Crisis*, 1 (1915), 46–77
Brown, H. C., 'Human nature and the State', *International Journal of Ethics*, 26 (1915–16), 177–92
Burns, C. D., 'The moral effects of war and peace', *International Journal of Ethics*, 25 (1914–15), 317–27
'When peace breaks out', *International Journal of Ethics*, 26 (1915–16), 82–91
'The idea of the State', *Mind*, 27 (1918), 180–97
Burns, C. D., Russell, B. and Cole, G. D. H., 'Symposium: the nature of

the State in view of its external relations', *Proceedings of the Aristotelian Society*, 16 (1915–16), 290–325

Cohen, M. R., 'Communal ghosts and other perils in social philosophy', *Journal of Philosophy, Psychology and Scientific Method*, 16 (1919), 673–90

'Positivism and the limits of idealism in the law', *Columbia Law Review*, 27 (1927), 237–50

Coker, F. W., 'The technique of the pluralistic State', *American Political Science Review*, 15 (1921), 186–213

Cole, G. D. H., 'Conflicting social obligations', *Proceedings of the Aristotelian Society*, 15 (1914–15), 140–59

'Loyalties', *Proceedings of the Aristotelian Society*, 29 (1925–6), 151–70

'Marx and the world situation today', in J. Middleton Murray *et al. Marxism*. London, 1935

Collini, S., 'Hobhouse, Bosanquet and the state: philosophical Idealism and political argument in England, 1880–1918', *Past and Present*, 72 (1976), 86–111

Croly, H., 'The future of the State', *New Republic*, 12 (1917), 179–83

Davidson, J., 'The Scottish Church case', *Political Science Quarterly*, 20 (1905), 91–110

Demos, R., 'Legal fictions', *International Journal of Ethics*, 34 (1923–4), 37–58

Ekrich, A. A., 'Harold J. Laski: the liberal manqué or lost libertarian?', *Journal of Libertarian Studies*, 4 (1980), 139–50

Elliott, W. Y., 'The pragmatic politics of Mr. H. J. Laski', *American Political Science Review*, 18 (1924), 251–75

'Mussolini: prophet of the pragmatic era in politics', *Political Science Quarterly*, 41 (1926), 161–92

'Pragmatic ethics, positivistic law and the constitutional State', *Economica*, 7 (1927), 1–26

Ellis, E. D., 'The pluralistic State', *American Political Science Review*, 14 (1920), 393–409

'Guild socialism and pluralism', *American Political Science Review*, 17 (1923), 584–96

Elton, G., 'Introduction', to J. N. Figgis, *The divine right of kings*. New York, 1965

Figgis, J. N., 'The Church and the secular theory of the State', *Report of the Church Congress* (1905), 189–92

'Ideal politics', *The English Church Review*, 5 (1914), 487–96

Follett, M. P., 'Community is a process', *Philosophical Review*, 18 (1919), 576–88

Forsyth, M., 'Thomas Hobbes and the constituent power of the people', *Political Studies*, 29 (1981), 191–203

Greenleaf, W. H., 'Laski and British socialism', *History of Political Thought*, 2 (1981), 573–91

Haldane, R. B., 'The nature of the State', *The Contemporary Review*, 117 (1920), 761–73

Hinton, J. 'G. D. H. Cole in the stage army of the good', *Bulletin of the Society for the Study of Labour History*, 28 (1974), 76–83

Jacks, L. P., Shaw, G. B., Burns, C. D. and Oakley, H., 'Symposium: ethical principles of social reconstruction', *Proceedings of the Aristotelian Society*, 17 (1916–17), 256–99

Laing, R. M., 'Aspects of the problem of sovereignty', *International Journal of Ethics*, 32 (1921–2), 1–20

Laski, H. J., 'The personality of associations', *Harvard Law Review*, 29 (1915–16), 404–26

'The apotheosis of the State', *New Republic*, 7 (1916), 302–4

'The responsibility of the State in England', *Harvard Law Review*, 32 (1918–19), 447–72

'The pluralistic State', *Philosophical Review*, 28 (1919), 562–75

'Man or the State', *Nation*, 110 (January 1920), 146–7

'Democracy at the crossroads', *Yale Review*, 9 (1920), 788–803

'Recent contributions to political science', *Economica*, 1 (1921), 87–91

'Lenin and Mussolini', *Foreign Affairs*, 2 (1923), 43–54

'Political science in Great Britain', *American Political Science Review*, 19 (1925), 96–9

'Machiavelli and the present time', *Quarterly Review*, 53 (1927), 57–70

'Bosanquet's theory of the general will', *Aristotelian Society Supplementary Volume*, 8 (1928), 46–61

'The prospects of constitutional government', *Political Quarterly*, 1 (1930), 307–25

'Reflections on the crisis', *Political Quarterly*, 2 (1931), 466–9

'The present position of representative democracy', *American Political Science Review*, 26 (1932), 629–41

'The obsolescence of federalism', *New Republic*, 98 (1939), 367–9

'Morris Cohen's approach to legal philosophy', *University of Chicago Law Review*, 15 (1947–8), 575–87

Laski, H. J. and Lippmann, W., 'Authority in the modern State', *New Republic*, 19 (1919), 149–50

Lindsay, A. D., 'The State in recent political theory', *Political Quarterly*, 1 (1914), 128–45

'The State and society', *The International Crisis*, 2 (1915), 92–108

'Sovereignty', *Proceedings of the Aristotelian Society*, 27 (1923–4), 235–54

'Bosanquet's theory of the general will', *Aristotelian Society Supplementary Volume*, 8 (1928), 31–45

Machen, A. W., 'Corporate personality', *Harvard Law Review*, 24 (1910–11), 253–67 and 347–65

MacIver, R. M., 'Ethics and politics', *International Journal of Ethics*, 20 (1909–10), 72–86

'Society and State', *Philosophical Review*, 20 (1911), 30–45

Malcolm, N., 'Hobbes, Sandys and the Virginia Company', *Historical Journal*, 24, 297–321

Martin, K., 'The return of the State', *Economica*, 6 (1926), 40–8

Mellone, S. H., 'The Scottish Church case and its ethical significance', *International Journal of Ethics*, 15 (1904–5), 361–9

Morrow, J., 'Ancestors, legacies and traditions: British Idealism in the history of political thought', *History of Political Thought*, 6 (1986), 492–515

Muirhead, J. H., 'Recent criticism of the Idealist theory of the general will', *Mind*, 33 (1924), 166–75; 233–41; 361–8

Oakeshott, M., 'The concept of a philosophical jurisprudence', *Politica*, 3 (1938), 203–22; 345–62

Oakley, H. D., 'The idea of a general will', *The International Crisis*, 2 (1916), 138–63

Peretz, M., 'Laski redivivus', *Journal of Contemporary History*, 1 (1966), 87–101

Russell, B., 'The ethics of war', *International Journal of Ethics*, 25 (1914–15), 127–42

Sabine, G. H., 'The concept of the State as power', *Philosophical Review*, 29 (1920), 301–18

  'Pluralism: a point of view', *American Political Science Review*, 17 (1923), 34–50

Spitz, D., 'Robert M. MacIver's contributions to political theory', in M. Berger, T. Abel and C. H. Page (eds.), *Freedom and control in modern society*, New York, 1954, 297–312

Stapleton, J., 'The national character of Ernest Barker's political science', *Political Studies*, 37 (1989), 171–89

  'English pluralism as cultural definition: the social and political thought of George Unwin', *Journal of the History of Ideas*, 3 (1991), 665–84

Tugwell, R. G., 'Guild Socialism and the industrial future', *International Journal of Ethics*, 32 (1921–2), 282–8

Urban, W. M., 'The nature of the community', *Philosophical Review*, 29 (1919), 547–61

Wadia, A. R., 'The State under a shadow', *International Journal of Ethics*, 31 (1920–1), 319–37

Weeks, J., 'The politics of pluralism', *Bulletin of the Society for the Study of Labour History*, 32 (1976), 59–66

Wilde, N., 'The attack on the State', *International Journal of Ethics*, 30 (1919–20), 349–71

Woolf, L. S., '*Magna latrocina*: the State as it ought to be and as it is', *International Journal of Ethics*, 27 (1916–17), 36–49

Wright, A. W., 'Guild Socialism revisited', *Journal of Contemporary History*, 9 (1974), 165–80

  'From Fabianism to guild socialism: the early political thought of G. D. H. Cole', *Bulletin of the Society for the Study of Labour History*, 22 (1976), 23–5

Zimmern, A. E., 'The supremacy of the State', *New Republic*, 12 (1917), 49–50

H. J. LASKI'S *NEW REPUBLIC* BOOK REVIEWS

'Realistic social philosophy', 11 (7 July 1917), 283–4
'An English radicalism', 13 (3 November 1917), 25–6
'The literature of politics', 13 (17 November 1917), 6–8 (of supplement)
'Lord Acton', 14 (23 February 1918), 117–19
'Industrial self-government', 14 (27 April 1918), 391–2
'Labour and the State', 15 (1 June 1918), 131–2
'What is history?', 15 (13 July 1918), 323–4
'The responsible State', 16 (14 September 1918), 203–4
'The new State', 18 (8 February 1919), 61–2
'National guilds', 18 (22 February 1919), 123–4
'The war State', 18 (8 March 1919), 188–9
'Constitutional documents', 18 (26 April 1919), 429–30
'Constitutional government', 19 (24 May 1919), 126–7
'Rousseau', 19 (16 July 1919), 363–4
'A great churchman', 20 (20 August 1919), 95–6
'The history of trade unionism', 22 (12 May 1920), 359–60
'Parliament and revolution', 22 (19 May 1920), 383–4
'Guild socialism and the State', 23 (30 June 1920), 154–5

UNPUBLISHED MATERIAL

Stapleton, J., 'Academic political thought and the development of political studies in Britain, 1900–1950', D. Phil. thesis, University of Sussex, 1985

Index

actions, 9, 16–18, 22–3, 114–15, 174, 250
actors, 7–8, 224–5, 227, 230–6, 238–43, 247–8, 252–6, 264
Allport, G. W., 225 n.5
Althusius, Johannes, 43–7, 48, 54, 57, 90, 130–1, 144, 218, 245 n.13
Amalgamated Society of Railway Servants (ASRS), 139, 141–2, 180
American Political Science Review, 198
anarchism, 80, 83, 190–1, 198 n.6
Aristotelian Society, 163, 166, 207
Aristotle, 3, 50 n.34
associationism, 212–13
associations, 3, 59–60, 160, 208
  as communities, 143–8, 186
  as fellowships, 35, 44, 46, 51–2, 55, 57, 58–9, 61–2, 131
  as persons, 3–4, 11, 14, 28–31, 37, 48–50, 51–3, 65–6, 89–90, 94–6, 105–10, 115–18, 136, 140, 151, 187–8, 215–17, 233–43, 244–50
  as schemes, 152–9, 215
  as sects, 143–8, 183
  'enterprise', 14, 147, 162, 171
  functional, 169–72, 175–6
  in law, 13–16, 25–31, 39–40, 48–50, 65–9, 89–90, 101–7, 108–12, 115–18, 131–4, 135–43, 215–17, 233–7, 240, 244–50
Aubrey, John, 15 n.19
Austin, John, 72–5, 78, 79, 80, 81, 82–3, 96, 112, 125–8, 132, 149, 155–6, 157–8, 180, 223, 257–8, 259
authority, authors, 7–8, 29–31, 93, 143, 174, 189–90, 224, 227, 230, 235–41, 252–6, 257–61, 264, 265

Bacon, Francis, 15, 79
Barker, Ernest, x, 166, 168–9, 259–61, 262 n.1
  and 'federalism', 80, 150
  and Figgis, 81–2, 150–1, 160, 217–18
  and the First World War, 161, 162–3, 259

and Gierke, 64, 65, 151, 211, 213–19
and Hobbes, 154–5, 158, 223–9, 230, 232–3
and Laski, 81–2, 178, 181, 187, 193–4
and MacIver, 211–13
as historian, 161
as political theorist, 151–2, 196
on personality, 151, 152–3, 164 n.7, 214–17, 224–9, 230, 231–7, 243–7, 250
on the state, 153–61, 162–3, 198, 213, 216–19, 227–8, 231–5, 251–3
Barker, Rodney, 196 n.5
Bentham, Jeremy, 73 n.16, 195
Bentley, A. F., 192
Berlin, Isaiah, 83 n.43
Bismarck, Otto von, 60 n.51, 61
Black, Antony, 54 n.39, 60 n.48, 61 n.52
Bodin, Jean, 15, 34, 158, 223
bodies, 21–4, 153
  'politic', 26–9, 74
Bolshevik revolution, 196
Bosanquet, Bernard, 76–9, 80, 82–3, 96, 150, 164, 166, 173–5, 208–9, 223, 257–8, 259, 265
Bradley, F. H., 208 n.42
Bürgerliches Gesetzbuch (1896), 62, 65
Burns, C. DeLisle, 164

Calvin, Jean, 15
Child Support Agency, 111 n.57
Church, Anglican, 132, 143, 182, 184
Church, Catholic, 51, 55
  in Britain, 66, 181–4
Church, Russian Orthodox, 140–1
churches, 97–8, 127, 132–3, 135, 139–41, 143–6, 147–8, 152, 168, 179, 180–6, 242–3, 262
Cicero, 225–6
civil disobedience, 147–8, 183
civil war, 12
civitas, 14 n.16, 21, 212, 215
  Dei, 47

275

IDEAS IN CONTEXT

Edited by QUENTIN SKINNER (General Editor)
LORRAINE DASTON, WOLF LEPENIES,
J. B. SCHNEEWIND and JAMES TULLY

Titles marked with an asterisk are also available in paperback